T0285030

The
BATTLE *for*
LOUDOUN
COUNTY

www.amplifypublishing.com

The Battle for Loudoun County: Inside the Culture War Between a "Woke" School Board and the Radical Right in America's Wealthiest Suburb

©2024 Wayde B. Byard. All Rights Reserved. No part of this publication may be reproduced, stored in a retrieval system or transmitted in any form by any means electronic, mechanical, or photocopying, recording or otherwise without the permission of the author.

For more information, please contact:
Amplify Publishing, an imprint of Amplify Publishing Group
620 Herndon Parkway, Suite 220
Herndon, VA 20170
info@amplifypublishing.com

Library of Congress Control Number: 2024909218
CPSIA Code: PRV0523A
ISBN-13: 979-8-89138-079-0

Printed in the United States

To Brenda,

You don't know anything until you almost lose everything.
I am so glad that I didn't lose you.

You are my everything.

The BATTLE *for* LOUDOUN COUNTY

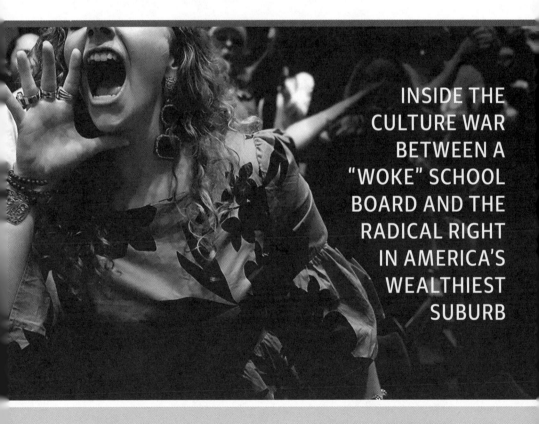

INSIDE THE CULTURE WAR BETWEEN A "WOKE" SCHOOL BOARD AND THE RADICAL RIGHT IN AMERICA'S WEALTHIEST SUBURB

WAYDE B. BYARD

amplify

an imprint of Amplify Publishing Group

CONTENTS

AUTHOR'S NOTE

A Warning

Loudoun County, Virginia, is the wealthiest, most-educated locality in America. It's diverse. It's home to cutting-edge technology. It boasts one of the most-honored school systems in the country.

It is also home to bigotry and cultural stupidity on an epic scale.

Loudoun is a template for how the Radical Right wants to reshape American politics, using a reasonable facade to push policies that were considered regressive a half-century ago. It also became the proving ground for how Republicans could swing an affluent, educated suburb just enough to secure a narrow electoral victory.

How did Loudoun become Fox News' go-to for an example of a "woke" school board and clickbait for the Alt Right and fringe media?

A combination of Dr. Seuss, the Underground Railroad, equity efforts, gender-identifying pronouns, a sexual incident in a high school bathroom, a veteran political operative, and politicians who were willing to distort minor incidents—and outright lie about them—when it suited their narrative. It also involves tone-deaf and naïve school officials and a dysfunctional school board that blundered into every trap the lunatic Right set for it.

I didn't enlist in the culture wars. I ended up on the front lines anyway. I became the center of a major media controversy and a high-profile

1

prosecution through a combination of location, circumstance, and political ambition—blind, ruthless political ambition.

I have some strong political opinions, but I don't share them online or casually.

When it comes to party affiliation, I identify as a Democrat. However, the only political campaigns I've been actively involved with were for Republican candidates for my local board of supervisors. These are people I know. I thought they'd do the best job.

Put me down as a raging moderate.

I'm not the type who becomes the subject of online tirades, reports on the evening news, or feature stories in *The Washington Post*.

But that's where I've ended up.

I'd say mine is a cautionary tale, but it's so bizarre that I can't tell you of what to be cautious. What I know is that your existence, however tangential to the swirling culture wars, can be upended by events the most active imaginations can't conceive of (and I have a wild imagination).

If you think living a good life will prevent you from being the target of a legal system tainted by national politics, you are naïve.

If you think the justice system is blind and impartial in the fractured, partisan society we live in, you are wrong. It may be incompetent and biased, but it is never blind.

Part of this narrative contains special grand jury testimony. This was given to my attorney, who gave it to me with no legal restrictions.

Accuracy has been the main thing missing from this story.

Until now.

PART I

The Battleground:
Loudoun County, VA

Setting the Stage

I've written this book by recalling what I experienced, adding context from information I discovered later through the grand jury investigation created after the sexual assaults as well as what came out during the trial. I hope that, by chronicling the insanity that led to my situation, my story will allow you to identify such behavior, call it out, and stop it before it reaches the levels I witnessed and experienced.

My Public Persona

I was a cultural accident.

Part of my job as public information officer for Loudoun County Public Schools (LCPS) was recording snow-day announcements. I recorded thirty-six messages each summer to cover every possible weather emergency. Even with this arsenal of possibilities, superintendents found "must-have" variations to the standard messages, so I often made new recordings—with the help of my faithful executive assistant, Kim Goodlin—as early as four-thirty in the morning. Each message had to be at least twenty-eight seconds long so that answering machines would pick them up. I also allowed for the fact that the messages had to be translated into Spanish, which would often make them 35 percent longer. I have a speech impediment, so I had to concentrate and enunciate each word slowly and clearly. This produced a leaden, deadpan tone that was easy for schoolchildren to imitate.

A lovely woman, Liz Scimonelli Campbell, created a Facebook page, "Friends of Wayde Byard," that grew to 17,000 followers based on the fun surrounding snow days. This page was soon flooded with memes depicting me as characters from *Game of Thrones*, *Batman*, beer ads ("The most interesting man in the world"), and my least favorite, my face on the body of Julie Andrews from the opening scene of *The Sound of Music*. Schools sold T-shirts with my name and likeness for fundraisers. There were Christmas ornaments featuring snowflakes and the legend "Waiting for Wayde." I agreed to have myself 3D scanned at the behest of a technology administrator, which resulted in small plastic busts that were given out at a technology conference. Soon my miniature, bald head was adorning desks all over LCPS. The two local weekly newspapers conducted annual "Best of Loudoun" polls, where I was routinely voted Best Public Servant.

Basically, I was a cottage industry without royalties.

My accidental celebrity has led to some odd "opportunities."

I was a guest caller at bingo nights.

I was a "dunkee" in the dunking booth. This activity ceased, however, after a toddler, disappointed he couldn't get me to splash, pushed the lever controlling the seat and triggered a surprise plunge that left me with a severely bruised midsection.

I was the pronouncer at spelling bees. This gig got nerve-wracking during the later rounds. Helicopter parents were always trying to say that their student missed a word because the pronouncer had pronounced it incorrectly. By the end, I was sweating as much as the kids.

I gave a graduation speech almost every year.

When I attended a school dedication (there are a lot of these in Loudoun) or some other school gathering, the superintendent or principal would introduce me, resulting in thunderous applause. I stood up like a trained monkey and waved. I was always mortified, but I tried to act bemused.

I was a cheap applause line.

But, mostly, I was a very odd subject for so much attention.

While some might have perceived that I had great power within the school division (school districts in Virginia are technically divisions of the state school board), I was, in fact, a third-tier administrator. (Remember how I recorded the snow-day announcements?) At the top of the org chart was the superintendent. Directly under the superintendent was the cabinet, which included my boss, Director of Communications and Community Engagement Joan Sahlgren. Then there was me. I had one employee under me, a secretary; no investigative powers; and no direct knowledge of the issues discussed in cabinet. In a military sense, I was a lieutenant colonel. I had a limited scope of operations that could only be conducted with the approval of those above me on the org chart.

"Limited scope" did not, however, translate to "not busy."

When I began my career as public information officer, a veteran principal, Wayne Mills, said I would be just another bureaucrat who hid in the central office and did nothing to help those working in the field. Wayne had reached an age where he felt free to dispense acerbic observations freely. I took this as a challenge and set out to be as visible and helpful as possible. One of my prouder career accomplishments was that, just before his retirement, Wayne admitted that his original assessment of me had been wrong.

A typical day for me began when I fired up the computer at six in the morning to see if anything dramatic affecting the school division had happened overnight. My phone was synched to my car's sound system so that I would get phone calls and emails on the way to work. Sometimes I wouldn't make it out of the driveway before the barrage began. Whenever a new message would arrive, the email would make a magical ping on the sound system. On busy days, the inside of my car sounded like Hogwarts. I had mapped out numerous stopping points along my route to work where I could pull over to type messages on my cell phone or have a phone conference with a principal facing a tough situation.

Sometimes, I wouldn't even make it to the office. I would often have to divert to a school that was having some crisis or another. LCPS had, and has, a lot of young principals who are inexperienced in emergency situations. Helping them was one of the greatest pleasures of my job.

I have a special affinity for principals.

My father was a high school principal in the 1970s. This job was incredibly stressful before social media, which examines, analyzes, and condemns almost everything a principal does, usually using "facts" that are no more than flimsy rumors.

Case in point: A middle schooler hears another student jokingly say he'd like to shoot up the school. He posts this musing on social media. By the morning, we've sent messages to seventeen schools assuring them that they're not under the threat of a school shooting.

Fake news and rumors can travel at light speed in Loudoun.

My messaging activities with principals ranged from the bizarre to the improbably routine. One principal—a diminutive, bespectacled woman with a fierce devotion to education and her school—always gave me a long, chronological account of what had led up to the need for an emergency message before actually describing the emergency. One of her most endearing qualities—when she was excited, her voice rose an octave, making her sound like a cartoon chipmunk. My end of those types of conversations usually consisted of:

"Wait . . ."

"Hold on . . ."

"Get to the point . . ."

"OK, your school is on fire. I think I have a template message that I can adapt."

LCPS has a long list of template messages in Google Docs form. There are dozens covering every bizarre situation we've been forced to address publicly. It is still not enough. The ability of students—especially middle school students—to do offensive, dangerous, and, mainly, stupid things was endless. The list of templates grew accordingly.

The first thing I would do on a typical day at the office, besides emergencies, was sort through an electronic clipping service and media sites to put together the first of a twice-daily report on media coverage of LCPS for senior management. Some mornings there were twenty or more articles and broadcasts concerning Loudoun's schools. Right-wing media had begun to use LCPS as an example of a "woke" school division and why "traditional" American values were going straight to hell. We seemed to be especially popular with a TV station in Jackson, Mississippi. Guess they didn't have enough problems in Mississippi; they had to import more.

I would typically write one media release per day for LCPS's website and social media. Facing an onslaught of negative reports, we had to generate some good news of our own. And there was plenty of good news regarding students and staff. LCPS is a high-performing school division. Students have started technology firms, sought to cure complex medical conditions (using science projects light years from the baking-soda volcanoes of my day), and performed incredible acts of kindness for the community at-large.

I would field ten to fifteen phone calls from media and schools per day and sort through, redirect, and reply to four hundred to six hundred emails. The IT staff told me that my email account was the busiest in Loudoun County. In fairness, a lot of this email was spam that my email's blocking function could never seem to block.

What little free time I had was filled answering Virginia Freedom of Information Act (VFOIA) requests. For my first fourteen years as public information officer, I averaged four VFOIA requests a year. Starting in 2014, this number jumped to 74, 127, 172, and then to more than 500 in 2021 and more than 400 in 2022. Some of the requests required the extraction and redaction of thousands of emails. It was time-consuming and tedious work. Most nights I would leave work at five thirty or six. Two Tuesdays a month I would have to stay for school board meetings that would last eight or more hours, resulting in me getting home well past midnight.

At home, my district-issued cell phone would stay on until ten at night. There were always members of the media and principals contacting me after hours as I would try to doze in front of the TV. Sometimes I would jump on a Microsoft Teams (LCPS's videoconference platform) call using the spare computer I kept set up on the kitchen table. These late-night meetings were frequent enough that senior administration got to know the look of each other's kitchens and sleepwear. Nighttime emergencies would center on rumors of violence. Some off-kilter, diplomatically speaking, student, usually a middle schooler, would be online posing with a gun, or a lookalike gun, threatening to go on a shooting rampage the next morning. Regardless of the veracity of such content, as soon as it hit social media, we would need to act before people started warning students and fellow parents not to come to school the next day, fearful that a possible mass shooting was planned.

We would send mass emails stating that the rumors were false, the schools were safe, and that extra law enforcement would be on campus the following day—simply as a precaution. Only then could we shut down our computers and return our kitchens to their normal state.

Before LCPS would post such a message, law-enforcement officers would be sent to the student's home to do a threat assessment. Was there a gun in the house? Was the student or their family in a state of mental distress? These scenarios always involved a lot of hurry up and wait as the process played out. The vast majority of the time, it was just a kid screwing around with a lookalike weapon.

Outside of these regular duties, my job also entailed dealing with some bizarre incidents that fell into the category of "You can't make this shit up."

The most unusual event I ever had to deal with involved a drill featuring the CIA and the Loudoun County Sheriff's Office. The CIA planted actual plastic explosives under the hoods of school buses parked at one of our high schools. The exercise was held during spring break. An assistant principal authorized the use of school property for the drill without the knowledge of the central office. The idea was that bomb-sniffing dogs would locate the explosives in a real-life setting. The CIA provided ten slabs of plastic explosive in a special container.

After the drill, it collected nine.

The fact that the CIA couldn't count to ten put a severe dent in my faith in our national security apparatus.

The wayward piece of plastic explosive traveled several hundred miles in the engine compartment of a special needs bus until the vehicle came in for routine maintenance. The mechanic who discovered it removed the explosive from the engine compartment and plopped it down on the desk of the transportation director. A career Army veteran, the director immediately knew what it was.

Of course, news of such a discovery didn't stay in-house. The tale of the plastic explosive on the school bus reached local reporters before I'd made the five-mile drive to the LCPS bus garage. News of the "shocking" discovery was online before I had a chance to find out the facts of the matter. The following days witnessed a reporter from CNN, Tom Foreman, and all the local news outlets exploring this imminent danger to LCPS students.

The CIA sent out an expert spokesman who assured us local spokesmen that the CIA would take full responsibility for this faux pas. He would be by our sides every step of the way as we dealt with the media. He explained that the plastic explosive was actually quite safe, as it could only be detonated by a special electrical charge. It was designed so that soldiers carrying such explosives in combat didn't wipe out their platoon if enemy fire struck them. Hell, the spokesman said, you could even use a slab of plastic explosive for a frying pan over a campfire.

Having imparted this knowledge, the CIA spokesman decided he'd done enough. As the sheriff and I exited the front door to face the media, the CIA spokesman snuck out the back, which I suppose was a very CIA-like thing to do.

Being ready for any and every strange, tragic, and just plain stupid incident schools can generate required constant readiness on my part. There was a constant stream of work; something that suited my workaholic nature perfectly.

Weekends meant that my phone was always with me along with a "go pack," a spare computer and Internet hot spot, in my car so that I could send emergency messages and deal with the media no matter where I might be, which was usually at the home of one of my two married daughters. Once, I had shut the phone off for a couple of hours on a Saturday to help a son-in-law move firewood in the wilds of West Virginia. Coincidentally, a message needed to go out that schools would be closed for activities (church services, recreational sports leagues) the next day because of an impending winter storm. The need for this message was deemed so urgent that it couldn't wait for the hour or two I had been devoting to my family. Kim Goodlin stepped up and sent out the message.

Social media lit up.

Who was this woman?

What happened to Wayde?

Had he been fired?

Was he dead?

The next time I sent out a phone message, I made sure to thank Kim publicly, lest anyone think something horrible had happened or that she had somehow usurped me.

I was foolishly proud of the fact that I hadn't taken a sick day since I had started working full-time on January 5, 1981. I came to LCPS on June 21, 2000, after a twenty-year career in newspapers. I accrued more than two hundred days of sick leave and unused vacation with LCPS. I suppose that I got my philosophy about sick days from gym class at Mahwah, New Jersey, Junior-Senior High School. This class was taught by a group of ex-Marines who did their best to recreate Camp Lejeune one hour at a time. I can still remember one of them, John Carty, bellowing, "There are two reasons for missing physical education at Mahwah Junior-Senior High School, the death of a close relative or your own." Carty was the school's head basketball coach. A seat belt had been attached to the bench to control his volatile sideline demonstrations. Carty coached until a few weeks before his death from cancer. He definitely practiced what he preached.

The payout for my unused sick leave, upon retirement, would be $19,054.39. I accumulated 3,659.5 hours of leave, meaning my leave was worth $5.20 per hour.

I am a workaholic. Note to workaholics: You will never get paid what you're worth.

Workaholism was promoted by the superintendent who hired me for Loudoun County Public Schools, Dr. Edgar Butler Hatrick III. As his name might imply, Dr. Hatrick was the product of upper-crust New York society (his grandfather had been a powerful figure in the Hearst news syndicate, back when William Randolph Hurst was a major force in American life). If there was one person who raised the quality of Loudoun's schools to that of a nationally recognized educational leader, it was the man I will always refer to as "Dr. Hatrick."

An imposing man, at 6'5", Dr. Hatrick was an amazing public speaker with a deep, resonant voice. He was a 1963 graduate of Loudoun County High School and came back to teach at his alma mater shortly after graduating from the University of Richmond. In short order, he became assistant principal of Broad Run High School, then principal of Loudoun County High School, and was then taken into the central administration. Dr. Hatrick became superintendent in 1991 after an outsider spectacularly flamed out. He was truly invested in Loudoun County, its schools, school staff, and, above all, its students. He worked incredibly long hours and oversaw the operation of schools during the day and one of the largest construction operations in Virginia at night. A nationally recognized educational leader, he was elected president of the American Association of School Administrators.

All of his accomplishments, however, did not keep Dr. Hatrick from effectively being fired in 2013 on a 5-to-4 vote. Dr. Hatrick was up for a four-year contract renewal and, with forty-six-and-a-half years of service to LCPS, wanted to pass the half-century mark. The board that fired him had come in on the Tea Party wave, a precursor of the hyper-partisan politics that followed. A charade was engineered whereby Dr. Hatrick would announce his "retirement" and leave at the end of the following school year.

The Tea Party board wanted to be involved at all levels of school operation, including selecting principals. A school division, however, can only have one master. If a school board member was constantly calling school-level employees to inject themselves into daily operations, the school employee had to wonder who their true boss was and to whom they needed to answer.

Ten Bosses Equals Nine Too Many

The interview process that sought Dr. Hatrick's replacement was a farce. Experienced candidates backed away when they learned of the restrictions that the school board wanted to place on the superintendent's authority. In the end, a weak, "reach" candidate that the school board could push around was hired.

And thus began the slow, board-inflicted decline of Loudoun County Public Schools. As a school board member noted in 2022: "When Dr. Hatrick left, unfortunately, Loudoun has become the Wild West."

As I look back on this, I can't be objective about Dr. Hatrick's replacement, Dr. Eric Williams. Having a familial relationship with Dr. Hatrick makes that impossible. The kindest way to view Williams is that he was in over his head where LCPS was concerned.

Williams did give me one incredible moment of glory/near heart attack, however.

At 3:45 a.m. on March 12, 2020, I was awakened from a dead sleep by the landline in my bedroom. Williams told me that he had decided to close school for two weeks because of the pandemic. We were the first school division in Virginia to do so. He had told no one, not even members of his cabinet, that this was going to happen. He needed me to send a message to all parents and staff by 5:15 a.m.

And the message, which was quite long, needed to be translated into Spanish for both an email and a phone message. Finding a translator at 3:45 in the morning was not easy. Recording a lengthy message after being woken from a dead sleep was no easy matter either.

As I had always done in such situations, I called Kim Goodlin, who oversaw the Blackboard Connect communication system. After we shared a joint freak-out, she jumped on the first major task of the pandemic. We secured a translator, loaded the text, and recorded and sent the message by 5:15 a.m.

That's who I am: the guy who gets things done in an emergency.

The first call when you're in trouble.

At least that's who I was.

The Road to Crazy Town

The story of how Loudoun County became ground zero for the national culture war over education involved a variety of factors: the evolving nature of Loudoun County and its changing population, how those changes affected its schools, Virginia politics in the 2020s, and the role of a seasoned political operative advancing himself by magnifying the insignificant into national news.

This journey also involved the school division and the school board that oversaw everything stepping on the "third rails" of societal rage—race, the pandemic, and gender-identity politics—repeatedly.

Loudoun County had been a sleepy exurb of Washington, DC, for decades, boasting more cows than people. That all began to change with the opening of Dulles International Airport in 1962. Slowly, population growth began to accelerate, eventually resulting in massive growth from 1990 on.

According to US Census data, Loudoun had 86,129 residents in 1990. By the end of 2022, this number had ballooned to 453,554. More than 10,000 people moved to the county every year, and the population routinely grew between 2 and 3 percent annually. Big tech blew into Loudoun in the 1990s and transformed the area's economy. Once known as "horse country," Loudoun was now a densely populated suburb where AOL could establish its headquarters off Waxpool Road, near Dulles. The time of the tech boom marked a migration of wealth from the eastern section of the county to the west and south.

Homeowner associations (HOAs) became Loudoun's de facto political parties. In addition to governing grass length and mailbox colors, HOAs lobbied aggressively for their residents to remain in certain schools. Given Loudoun's record population growth, this was impossible. However, school boards sometimes adopted these HOA-generated plans, which led to odd-shaped boundaries that forced less-powerful HOAs or unaffiliated residents to make long trips to school.

Given this record growth and its proximity to DC, the county was now home to tech giants like Amazon, Verizon, Telos, and Orbital Sciences, all supported by seventy data centers and counting. A surge in US Department of Homeland Security personnel, including current and former military and intelligence workers, filled up the generic-looking high-rise buildings ringing the Beltway. Many were drawn to Loudoun because of the (relative to Fairfax) cheap housing and high-quality schools.

Loudoun's growth was accompanied by a huge influx of wealth. Starting in 2008, the IRS ranked Loudoun as the wealthiest county in America with a population of more than 65,000. Such wealth often led to strange behaviors, such as baby-producing contests. Some families in the county sought to have four or more children with a stay-at-home mom to display just how wealthy they were. And wealth brings with it entitlement. Parents expected high grades (nothing less than a 4.2), stardom in athletics, and cutting-edge facilities. This led to the construction of schools with truly breathtaking amenities (maker and collaboration spaces, dramatic lighting, college-grade athletic training facilities, coffee shops).

Loudoun was once reliably Republican. For decades, it had elected conservative congressmen like Frank Wolf and George Allen and sent service-oriented representatives such as Delegate Joe May to the General Assembly. Wolf was someone who could work across the aisle to serve the public good and a man of great human decency. He cared about the poor and downtrodden of this world, exhibited by his leadership of the gleaning of local orchards to find fruit for local food banks. He also personally investigated the genocides in Darfur by visiting that embattled region of Western Sudan. Joe May, a self-made millionaire, built a leading technology company from scratch. In the General Assembly, he championed legislation to enhance the technical capabilities of the poorest parts of Virginia. As a sign of our fractured times, May was primaried by an ultra-Right candidate who did not share his sense of public service.

Frank Wolf was replaced by a protégé, Barbara Comstock, a never-Trumper who was defeated by progressive Democrat Jennifer Wexton after two terms. Stripped of its moderates, Loudoun's Republican party turned increasingly toward crazy conspiracy theories and race-mongering as its numbers shrank—resulting in dire consequences for LCPS.

Majority Minority

On June 21, 2021, then-Superintendent Dr. Scott Ziegler presented "Promise and Progress: Report on Equity 2021" to a work session of the school board. While not one member of the media showed up and very few members of the public attended, it was a revelatory moment.

For the first time, an LCPS superintendent highlighted the fact that LCPS had become a majority-minority district. This demographic shift was, I believe, at the bottom of much of the turmoil surrounding the school division. According to numbers from the LCPS Research Department, LCPS had 19,927 students, 84 percent of them White, in 1995. By 2021, that number had ballooned to 81,703, with only 43.4 percent of the student population describing their ethnicity as White. Sixty-two of the LCPS schools had become majority-minority (Asian and Hispanic students made up the major minorities), with several more nearing a tipping point for this status.

Additionally, wealthy, academically inclined Indians made up the fastest-growing minority group. These tectonic shifts in demographics led to stresses and strains on school populations, as students and parents grappled with limited competitive college slots; a recipe for increased scrutiny of school educational policies.

A Troubled History with Race

The sins of Loudoun County's racist past are many and well-documented.

When Virginia made public education mandatory in 1870, it was, in fact, mandatory for White people only. What education was available for Black students was offered at standards far below their White peers.

Loudoun County was certainly not an exception to this practice.

Despite its reputation for refinement, Loudoun County history is littered with racial aggressions, including a lynching on the grounds of Leesburg High School in 1917. As with many Southern towns, a Confederate soldier statue was placed in front of the county courthouse in 1908. It wasn't removed until 2020.

LCPS records show that, in 1925, the annual salary of a White teacher was $836.10, while Black teachers were paid $358.12. The same year, the county spent an average of $29.27 to educate a White student and $9.81 for a Black child.

The integration of schools mandated by the Supreme Court's *Brown v. Board of Education of Topeka* decision in 1954 remained only a suggestion in Loudoun. In 1957, the school board hired Clarence Bussinger, an expert in fighting integration, as LCPS's superintendent. Bussinger spearheaded a legal effort that kept LCPS from fully integrating until 1968.

Over the years, racial animus continued to bubble up time and again over things like Confederate mascots and logos. Battles moved back and forth, with community members across the political spectrum fighting over the line between remembering history and acknowledging racism.

LCPS's 2020 racial reckoning, however, went far beyond changing mascots.

The 2020–2021 LCPS Employee Handbook contained the "Superintendent's Equity Statement." In part, it read: "When students and staff experience racial insults, slurs, and/or other hate speech, we lack the positive culture and climate that supports students' growth."

So far, so good. Nobody supports hate speech.

But then the language went over the top. "LCPS calls for all students, staff, families, and other members of our community to engage in the disruption and dismantling of white supremacy."

This apparently radical bit of prose came back to haunt LCPS again and again. Disrupting and dismantling White supremacy was far beyond the reach of the school division, and the language inflamed those who deny that there is such a thing as White supremacy. It was a shot in the culture war that never should have been fired.

Cultural Flashpoints

There are several key incidents that turned Loudoun into a political and cultural battleground. They involved race, the worldwide pandemic, and gender equity. While not unique to Loudoun, these combustible ingredients combined in this venue to produce an absolutely toxic political environment.

The Underground Railroad Jumps the Tracks in 2019

As part of Black History Month, three physical education teachers at Madison's Trust Elementary School conducted an "Underground Railway Simulation." This simulation had been around for decades and was sometimes used as a team-building exercise. Basically, one group of participants was dubbed escaped slaves. Another group was tasked with playing the role of the conductors along the Underground Railroad who helped the escaped slaves overcome obstacles.

This lesson was once endorsed by the Virginia Association for Health, Physical Education, Recreation, and Dance (VAHPERD), which is the professional association for Virginia's physical education teachers. But this endorsement was dated by the time the simulation was used at Madison's Trust; society's views of such exercises had definitely changed. This exercise was done in third-grade gym classes. About ten families complained about it.

Was the timing of the Underground Railway Simulation at Madison's Trust tone deaf and insensitive?

Yes. It couldn't have been worse.

It came on the heels of the revelation that Virginia Governor Ralph Northam had posed in blackface for a photo featured in a long-ago yearbook. With tensions high, the community sought other examples of racism.

Realizing its error, Madison's Trust Principal Dave Stewart emailed the community apologizing for the exercise on February 12, 2019. "The lesson was culturally insensitive to our students and families. I extend my sincerest apology to students and the school community."

The official messaging seemed to have quieted things down until late on the evening of Thursday, February 21. That's when I received a furious phone call from Shomari Stone, a WRC-TV reporter. He wanted a statement on the racist game played at Madison's Trust and was going on air in a few minutes. I, politely, let Stone know that I would not be making a statement until I knew what, specifically, LCPS was being accused of. A few minutes later, I switched on Channel 4 and saw Stone talking to Michelle Thomas, also known as "Pastor Michelle."

Pastor Michelle dubbed the Underground Railroad Simulation the "Runaway Slave Game," which the media ate up. Rumors started circulating that Black children were deliberately assigned the role of slaves and that White students had chased them in the guise of "slave catchers."

"Loudoun County has a history of misleading kids, number one, and perpetuating racist things among our students," Pastor Michelle told the media. "This is not the first one."

The next day, I turned on the morning news and saw three reporters working live in front of Madison's Trust. I drove more than fifty miles at breakneck speed, reaching the school before the morning news programs ended. Schmoozing the reporters (all amiable types I was acquainted with), I deployed the official statement that I had used with the increasing number of media outlets calling for comment. "We tell our children to be responsible for their mistakes. We made a mistake. Slavery is never a game." Most media outlets seemed satisfied with this observation, and things died down again for a week.

Then the "Black Panthers" showed up.

As students and parents entered Madison's Trust on March 1, a van pulled up. Six African Americans, clad in black, headed for the main entrance. A parent entering the building with a tardy student held the door open for these "visitors," a clear violation of safety protocols.

The six unauthorized visitors entered the main office.

They identified themselves as members of the Black Panther Party of Virginia and said that they had traveled from Roanoke, a distance of 181 miles, to demand the firing of the teachers who had conducted the Underground Railroad Simulation. The group at Madison's Trust bore no resemblance to the original Black Panther Party, which had actually disbanded way back in 1982.

One "Black Panther," a small woman, carried a large stick, which she dubbed the "Staff of Truth." Dave Stewart met the unwelcome visitors and calmly defused the situation. A video taken by the "Panthers" showed a peaceful, impromptu meeting, albeit one with an air of underlying tension. The "Panthers" wanted the gym teachers fired, and Stewart firmly stood his ground. After a few minutes, the conversation fizzled, and the Panthers left.

Unbeknownst to Stewart, one of his employees had called the sheriff's office about people "possibly being disorderly inside the office of the school." As the "Panthers" were leaving, nine sheriff's office cruisers rolled up to Madison's Trust—the expected response when a call for help goes out from a school. It was appropriate in scale because "disorderly" could have meant anything, up to and including the display of a weapon. There was no confrontation between the deputies and the "Panthers." They got in their van and drove into oblivion.

Both LCPS and the sheriff's office put out messages about a brief disturbance at the school; there had been no threat to the overall safety of the school community.

The school seemed to have dodged a bullet until late in the afternoon, when what I can only describe as a highly fictionalized article about the Black Panthers and Madison's Trust showed up on the right-wing blog, *The Bull Elephant*. The author, Jeanine Martin, was a Republican activist in the wilds of western Loudoun County. Martin's article contained alarming "details" that bore virtually no connection to reality. "This morning two black vans, with darkened windows, pulled up to the school, ran over safety cones, and unloaded a large group of Black Panthers. Children were arriving and seven or eight Panthers simply followed the students into the school. The Black Panthers were dressed all in black, stormed the principals [*sic*] office, brandishing huge sticks as weapons, yelling and threatening Principal Dave Stewart. The Panthers filmed the incident. The sheriff's office was called and 15 deputies, in marked and unmarked cars, arrived on the scene."

The article caused political panic. The board of supervisors pressured the sheriff's office to put out a second statement, which it did late on Friday night. By Saturday morning, Superintendent Dr. Eric Williams decided that a community meeting would have to be held Sunday afternoon at Madison's Trust.

The Sunday afternoon meeting came on the cusp of a blizzard, resulting in a hard stop time of three in the afternoon. The faux Panthers seemed to have created the desired effect, as they scared the living shit out of Ashburn's White population. Several hundred adults—overwhelmingly White—packed the multipurpose room.

Dave Stewart and central office representatives, including Superintendent Williams, sat at the front of the room and fielded questions from the audience. Armed with microphones, Director of Elementary Education Mike Martin and I roamed through the audience.

For the first hour or so, the discourse was civil, if somewhat awkward. Then I noticed three people standing silently at the front of the room. They turned out to be the gym teachers who had staged the Underground Railroad Simulation. The superintendent did not wish to give in to their dramatic appearance at the front of the gathering by allowing them to speak, a decision I agreed with. This meeting was for parents, and they had time limits on their questions, no follow-ups allowed. At length, then-school board Chair Jeff Morse instructed the superintendent to let the teachers speak.

What followed, according to those with intimate knowledge of the whole Underground Railroad fiasco, was a fictionalized version of the teachers' actions. As one teacher watched silently, the other two read from a seven-page, typewritten lesson plan that no one else seemed to recall. They listed, in excruciating detail, all of the pedagogical reasons that their lesson was sound. At the end of their presentation, which far exceeded the time offered to other speakers, the audience broke out in loud, sustained applause.

Order broke down.

That blizzard-imposed stop time worked out well, as things quickly began to escalate out of control.

At the front of the room, a Black sports journalist tried to refocus the gathering on its original intent. He was heckled from the audience by people talking in stage whispers; they could be heard by the journalist, but not the audience at-large. One man, a blond, crew-cut government type, whispered, "Your people are the majority of the prison population." The Black journalist exploded in reaction to such an extent that his wife walked out of the room in frustration.

The aftermath of the Madison's Trust episode far outlasted the initial drama.

Dave Stewart was unfairly vilified and assaulted by all points on the outrage spectrum. A boyish-looking man as he entered middle age, Stewart had been the principal of one of LCPS's most-disadvantaged schools,

Guilford, before he came to wealthy, suburban Ashburn and Madison's Trust, which he opened. Stewart was scheduled to be named LCPS's Principal of the Year in April 2019, an honor that was quickly rescinded after this episode.

Eighteen months after the events of February 2019, Dave and I held an unofficial, informal "debrief," and my key takeaway from the discussion was my sadness at the lasting trauma inflicted on a good man.

Emboldened by the media attention she received from Madison's Trust, Pastor Michelle became a constant presence on Loudoun's landscape. She developed the habit of staging press opportunities, unannounced, at the Administration Building. She would show up, commandeer a room or hallway, and set up shop. The media always attended, knowing Michelle would provide a controversial sound bite.

The Equity Collaborative

To deal with its perceived problems with race, LCPS hired the Equity Collaborative of Hillsborough, North Carolina. The Equity Collaborative held twenty-four focus groups and interviews at LCPS schools between mid-April and the end of May 2019. This work cost LCPS $120,000. On June 6, the Equity Collaborative presented its report, *Systematic Equity Assessment: A Picture of Racial Equity Challenges and Opportunities in Loudoun County Public School District*, to the school board.

The five themes the focus groups reflected on were generic concerns you could find in Anytown USA:

1. People were unclear and fearful about how to participate in conversations about race, let alone respond to racially charged incidents.
2. Educator focus groups indicated a desire to recruit and hire diverse school staff that reflected student racial and language backgrounds.

3. Economic diversity across the county/division complicated the discussions about race, leading many people to steer the conversation away from race to focus on poverty.
4. Discipline policies and practices disproportionately negatively impacted students of color, particularly Black/African-American students.
5. Many English learners, Black/African-American, Latinx, and Muslim students had experienced the sting of racial insults/slurs or racially motivated violent actions.

The report did not include recommendations for the unique needs of LCPS.

The Equity Collaborative then gave the school board four primary recommendations to deal with these problems.

1. Produce and publish on the "Superintendent's Message" page a new division-authored statement defining and condemning White supremacy, hate speech, hate crimes, and other racially motivated acts of violence. Require individual school sites include this message on their webpage and in communications to parents twice a year (not only in response to an incident).
2. Review the current/establish a clear policy with built-in accountability for addressing racially motivated acts and create proactive leadership measures to address the use of racial insults. Name that the N-word is not tolerated by anyone in LCPS.
3. Design additional opportunities for LCPS educators to engage in professional learning about color consciousness and instructional efforts across the division.
4. Revise the current/establish a short- and long-range action plan to address challenges related to hiring for diversity, equity, and inclusion.

I couldn't help but feel disappointed. Despite the money spent, here it was: the best generic advice money could buy, cut-and-paste solutions to unique local problems.

This was not a sentiment shared by LCPS. Pleased with the initial product from the Equity Collaborative, LCPS contracted for more services, particularly instruction for upper-level personnel so that they could impart the wisdom they received to their subordinates for further dissemination to the masses. One of the training modules for upper-level LCPS staff included this description: "follow up meetings focused on Critical Race Theory Development." The right-wing media had a field day with this language—here was proof of LCPS introducing Critical Race Theory (CRT) training at its highest level so that it could be forced down into the student curriculum.

Altogether, LCPS paid the Equity Collaborative $348,167, generating public uproar and proving the kind of generic work you get from a consultant is never a bargain.

Equity in the Center

Part of the Equity Collaborative's June 6, 2019, report on LCPS stated the need for increased professional development regarding race and the changing nature of Loudoun's student population. "While LCPS has a long history of providing educators with high-quality professional development and support on instructional matters, few LCPS educators have had formal training or support on appropriately weaving social and cultural differences into the fabric of schools and classrooms. Hence, issues such as poverty, race, gender identity, and sexual orientation are perceived as not only difficult to traverse or poorly traversed, but better left untouched or ignored."

In response, LCPS's Department of Instruction developed a three-part training module entitled "Equity in the Center." This training was developed hastily and presented at the August 2019 Administrative Leadership

Team (ALT) meeting. It was ill-received on virtually all fronts. I will say, up front, school personnel do need to learn about diversity. Like most school systems in America, LCPS's teachers are overwhelmingly White and female. While the vast majority of LCPS teachers are not deliberately callous or discriminatory toward minority students, some are not as culturally sensitive toward, and informed about, minority students as they should be. Such was the case of a White teacher who told a student of Middle Eastern heritage, "I don't negotiate with terrorists." While the Equity in the Center module sought to alter such behavior, it was heavy-handed and simplistic. Using crude graphics and videos and concepts rife with diversity buzzwords not tied to actual research, it didn't enlighten administrators, but rather, angered many. When the Equity in the Center training reached the teaching ranks, the results were even worse.

One chart used in the training separated groups into "experiences privilege" or "experiences oppression." Among the groups experiencing privilege: Christians. An animated video, "The Unequal Opportunity Race," depicted White people getting a head start while people of color waited before facing a series of deliberate obstacles. This training explored concepts such as "White Privilege," "White Fragility," and CRT. CRT had already become a lightning rod nationally, and now the term was being thrown around in Loudoun County. Simply put, CRT examines social, political, and legal structures and power distribution through the lens of race. It examines bias in laws and legal institutions that result in the highly disproportionate rate of incarceration for minorities. CRT is usually taught at the graduate school level, and then in great depth. A two-hour, staff-development session was not going to be able to explain all of its nuances. Giving a shallow explanation of CRT was begging for trouble.

And indeed, LCPS was soon in trouble. Parents charged that LCPS teachers were being indoctrinated into CRT-thinking and then subtly changing their curriculum to indoctrinate students in this "radical" philosophy. While there was no actual course labeled CRT, critics argued that its tenets were seeping into Loudoun's curriculum.

Superintendent Eric Williams didn't exactly dispel this notion in a September 18, 2020, email to a stakeholder that eventually found its way into the public. "While LCPS has not adopted CRT, some of the principles related to race as a social construct and the sharing of stories of racism, radicalized oppression, etc. that we are encouraging through the Action Plan to Combat Systematic Racism, in some of our professional learning modules, and our use of instructional resources on the Social Justice standards, do align with the ideology of CRT." It would be hard to find a better example of nuanced educational gobbledygook. Employing nuanced educational gobbledygook in a culture war was like bringing the proverbial knife to a gunfight.

Personally, I sloughed off the Equity in the Center training's inadequacies because my bar for bad lectures was pretty high. While I was inclined to let the Equity in the Center training slide as a misfire, other LCPS employees weren't nearly as forgiving. Monica Gill, an American history teacher at Loudoun County High School, was among the most vocal critics.

She expressed her views at school board meetings and in articles in conservative media. "I didn't grow up in white privilege. I worked hard to get through college, and it wasn't handed to me by any stretch. It seemed to me that this whole thing they were pushing was very shallow." In this, I did agree with Monica Gill; meaningful discussions of concepts such as Critical Race Theory, White privilege, and White fragility can't be had in a few hours of professional development. Even when discussed at great length in graduate school, they can cause controversy between different factions highly educated on the topic.

Equity Ambassadors

Moving on from shallow professional development, LCPS created the Equity Ambassador program. As well-intentioned as the program may have been, it was interpreted by the Right as an assault on conservative values. The vague mission of the Equity Ambassador program didn't help the school division defend it.

Originally, the Equity Ambassadors were meant to be a small group of minority students representing LCPS schools who would consult with the director of equity's office to discuss school climate concerns. When people complained that only minority students could serve as ambassadors, the program was opened to students with a "passion for social justice." Of course, the Right saw words like "passion for social justice" as code for "woke social warriors intent on attacking the American way of life." Fueling this paranoia was the Bias Incident Reporting System. This consisted of an online form that allowed students to anonymously report alleged incidents of bias involving students and teachers and request an administrative investigation. Panicked parents on the Right promoted the specter of "hit lists," with students and teachers who voiced unpopular views on race and gender being singled out for retribution. They also claimed that the existence of this reporting system would have a "chilling effect" on those exercising their First Amendment rights.

For its part, LCPS said that the information collected by the Bias Incident Reporting System was used only to inform discussions by the Equity Ambassadors. No disciplinary actions were taken as a result of these reports. Such reassurances fell on deaf ears. The Liberty Justice Center sued LCPS, and the Equity Ambassador program was soon the object of favorable and unfavorable court rulings that ensured it would be debated by the judicial system for years.

The Attorney General Calling Loudoun County Public Schools Racist

Heading into the 2020s, Loudoun started to see the impact of the culture wars on individual political races. On November 18, 2020, Virginia Attorney General Mark Herring signed a finding by his office's Division of Human Rights that

LCPS had discriminated against minority students applying to its Academy of Science. For the 2018 to 2019 school year, 2,116 students had applied to the Academy of Science, including 65 Black students. Only one Black student and two Native Americans and/or Pacific Islanders had been accepted for admission. The incoming class had 353 Asians and 104 White students. The attorney general's office recommended a sixty-one-page conciliation process.

Knowing Mark Herring, and his wife, Laura, personally, I respected his opinion.

Raised by a single mom, Herring graduated from Loudoun Valley High School and worked construction to put himself through college. He served as attorney general between 2014 and 2022. In 2019, Herring became embroiled in Virginia's blackface scandal. An old yearbook showed that Governor Ralph Northam had dressed in blackface during medical school. Northam waffled about whether the photo was really him. Herring called for Northam to resign. Then it turned out that Herring had his own past appearance in blackface.

To his credit, Herring owned up to the incident: "In 1980, when I was a 19-year-old undergraduate in college, some friends suggested we attend a party dressed like rappers we listened to at the time, like Kurtis Blow, and perform a song." The damage had been done and, with a weak top of the Democratic ticket, Herring's campaign was in trouble as the 2021 election approached.

On November 2, 2021, Herring lost his bid for a third term, 50.4 percent to 49.6 percent, to Jason Miyares. They were separated by only 26,536 votes out of 3,267,664 cast.

When Herring conceded the next day, I felt very bad for him.

Looking back at this from a 2024 vantage point, I feel very bad for me.

How the Pandemic Heightened
Culture War Tensions

The new school board's fate was effectively sealed on March 12, 2020, when Superintendent Eric Williams closed schools for two weeks because of the looming pandemic. This was the first of many such closures in Virginia. In retrospect, Williams made the right call. Only one LCPS employee, an older substitute teacher, died from COVID-19. Cases among LCPS students and staff were low. LCPS became a model of communications transparency regarding the pandemic. Letters were sent to school communities each time a case was reported. Graphics on the LCPS website, updated daily, showed the number of COVID-19 cases the school division was aware of.

The initial closure coincided roughly with LCPS's spring break. The school division's buildings were scrubbed floor-to-ceiling, as was the Administration Building. An emergency school board meeting was held the following Friday. As I departed the Administration Building, I assumed I would be back in two weeks.

Of course, I couldn't have been more wrong.

During the next eighteen months, there were heroic efforts and epic failures dealing with the pandemic where LCPS was concerned.

LCPS accomplished some amazing things in response to the pandemic.

The school division distributed thirteen million meals; setting up drop-off points throughout the county and using school buses to deliver food. In addition, parents and students could drive up to schools to receive meals.

LCPS distributed twelve thousand computers for online learning and was able to navigate supply chain issues through efficient procurement, supplying enough computers and hot spots so everyone could work online.

The school division set up a clinic at Brambleton Middle School that administered 21,000 COVID-19 vaccines to school staff during a seven-week period in early 2021, which allowed staff to prepare for schools to reopen.

However, the school division and school board failed miserably at executing the primary thing parents were seeking: formulating a plan to get students back in school. Of course, Loudoun was not alone in this failure, and circumstances far beyond the control of the board fueled its futility. While the country's president talked about ingesting bleach as a potential cure, the federal Centers for Disease Control and Prevention and state and local health departments constantly revised standards as to when it would be safe to resume public gatherings. LCPS's failure involved gathering a great deal of data with great public fanfare and then doing absolutely nothing. It advertised "sprints" during which it took polls and held focus groups, gathering data intended to shape a policy to reopen schools. It presented this data to the school board at regular meetings and special meetings. It was discussed at length.

And then LCPS did nothing.

After the initial scrubbing of schools, classroom doors were sealed to prevent contamination. Furniture was moved out of schools and placed in specially rented containers. Millions were spent on plastic shields to be placed around desks and millions more on personal protective equipment (PPE). Still, schools remained closed to all but a few special needs students.

A continually changing set of metrics for when in-person instruction could start frustrated parents on all sides of the educational spectrum.

In retrospect, I think we could have placed students on alternating-day schedules, with half the students attending at one time while the other half attended virtually. Some of the smaller school divisions in Northern Virginia did this with no calamitous results. Keeping students out of school for a long period of time did produce calamitous results regarding their mental health. After school resumed in-person instruction for the 2021–2022 school year, principals told me that there was a marked change in student behavior. This was especially evident at the middle school level.

Students who physically left school as fourth- and fifth-graders came back as sixth- and seventh-graders with no idea how to act like a young adult. They spoke in a manner that they had become accustomed to online. This did not go over well face-to-face.

How *The Cat in the Hat* Struck Back

If you're going to pick a hill to die on, make sure it's not occupied by Dr. Seuss. Taking on a cultural icon, even through an earnest memo, is a very bad idea.

In 2017, the National Education Association (NEA) suggested that schools de-emphasize Dr. Seuss and read more culturally inclusive works. Minority characters in his works tended toward racist stereotypes, and Seuss had drawn overtly racist cartoons during his early career as an advertising artist and cartoonist. Dr. Seuss later admitted that his earlier work did not reflect the philosophy of the bulk of his children's literature.

The NEA did not renew its contract with Dr. Seuss Enterprises, the entity that oversaw the author's estate.

In February of 2021, a member of LCPS's central administration issued a memo reminding building-level administrators that Read Across America Day should include stories that reflect the diverse nature of students. "Realizing that many schools continue to celebrate 'Read Across America Day' in partial recognition of Dr. Seuss' birthday, it is important for us to be cognizant of research that may challenge our practice in this regard. As we become more culturally responsive and racially conscious, all building leaders should know that in recent years there has been research revealing racial undertones in the books written and illustrated by Dr. Seuss. We continue to encourage our young readers to read all types of books that are inclusive, diverse, and reflective of our student community, not simply celebrate Dr. Seuss."

The memo leaked to right-wing media, including the *Daily Wire* and Fox News. LCPS made headlines for "canceling" Dr. Seuss. On February 27,

LCPS issued a memo that began, "Dr. Seuss Books have not been banned in Loudoun County Public Schools." In conversations with CNN, *The Washington Post,* and *USA Today*, I drove home this point, which these outlets accepted and magnified. However, social media picked up the Right's echo-chamber talking points, and amplified the furor around the story with vitriolic posts. Dr. Seuss Enterprises announced on March 2, 2021, that it would no longer print titles featuring the most egregious insensitivities. To the great relief of Western Civilization, *The Cat in the Hat* was spared.

Anti-Racism's Bad Name

I circle March 12 on my calendar annually. By some celestial dictate, bad or dramatic things tend to happen on this date.

In March 2020, a group dubbing itself Concerned Parents of Loudoun County sent out a mailer claiming that LCPS "recently teamed up with an extremist organization to teach your children to hate you." In most places, this would have been a huge controversy. In Loudoun, it was just another temporary outrage in a long string of temporary outrages.

In response to the mailer, a Loudoun parent, Jamie Neidig-Wheaton, formed the Facebook group, Anti-Racist Parents of Loudoun County, which grew to 624 members by March 2021.

On March 12, 2021, a member of this group, using the screen name Jen Morse, posted the following:

> *This is a call for volunteers to combat the anti-CRT activities of the P.A.C.T. folks, the stoplcpscrt website, and the like. Looking for folks who are interested in volunteering to organize, lead, execute, and donate regarding the following points:*
>
> *Gather information (community mailing lists, list of folks who are in charge of the anti-CRT movement, list of local lawmaker/ folks in charge)*

Infiltrate (create fake online profiles and join these groups to collect and communicate information, hackers who can either shut down their websites or redirect them to pro-CRT/anti-racist informational webpages)

Spread information (expose these people publicly, create online petitions, create counter-mailings)

Find a way to gather donations for these efforts. Volunteering is great, but these activities can be costly and not everyone has extra funds readily available

Anyone who is interested in this, please feel free to comment here or PM me directly and indicate what you can help with. Then we can hold a kickoff call and start action items

The genius who believed this public site was the ideal place to answer such a plea was a former Latin teacher from Potomac Falls High School, Hilary Hultman-Lee. Hilary wrote: "Regarding the anti-CRT movement, we'd like to compile a document of all known actors and supporters. Please comment below with the legal names of these individuals, area of residence or School Board Rep known, known accounts on social media, and any other info that you feel is relevant."

Amazingly, some people began to—publicly—compile a list.

After a couple years of venting venom and drawing attention to themselves, the fearless culture warriors on the Right were horrified and amazed that the group they dubbed the "Chardonnay Antifa" was fighting back. Complicating the matter, six school board members (Brenda Sheridan, Atoosa Reaser, Ian Serotkin, Denise Corbo, Leslee King, and Beth Barts) joined the Anti-Racist Parents of Loudoun County Facebook group. The board members reasoned that they were seeking to gather input from all elements of the community. They belonged to many Facebook groups in which they were not active participants. This was true in the case of Anti-Racist Parents of Loudoun County, with one notable exception.

Beth Barts posted: "I am very concerned that this (anti-) CRT 'movement' for lack of a better word is gaining support. It is difficult for me to bring attention to it without calling out specifics which may violate our code of conduct." Barts later reacted to a posting about her post. "Thank you for the response to my posting this morning. Silence is complicity."

The school board's membership in this Facebook group, and Barts's participation in it, led to a claim that the board was holding an illegal electronic meeting online. It wasn't; they conducted no business in this forum. Board members are allowed, under Virginia law, to belong to political groups and social organizations, and to interact in such venues, without violating the commonwealth's open-meeting laws. Detractors also claimed that the school board used the Anti-Racist Parents of Loudoun County group to compile a "hit list" to punish its enemies. The Loudoun County Sheriff's Office inaugurated an investigation. In August 2021, it declared that nothing had come of it.

LCPS's Communications and Community Engagement Office created an even-handed message designed to calm the waters—in retrospect an exercise in hopeful naivety—that went out under Superintendent Scott Ziegler's signature on March 19, 2021. "It has come to my attention that individuals, including some identifying themselves as LCPS employees, have made statements across social media about parents and their thoughts about the school division's equity work. LCPS recognizes the right of employees to free speech, but does not condone anyone targeting members of the community for their viewpoint."

As for Jamie Neidig-Wheaton, the founder of Anti-Racist Parents of Loudoun County, in the face of the county's ever-escalating cultural wars, she jumped ship, moving to the West Coast. "It's destroyed my faith in people who claim to be neighbors," Neidig-Wheaton said of the backlash she faced in Loudoun. "I spent months having to worry about my children's safety, while listening to people whose home addresses were never disclosed support the people who publicly tweeted mine."

There are lessons to be learned about the consequences actions on social media bring with them, but few in Loudoun County have taken this course.

Potential Policy 8040

Loudoun County's most-controversial school board policy was the result of an action in 2020 by Virginia's General Assembly under House Bill 145 and Senate Bill 161. The state superintendent informed Virginia school boards that they would need a policy regarding the rights of transgender and gender-expansive students by the beginning of the 2021–2022 school year.

Loudoun's policy (number 8040), which the school board's Legislative and Policy Committee crafted, included the following language:

"Students shall be allowed to use the facility that corresponds to their consistently asserted gender identity (in relation to bathrooms and locker rooms)."

"LCPS staff shall allow gender-expansive or transgender students to use their chosen name and gender pronouns."

The potential policy language inflamed the Right. And unknown to anyone at the time, it was also language that would impact the firestorm to come around bad student behavior in school bathrooms.

Tanner Cross and the School Board

Tanner Cross, a physical education teacher at Leesburg Elementary School, let the world know that he wasn't about to obey any school board policy dictating that transgender students be addressed by their preferred pronouns during public comment at the board's May 25, 2021, meeting. Cross said, "I'm a teacher, but I serve God first. And I will not affirm that a biological boy can be a girl and vice versa, because it's against my religion. It's lying to a child. It's abuse to a child . . . I love all of my students, but I will never lie to them, regardless of the consequences."

At thirty-eight, Cross was a handsome, muscular man who exuded sincerity. He looked like a model gym teacher.

An open face and a closed mind.

I believe Cross spoke anticipating that the school division would take some sort of action against him. In the first of what would be many subsequent tactical errors, Scott Ziegler took just such an action. The superintendent suspended Cross, with pay. Scott told me that there were legal precedents for this action based on court rulings in similar cases in other states. I helped compose a media release stating the school division's stance on the suspension. "Many students and parents at Leesburg Elementary have expressed fear, hurt and disappointment about coming to school." The statement went on to say that while LCPS "respects the rights of public school employees to free speech and free exercise of religion, those rights do not outweigh the rights of students to be educated in a supportive and nurturing environment."

Cross reacted to the suspension with a swiftness that told me that he knew it was coming. Alliance Defending Freedom, a conservative Christian legal group, quickly filed an injunction seeking to void his suspension. On June 8, Loudoun County Circuit Court Judge James Plowman granted Cross's injunction and reinstated him immediately. LCPS appealed Plowman's ruling to the Virginia Supreme Court believing, in the first of many such failed court actions, that more rational minds would prevail at another level of the judiciary.

On August 30, the Supreme Court upheld Plowman's ruling.

The Perfect Political Storm

Loudoun's wealth, diversity, and proximity to Washington provided the ideal ingredients for those seeking political power or the development of a national template for those seeking political power. In the spring of 2021, those swirling cross-currents came together to form the perfect storm after a sexual assault took place in a school bathroom.

The following provides insight into the key players that made Loudoun the centerpiece of America's culture war.

Ian Prior and Fight for Schools

Ian Prior is a parasite on the body politic.

On Fox News, he regularly portrayed himself as a concerned parent first and activist second. "My driving motivation is not the fact that I'm Republican; it's the fact that I'm a parent and I have to send my kids to these schools that I pay for, and I don't want them coming home with a clouded view at a young age when they're not ready to critically think for themselves."

In Loudoun, he billed himself as the executive director of Fight for Schools, a "grassroots" organization dedicated to the recall of the school board. In addition, he was cofounder of the *Daily Malarkey*, CEO of Headwaters Media, and vice president of Mercury Public Affairs.

In reality, Prior was involved in planning political strategy and fundraising on a state and national level for the Republican Party—a very far cry from your average "concerned parent."

The wildest distortion about Fight for Schools was the mission statement on its website: "Fight for Schools is a non-partisan political action committee focused on electing common sense candidates that commit to policies

that support equal opportunity, tolerance, meritocracy and achievement."
It's the only parent activist website that I have ever seen that featured donation buttons: $10 to $250, with an "Other" button for those for whom $250
was not enough.

The first time I met Prior in person was when he collected FOIA documents. He was wearing a "Goonies" T-shirt and shorts.

Prior rebuilt his career after his brief stint working for the Trump administration by vaulting Loudoun to national prominence as the poster child
for what he described as "woke" school policies; he portrayed himself as
the leading voice of sanity protecting parent rights. He was often spotted
outside school board meetings editing scripts and choreographing speakers
for the public comment section. Prior was conspicuously absent from the
calamitous June 22, 2021, school board meeting, which I will detail later in
this book. Occasionally, Prior would take the microphone to threaten school
board members with various legal consequences unless they acquiesced to
his demands.

Prior's efforts went far beyond verbally harassing the school board.

Fight for Schools obtained enough signatures to start a recall hearing
for six school board members in Loudoun County Circuit Court. Virginia's recall laws are fairly complex, justifiably so since such an action seeks to
overturn the results of a general election. To initiate a recall in Virginia, you
must first obtain an amount of signatures equal to 10 percent of the people
who voted in the election that elected the official who is the target of the
recall. The signatures must be those of registered voters in the district from
which the official was elected. The commonwealth's attorney (prosecutor or
district attorney for you non-Virginians) must then determine if the alleged
crimes of the elected official are sufficient to warrant a recall election. The
bar for calling a recall election is very high: misusing or theft of public funds
or the commission of a serious crime.

Fight for Schools alleged that the six Loudoun County School Board
members should be recalled because they "violated state open meeting laws

by joining two closed Facebook groups in which participants discussed issues including school closures and re-openings." The investigation of alleged sexual assaults was a secondary reason for the recall.

Months went by without the necessary signatures being collected, despite Prior saying that an army of volunteers was constantly working on the project. Fight for Schools finally passed the threshold for signatures after haunting polling places during the 2020 election. Petitions for recall were soon filed for school board Chair Brenda Sheridan and Vice Chair Atoosa Reaser. All Loudoun's circuit court judges and the commonwealth's attorney recused themselves from the cases. The impartial substitutes brought in from other jurisdictions to fill these roles decided on May 24, 2021, that there were no grounds for a recall.

The decision on Loudoun's school board mirrored the fate of school board recall efforts nationwide. According to Ballotpedia, there were ninety-two school boards and 237 school board members who faced recall efforts in 2021. The success rate for the recalls was 0.42 percent. In 2022, fifty-one school boards and 117 school board members faced recall. Perhaps due to more focused efforts and lessons learned from past losses, the successful recall rate rose to 6.8 percent (still far short of a wave of removals).

WRC-TV reported on what Fight for Schools planned to do after Loudoun's recall effort failed. "Fight for Schools said it will likely change gears and work to help conservative politicians win elections, focusing first on Virginia's 10th Congressional District." In that election, progressive Congresswoman Jennifer Wexton was reelected, marking another Fight for Schools failure.

Prior was one of the Loudoun County figures prominently featured in the October 30, 2022, CNN documentary *Perilous Politics: America's Dangerous Divide*. During the broadcast, CNN noted that Fight for Schools raised $612,756. Among its backers were prominent Republican political action committees, such as 1776 Action and American Majority.

CNN Senior National Correspondent Kyung Lah asked Prior if he felt responsible for the breakdown of civil political discourse in Loudoun. His reply: "No. I can only speak my mind. I take responsibility for what I say, and for what I do. We condemn threats whether it's to the School Board or the community."

Lah also noted that many people viewed Prior as the villain in the Loudoun County School Board drama. His reply: "Maybe a villain to them, but to others I think they have a very different idea. I'm the person that's basically allowed people to understand that they have a voice and that their voice matters."

Glenn Youngkin

Glenn Youngkin's career was the ultimate product of political opportunism; the place where wealth, social anger, fear, and a weak party infrastructure intersected.

With a fortune estimated at $470 million by *Forbes* at the time of his election, Youngkin spent $20 million of his own money to become governor. He spent $5.5 million of his own money to win a Republican primary in a chaotic field of six candidates.

Like Donald Trump, Youngkin had zero political experience before seeking high elected office. His professional experience encompassed twenty-five years with the Carlyle Group, where he became co-CEO in 2018.

Despite his immense wealth, Youngkin portrayed himself in one ad as a teenager who had to go to work when his father lost his job. The family had enough money to send him to Norfolk Academy, a private school in Virginia Beach for White children whose parents didn't want them to attend integrated public schools. Youngkin went on to attend Harvard Business School.

Depictions of an impoverished youth were political nonsense.

To the general public, Youngkin was the moderate who wanted to govern for all Virginians. On right-wing media, he stoked the cultural fears of frightened White people. Youngkin's ultra-conservative bona fides included the fact that he was an evangelical who started the nondenominational Holy Trinity Church in his basement in 2011.

Youngkin ran a campaign based on the support of Trump supporters while trying to keep Trump at arm's length—MAGA lite.

During his campaign, Youngkin adopted a red fleece vest as his favorite wardrobe accessory, a choice that gave him the air of a suburban dad you might bump into at Costco.

Youngkin's opponent in the general election was former Democratic Governor Terry McAuliffe, who served from 2014 to 2018. With a large head start in the polls, McAuliffe did not appear to take things seriously until the race was almost in a dead heat.

During a debate on September 28, 2021, McAuliffe made a verbal gaffe on par with Hillary Clinton's "basket of deplorables." Asked about removing controversial books from the school curriculum, McAuliffe said: "I'm not going to let parents come into schools and actually take books out and make their own decision . . . I don't think parents should be telling schools what they should teach." McAuliffe's campaign never recovered from the blunder. On November 2, 2021, Youngkin defeated McAuliffe 50.58 percent to 48.64 percent, becoming the first Republican to win a statewide election in Virginia since 2009.

Barely in office, Youngkin started a "quiet" campaign for president that was anything but quiet. Virginia limits its governors to one term. A governor can run for office again after a hiatus of four or more years. Such a return has only been done once. Some governors—Chuck Robb, George Allen, Mark Warner, and Tim Kaine—eventually moved on to the Senate. Given such a limitation, most governors try to make their mark quickly to sustain their political careers. Democrats tended to seek legislation limiting the sale of guns and the expansion of citizens' rights. Republicans enacted tax cuts on everyday necessities such as groceries and cars.

During his first year in office, Youngkin met with mega donors in New York and Utah. He formed a political action committee and a dark-money "social welfare organization." In September 2022, Youngkin hosted a two-day retreat, dubbed the "Red Vest Retreat," outside Charlottesville to map out his political future, Newt Gingrich on hand to help the governor woo major Republican donors.

The quiet campaign did not garner much support.

On February 26, 2023, Youngkin's chief political strategist, Jeff Roe of Axiom Strategies, said that the contest for the 2024 Republican presidential nomination was a "two-person" race between Donald Trump and Ron DeSantis. "There's simply no room for a third or fourth, or even fifth person in this race." (At that time, Fox presidential polling had Youngkin at 1 percent.) Shortly thereafter, Roe departed to join DeSantis's Never Back Down organization. At a subsequent donor retreat in Sea Island, Georgia, Youngkin was uninterested in questions about a possible presidential run.

Reality had set in.

From his quiet presidential campaigning, which effectively ended with his loss of the 2023 General Assembly elections, to his maniacal focus on identity politics and parental rights, it was clear to me how these forces would shape the role Youngkin was to play in the fallout from the sexual assaults involving LCPS.

Jason Miyares

Jason Miyares defeated Mark Herring, a two-time incumbent, in the 2021 attorney general race. A former assistant commonwealth's attorney in Virginia Beach, Miyares was elected as a delegate from that jurisdiction in 2015. He was the first Cuban American elected to the General Assembly (his mother immigrated in 1965).

Shortly after assuming office, Miyares fired seventeen attorneys and thirteen other employees in the attorney general's Office of Civil Rights. He also fired employees working on housing conditions and human trafficking.

Miyares left no doubt about where he stood on the controversies surrounding Loudoun County Public Schools. On November 13, 2021, he held a press conference with Loudoun County Sheriff Mike Chapman at his side. The attorney general-elect announced that he and the governor would change the Code of Virginia so that the attorney general could step in when local officials didn't think that the commonwealth's attorney was doing an adequate job. Miyares also said that he would investigate the sexual assaults involving LCPS.

On January 14, 2022, Miyares laid out his case against LCPS in a media release in advance of Youngkin bringing a special grand jury into existence: "Loudoun County Public Schools covered up a sexual assault on school grounds for political gain . . . Virginians have dealt with the horrific aftermath of these scandals . . . Virginians deserve answers."

Miyares had a pithier observation for Sean Hannity in a January 2022 interview: "What we saw is a school board that went woke, and I like to say, once you go woke, you go broke." There were no financial implications for the school board here, but, when you're spewing catchy jargon, why let facts get in your way? Facts were never what the upcoming investigation was about.

Theophani "Theo" Stamos

The attorney general appointed Theophani "Theo" Stamos as his special assistant overseeing the Loudoun County special grand jury.

A moderate Democrat, she came from a journalism background. Growing up on Chicago's South Side, Theo came to Washington to work for media outlets such as *The Washington Times*, a publication founded by the infamous cult leader Sun Myung Moon. She then worked her way through law school nights at American University.

Theo was a prosecutor for twenty-five years in Arlington County, a suburb of Washington, before being elected its commonwealth's attorney in 2011. During her tenure, she established a drug court and supported a second-chance program for young offenders.

Theo never had a conviction overturned as erroneous during her time as the commonwealth's attorney. Upon further research, that last statement might seem a bit disingenuous. In her last, failed, reelection campaign, more than one hundred lawyers signed an open letter critical of Theo, noting that nearly 98 percent of felony convictions in Arlington came from plea bargains, a much higher percentage than in neighboring jurisdictions. "The number of charges that are brought are insane," lawyer Patrick Anderson told *The Washington Post*. This gave some context for the situation I would find myself in. If you want to pressure someone into a plea agreement, Theo Stamos was the prosecutor you wanted.

Her 2019 bid for reelection exhibited more examples of Theo's misplaced prosecutorial zeal.

As an assistant commonwealth's attorney in 1999, she charged two ten-year-olds—fifth graders—with felonies for allegedly pouring soap into a teacher's drinking water. Theo said that she had brought the charges at the behest of the alleged victim. "The teacher wanted to make sure that those children understood the gravity of what they had done." The ten-year-olds' principal disagreed and said so in a letter to the editor. "I do not believe prosecuting these children helped in any way, nor did it conform to our values in Arlington. Such prosecutions have life-long negative, and sometimes dire, consequences."

Theo charged a fourteen-year-old who tried to open a locked door on a trailer at the county fair with breaking and entering. Theo cited the Florida woman who owned the trailer as the justification for this prosecution. "She felt violated by the fact that someone was trying to get into her home."

These cases stiffened my resolve not to accept a plea deal from Theo Stamos.

After serving out her term of office in Arlington, Theo joined the Trump Justice Department in January 2020. Miyares hired her as special counsel to the attorney general of Virginia for Cold Cases, Actual Innocence and Special Investigations. In a media release announcing Theo's appointment to the Loudoun County special grand jury, Miyares's spokesperson, Victoria LaCivita, stated the rationale for the move: "The Attorney General's Office has every confidence in her ability to conduct a fair, impartial investigation that will provide parents with the explanation and answers they deserve. She has a long track record with conducting investigations and applying the law equally."

During her questioning of witnesses before the special grand jury, Theo made it clear that she had no love for school administrators. She made the following statement on July 12, 2022, evidence of what I believe was inherent bias on her part. "Let me digress a moment by saying when I was in the Commonwealth's Attorney's Office for thirty-two years, we often had concerns with our school system being reluctant to provide information, as they were required to do, about criminal activities at the schools because they don't want to besmirch their individual school, and they don't want to besmirch the Loudoun County school system or Fairfax."

Carlton Davis

Carlton Davis's title was special assistant for investigations, Office of the Attorney General. The son of former Virginia Congressman Tom Davis, he probably got ahead through his familial connections and had never before—at least according to one attorney involved with the special grand jury—handled a criminal case in court. This was evident from some of the stupidities I discovered when reading through the special grand jury transcripts. Davis would make a legal mistake, then call it to the attention of the jurors.

Evidence of Davis's partisanship can also be seen when he lobbied for a position at the University of Virginia. Two Democratic members of the General Assembly called for an ethics probe of the Virginia Attorney

General's Office after they obtained an email in which Davis lobbied for the position the same day that the position's occupant was fired (January 23, 2022, a few days after the Youngkin administration took office).

The position had opened up as a result of the firing of the university's chief counsel, Timothy Heaphy, after he served on the Congressional committee probing the January 6 insurrection. Miyares stated that Heaphy's affiliation with the January 6 committee had nothing to do with his termination. Davis immediately emailed Chief of External Affairs and Policy Klarke Kilgore, lobbying for the University of Virginia job. "When the Loudoun County investigation wraps up in a few months, assuming it is done well and the AG looks good (as is the hope/expectation on my end), as mentioned a couple of times, I'd be very interested in working in the University's Counsel's office."

State Senator Jennifer Boysko asked at the time: "How can we trust any kind of outcome when we know this has all been politically motivated by a staffer who is trying to get a job, a plum job at U.VA?"

Having Carlton Davis working for the prosecution was like having an extra member of the defense team. He would often go on long rants while questioning witnesses before the special grand jury that amounted to improperly offering evidence in the form of his own unsworn commentary. One such rant implied that LCPS's prime motivation was to protect itself: "The system was whatever rules and rationale it deems necessary to protect its own interests, not the interests of the students, not student privacy, not the interests of teachers, not the interest of parents, not the interests of the community, certainly not, you know, the interests of consistency or principle, but really just the interests of Dr. Ziegler and the administration, you know, I just think that's wrong on so many levels.

"I mean, do you have any—I realize I'm testifying here, but do you have any comments in response to that?"

In later court proceedings, it was revealed that the attorney general's office destroyed Davis's official emails thirty days after he left employment there in January 2023.

So much for prosecutorial ethics.

Mike Chapman

The first thing Sheriff Mike Chapman would want you to know is that he was not your typical "County Mounty." After starting his law enforcement career with the Howard County, Maryland, Police Department in 1978, he joined the federal Drug Enforcement Administration (DEA) in 1985 and remained with the DEA until 2008. The first time LCPS administration met with Chapman after his 2012 swearing in, the sheriff made a point of stressing all of the federal law-enforcement experience he and his chief lieutenants had.

Besides his federal background, Chapman could be chiefly characterized by his love for publicity. He never met a camera that he didn't like and made a special point of publicizing any investigation involving the schools his office had undertaken. The first time this happened was when the sheriff's office issued a media release about "magic brownies" found at one of the county's middle schools. The end result of this misadventure? Several panicked middle schoolers showed up at the nurse's office when the effects of the brownies were not as magical as advertised.

Chapman was reelected in 2015, 2019, and 2023. As the years went by, I developed a great working relationship with his primary public information officer, Kraig Troxell.

However, the events of June 22, 2021, would go on to severely damage the relationship between the sheriff's office and LCPS.

Everyone I have talked with who had a working knowledge of Chapman's administration stated that he had been the most political sheriff they had ever seen. He was a Republican, and the local Republican leadership was MAGA, so this shouldn't have been at all surprising.

As the special grand jury would later document, the sheriff's office shared the blame for the fiasco that arose from the 2021 assaults at Stone Bridge and Broad Run high schools. However, the mentions involving law-enforcement agencies were fleeting. The schools were the Youngkin administration's target from the beginning, and the misdeeds of others were not going to stand in the way of that.

The LCPS "Family"

To understand the events in Loudoun, you have to know the people involved from the school division side. Over the following pages, I outline a roster of the staff and elected officials involved.

Dr. Scott Ziegler

When I interviewed Scott for his introductory article as LCPS superintendent, he told me that he would not be afraid to make decisions and that he knew that some of his decisions would result in mistakes, a prophetic insight. A stand-up guy, Scott faced an unprecedented and unjustified torrent of public vilification and insider backstabbing during his tenure as the school division's chief executive.

Scott became interim superintendent in January 2021 after the previous superintendent, Dr. Eric Williams, left unexpectedly. A superintendent leaving midyear during a national health emergency was a clear sign that the school division was in a state of crisis. At the same time, the second in command, Chief of Staff Nyah Hamlett, left to take a superintendency in North Carolina. The top two administrators gone in quick succession was a huge red flag for anybody applying for the top post.

School board member Beth Barts testified to the special grand jury about the difficulty of finding an interim superintendent. "Nobody wanted the job.

Not a single person wanted the job. So, Dr. Ziegler, who had just come to Loudoun as our HRTD (Human Resources and Talent Development) director; he said he would do it, and we were so grateful."

In short order, Scott oversaw the setup of a fantastically efficient vaccination clinic for employees and a plan for returning at least some students to in-person learning. Loudoun's schools began offering in-person instruction four days a week on March 17, 2021. For these efforts, the school board named him the permanent superintendent in June.

When Scott was appointed LCPS's permanent superintendent on June 8, 2021, the vote for his hiring was listed as unanimous. At the time, Barts was effusive in her praise of the new superintendent. "Ziegler has shown us what it means to be [a] strong leader, in the areas of communication, tough decision making and in providing a safe, empathetic, respectful, and supportive learning environment for all."

In a standard personnel move often undertaken by the military and private industry, Scott began moving assistant principals between schools. It was a move that ruffled feathers, but some school cultures can become stagnant, and assistant principals lacked experience with different school populations, cultures, and managerial styles. Sometimes, such a shakeup is needed.

In another snag, when Scott assembled a small group of senior principals to bounce confidential ideas off of, these ideas didn't stay confidential for long. Some principals ran to school board members, and public blowups followed.

While his tactics may not have had the best success with administrative staff, students responded much better to his frank and open conversations.

Scott truly shined during school visits. Each Friday, he would visit two or three schools to talk with small groups of students. During these visits, he would answer any and all questions. When students asked why lunch menus were being changed at the last minute, Scott would move into teacher mode and explain supply chain issues caused by the pandemic. Scott also gave insights into his personal life, such as the fact that he was taking Spanish and piano lessons in an effort to broaden his academic horizons.

That off-kilter approach was one that Scott also took to his appearance, from full arm-sleeve tattoos to steadfastly refusing to wear a tie. There was a general casualness to his attire. While I had my reservations about such dress among staff and students, I ditched my tie to follow the superintendent's lead and adopted the least casual iteration of "business casual" that I could.

Scott's personality can be hard to fathom from casual conversations. It's only when you get to know him that you understand his motivations, which, for the most part, were very sincere.

Misunderstood for some of the initial actions he took, and blamed for things he had no control over, Scott absorbed an unbelievable amount of abuse during his tenure. Outwardly, he maintained a facade, thin though it may have been, of detached cool. As the controversy surrounding LCPS grew and detoured into very dark places, Scott installed an elaborate security system at his home and began carrying a concealed 9-millimeter pistol—an ominous response to the emotional trauma he experienced.

Joan Sahlgren

In 2021, Joan Sahlgren and I competed for the position of director of public information. Joan was chosen. The selection committee made the right choice.

Joan began her new role on March 1, 2021, just as controversial events around LCPS had begun to ramp up.

Joan's résumé was varied: aide to former Virginia First Lady Lynda Johnson Robb, fashion-show coordinator, community college adjunct professor, and public-relations guru for the paper industry. She was blonde and trim, with an impeccable sense of fashion and an open, engaging smile. Joan tended to be a little too effusive in offering praise for routine work, a complement to me, as I tended to be too withholding in that department.

Joan changed the name of the Public Information Office to the Office of Communications and Community Engagement. She quickly brought on positions that I had lobbied for years to obtain: a social media specialist, a graphic artist, a trio of communications specialists, and an extra videographer. She set up a communications strategy that moved LCPS toward the standardized methods it had sorely lacked—and desperately needed—for years. She oversaw our move from a cave-like office on the first floor to an airy, spacious suite on the second.

Joan and I quickly reached a working arrangement: she would handle the administrative side of the operation, and I would take on the day-to-day and "emergency" situations. We acted as "thought partners" in formulating plans of work, checking to make sure neither of us went off on a tangent. Our skill sets complemented one another, and we quickly became collegial friends.

Dr. Mark Smith

Dr. Mark Smith came to Loudoun, after being named the 2017 Principal of the Year by the Virginia Association of Secondary Principals, to work in personnel. Like a lot of staff, he was thrust into a position of greater responsibility when Eric Williams departed the scene.

I found Mark personable and professional when I worked with him on personnel issues. There was a lot of trepidation on the part of my coworkers when he was named chief of staff.

Unfortunately, through a combination of factors, many beyond Mark's control, their fears were realized.

The School Board

The school board that handled, and mishandled, the political firestorm that overtook Loudoun County from 2020 to 2023 was elected to a four-year term in November 2019. In this section, I'll share, not only my observations of these important figures in the upcoming controversy, but also snippets from their special grand jury testimony to round out their character and backgrounds.

Only two members from the previous board, Jeff Morse and Brenda Sheridan, returned. In Loudoun, all nine members of the school board were elected at once—a very bad idea. Finally, in January 2023, the school board drew lots that designated five seats for two-year terms in the November 2023 election. After that, all four-year terms would be staggered.

Of the nine school board members, eight represented electoral districts with one member elected at-large.

The 2020–2023 school board experienced an unbelievable level of internal and external chaos that began with the pandemic and moved well beyond it. In the past, it had been routine for at least one member of the board to be unable to fulfill their full term. People move out of their electoral districts to pursue new jobs. One member of a previous board died. This board experienced extreme turnover. It was the first to have three people occupy one seat during a four-year term—not once, but twice—and saw a member resign and another die during the same term. The board also oversaw two interim superintendents and hired two more on a permanent basis.

In Virginia, school boards technically have one employee, the superintendent. All communication to central-office and school-level administrators is supposed to go through the superintendent. This rule was widely ignored, however, leading to school board members creating havoc by meddling in areas in which they had no expertise, often at the behest of parents, who had a very narrow, and self-serving, focus.

The inexperienced board elected its most-experienced member, Brenda Sheridan, who represented the Sterling District, as its chair.

Any mistakes Sheridan made were from the standpoint of what she believed was best for students. The amount of abuse she endured during her two years as chair would have broken most people.

Sheridan's childhood was marked by domestic strife. Her parents divorced, and she lived for a time on welfare. Sheridan's compassion for those in need came from experience, not "wokeness." Once-prosperous Sterling was now the most economically depressed district in Loudoun. Sheridan fought tirelessly to make sure Sterling's students were given the opportunities and amenities given to LCPS's wealthy students.

Because she was outspoken and overweight, the lunatic Right focused its most vitriolic online attacks on her appearance. The threats against Sheridan were so violent that a sheriff's cruiser was stationed outside her house, and the FBI launched investigations into some out-of-state stalkers who listed specific characteristics about her home and traced the movements of her family.

Sheridan's visibility made her the face of school controversy; a face that the media sought as a spokesman for sanity. Part of my job, which I gladly performed, was acting as Sheridan's de facto press agent. I arranged appearances on MSNBC, *Don Lemon Tonight*, a CNN special report, and *Meet the Press*. She always came across as knowledgeable, firm in her convictions, and compassionate.

Before the special grand jury, Sheridan gave as true an account as I have ever heard about what it was like to be a school board member in the middle of a culture war.

"So I'm going to get real with you for a second if that's OK. Is that OK with everybody? I spent over a year clearing my name because citizens in my community signed a petition to have me removed, and what I have left is my name. My dignity was stolen from me, my integrity. I still have my integrity because I keep . . . what people tell me is confidential and I keep the closed sessions confidential and I stand by that."

Jeff Morse of the Dulles District was the board member who consistently made the most sense. He served as chair on two different boards and weighed in only when he thought his input mattered. While conservative, Morse, a Republican of the old school, would listen to reason and vote accordingly.

A retired Navy commander, Morse represented a district that experienced explosive population growth with increasing diversity to match. He ran unopposed for a third term to be a part of this board, garnering 97.2 percent of the vote.

Before the special grand jury, Morse detailed the reasons he wouldn't run for a fourth term.

"I can't see the middle ground, it's gone . . . There is no satisfying this board. We are divided."

Beth Barts, Leesburg District, was the school board member from hell, in my opinion. Addicted to social media, Barts generated more controversy, chaos, and confusion than any of the thirty-seven board members I experienced in twenty-three-plus years of working for LCPS. Originally, I had been optimistic about Barts's election because she defeated a hard-right candidate. She came on the school board describing herself as an "activist" and never moved away from that perception of herself. "Activists" make lousy school board members, if you ask me. Once you're on a board, you have to function as part of a whole and funnel your passions through official channels, which is slow and dull, but it is how effective governing is done. Barts was not interested in effective governance. She inserted herself into the middle of every situation at every school in her district. "I'll be honest, I was a snooper," Barts told the special grand jury. "And so I had to recuse myself once or twice from hearings, because I decided—yes, I decided to find information. And I didn't know you couldn't do that. I mean, I thought it was part of our job as being an elected representative, to get all the information. And, you know, but I found out that's not the way it works."

Barts became notorious for her constant posts on Facebook. Critics pointed out that her time stamps showed that she was actually posting during school board meetings. I can attest to the fact that she wasn't paying attention. A Virginia Freedom of Information Act request showed Barts communicating with another board member online during a meeting. She laughingly asked what was going on since she hadn't been paying attention during the last three votes.

Barts regularly violated the confidentiality of executive sessions, which led the school board to censure her on March 4, 2021, after, ironically, an executive session. "This is not in reaction to any one event," Sheridan said of the censure. "This is a response to a culmination of behaviors over the last 14 months, from the beginning of this term until today."

Barts became the focal point of the effort to recall the school board. Facing mounting internal and external pressure, she resigned on November 2, 2021, my sixty-fourth birthday. I suspect that she had cut a deal to resign if Ian Prior and his followers would lay off her. This line of thought stems from a conversation after I sought to charge her the going rate to obtain information she sought through a FOIA request. While whining about the estimated fee, Barts said, "Do I have to tell Ian Prior about this?" During a 2023 interview with *The New York Times*, Barts confirmed that she had a cordial relationship with Prior.

After resigning, Barts continued posting on Facebook from the perspective of a former school board member. Many of her posts featured confidential information given to the board after her departure. It was clear that a sitting member was violating ethical standards by leaking documents meant only for school board review.

The school board appointed Tom Marshall as Barts's replacement on December 14, 2021. Given the field of candidates the school board had to choose from to fill this vacancy, including the woman who eventually won the seat in a special election, I was amazed that Marshall was chosen.

Past eighty years old, Marshall ran for the school board four times and won twice. Quite the wit, Marshall had been known to remark, "I hope my term expires before I do."

Marshall sometimes appeared confused on the dais, but he had moments of clarity during which he offered keen insights. In the end, his last service on the school board contributed little concrete good. At least he didn't do any harm.

Erika Ogedegbe won a special election to fill out the last year of Barts's term in November 2022 by capturing 38 percent of the vote in a three-way race. She seemed like a genuinely nice, competent person. She was not reelected in 2023.

Denise Corbo, the at-large member, reinforced my opinion that teachers make shit school board members. As a former Teacher of the Year (2018), Corbo was a particularly lousy member of the school board.

Corbo stated that it was the school board's responsibility to oversee the day-to-day operation of the schools. Having a teacher thinking that they have the administrative knowledge to run a school division is like having a carpenter thinking they can build a skyscraper.

An extremely attractive woman with flowing, blond hair, Corbo obsessed over her official school board portrait, even though it was clearly the best of the bunch. Corbo set herself apart from her fellow board members by continuing to attend meetings virtually while all the other members were in-person as pandemic restrictions eased. She received an Americans with Disabilities Act (ADA) accommodation for the lingering effects of an undesignated disease, which Corbo maintained made her more vulnerable to the effects of COVID-19.

The Code of Virginia allowed members of public bodies to attend a percentage of a body's meetings remotely. For the Loudoun County School Board in 2021, this meant a member could invoke an exemption—no questions asked—for thirteen of fifty-two meetings. Corbo rarely used her exemption, which meant regular drama at the beginning of school board meetings as members voted on whether to allow her to participate remotely.

The general consensus was that Corbo was afraid to be in the board room with the public present. This assumption was bolstered by an email she wrote to the school board on July 10, 2021.

"We allow anyone in the world to attend our meetings. There's no screening for IDs, weapons, and there is no bulletproof protection. I don't believe it's safe for the school board to have any in-person meetings until more robust safety protocols are in place and the threats have stopped. I hope the threats will stop after the politically-charged November elections. As of now,

I do not plan to attend any committee board members [*sic*] until it's safe." All of these safety practices and physical barriers were in place in the board's meeting room and had been since August 2021. The last time Corbo attended a board meeting in person was for a closed session on August 5, 2021.

Corbo's claim of being too health-compromised to attend board meetings was destroyed by something that popped up on social media. She attended a swank charity event, the 20th Annual JustWorld Gala, on January 27, 2023, at Belle Herbe Farm in Wellington, Florida. Photos of Corbo among the seven hundred guests at this posh event were posted. On March 25, Corbo announced that she wouldn't be running again.

Atoosa Reaser, Algonkian District, was a calculating progressive. An immigrant and lawyer, Atoosa would appear to stand for the right thing, but only to a point.

The school board's vice chair for the first two years of her term, Atoosa seemed to make decisions with an eye toward her political future. She announced a run for a newly formed House of Delegates seat midway through her school board term, and, in November 2023, she was elected to that seat.

Atoosa Reaser came to America from Iran in 1979 at age eight and learned English as her second language. She changed schools eight times before graduating high school in Fairfax County. Atoosa was the image of a successful, attractive suburban mom. Her manner was girlish and bubbly, turning business-serious when necessary.

Still, she had been known to waffle on controversial issues and make a decision that was the most politically expedient. My assessment of Atoosa changed after I read her special grand jury testimony from October 17, 2022.

During this testimony, she slammed prosecutor Carlton Davis. Davis asked Atoosa repeatedly about her role on the school board. She, repeatedly, tried to give a lawyerly answer, which clearly frustrated Davis.

"I asked the question four times. You didn't answer. So now I'm just going to skip that question."

"Actually, you interrupted me four times," Atoosa answered. "So I'm going to finish my answer."

As the questioning proceeded, Atoosa came across as polished and Davis as increasingly sarcastic and desperate. It got to the point where Davis's tone turned threatening. "We know a lot. We know a lot more than you think we do."

Atoosa did not back down. "I've spent my life in public service and I'm being accused of covering up the rape of a woman . . . That's been the narrative that's out there, the School Board covered up."

In a response to a juror's question, Atoosa laid out her thoughts about the special grand jury's investigation. "I don't think the result of the investigation is going to do anything to make anybody feel better. I think it's going to make people feel worse, because I feel like . . . that was the whole purpose of it because the way the order was written was to say to investigate the cover-up done by the School Board. So the conclusion was already made."

As I finished reading Atoosa's testimony, my esteem for her had grown immeasurably.

Harris Mahedavi, Ashburn District, was a nice guy who appeared to have no idea what he was doing.

An assistant Boy Scout scoutmaster and soccer coach, Harris's main contribution to the school board was that he defeated its former chair, Eric Hornberger, in the 2019 election.

A practicing Muslim, Harris brought much-needed diversity to the board, but that was about it in my opinion. He lobbied to have ethnic holidays, such as Diwali, Eid al-Fitr, and Lunar New Year added to the school calendar, which led to the 2022–2023 school year dipping below 180 days.

As chair of the Communications Committee, Harris's main goal, it seemed, was to find technologies that would lessen the amount of emails he had to read. While he didn't like reading emails, Harris had no trouble lengthening board meetings. On virtually every item, he asked to be recognized ("Chair?") and would then launch into a word salad that showed he was totally unprepared for the meeting.

Harris ran for reelection in 2023 and was defeated.

I like Ian Serotkin, Blue Ridge District, even though he could be a true pain in the ass. He was a concerned dad whose children attended one of LCPS's two public charter schools. He was also an Odyssey of the Mind coach.

The pain-in-the-ass part pertained to his constant grandstanding and attempts to legislate from the dais during school board meetings. He was always trying to tweak verbiage on policies that had already been passed by committee, which caused endless confusion and lengthened board meetings as members debated granular wording differences that really didn't make a difference.

Shortly after my future suspension, Serotkin was elected school board chair. I supported this. In a political world filled with idiots and idiotic ideologues, Serotkin is sane, which is as good as you're going to get in the present political climate. Soon after being elected chair, Serotkin announced that he wouldn't seek reelection, a realistic decision. He couldn't get the signatures he needed to run in a newly redrawn district. And even if he did, he had little chance of being elected.

Leslee King, Broad Run District, was a kind, gentle, thoughtful woman who represented an ideal for school board members. Past seventy, she ran for the school board because her vast life experience led her to believe that she could make a positive contribution to local education. Among the things on Leslee's résumé: teacher, pioneer in the field of technology, defense contractor, and single mom to three children. A prototypical grandmotherly type, she knitted scarves for fellow board members and staff. (The blue-and-white one she made for me has a place of honor in my office.)

Something that I learned at her funeral was that she had found out about a life-threatening heart condition while walking to the Capitol for President John F. Kennedy's inauguration. Despite multiple surgeries, warnings not to have children, and other restrictions doctors wanted to place on her, Leslee led a full life and wanted to give back to the community at its end. Her heart finally gave out on August 31, 2021.

The school board replaced Leslee with Andrew Hoyler, a young man in a hurry for the sake of being in a hurry. Hoyler ran against Leslee for the Broad Run seat and was trounced (61 percent to 37 percent). School board elections were supposed to be nonpartisan, but candidates routinely sought the endorsement of local political parties. Hoyler, running on principle, refused to take an endorsement. The Democrats endorsed Leslee King in a heavily blue district.

Principle took a predictable beating.

The school board appointed Hoyler as Leslee's replacement on October 12, 2021. He was the youngest member of the board at twenty-five and its first openly gay member. A graduate of an LCPS high school, Hoyler told the media that he struggled with suicidal thoughts in high school and that mental health would be one of the focal points of his tenure on the board.

I, along with just about everyone else who viewed the interview to fill the vacant Broad Run seat, was surprised by Hoyler's appointment. The majority of the school board members were Democrats. The Loudoun Democratic Committee endorsed Katrece Nolen for the seat. A bright (engineer), attractive African-American woman, the parent of LCPS students, and a breast cancer survivor, Katrece was also a past chair of the Minority Student Achievement Advisory Committee (MSAAC). She could be confrontational at times, but Katrece had the makings of a good school board member. Some viewed her snub as an act of overt racism. I think it was more a case of Democratic party infighting.

Whatever the reason, an injustice had been done.

A commercial airline pilot in training, Hoyler often attended meetings remotely. Because the Federal Aviation Administration (FAA) limits the amount of time a pilot can fly each month, he signed on as a substitute teacher to better learn what educators face in the classroom. On the dais or online, Hoyler tried very hard to point out incorrect language in virtually every policy that came before the board for a vote. He refused to vote for proclamations (Mental Health Awareness Month, School Counseling Month, etc.) because he deemed them a waste of time. This led to a great deal of wasted time at board meetings through the reading of routine proclamations. Ironically, the first proclamation he voted against was one celebrating LGBTQ history month.

Not learning from his earlier defeat, Hoyler refused a political endorsement in a November 2022 special election to complete Leslee King's term and finished third in a three-way race.

The first thing I was struck by while reading Hoyler's special grand jury testimony was the reason Hoyler sought to become a school board member in the first place. "And I recognize while LCPS was great for me, there are a lot of things I struggled with, primarily my mental health, with bullying, to the point where I had written my goodbye letters to my family and was going to burn my house down while I was home alone." I don't know if anyone so recently removed from this intense emotional experience should be serving on a school board or flying a plane.

Tiffany Polifko, Hoyler's elected replacement, was a hard-right overprotective mom who took advantage of running in a three-way race against two gay, twenty-something men. As she said over and over and over, she was the only parent in the race. That was enough to get her 33 percent of the ballots cast and a victory margin of ninety-eight votes. Affiliated with the lunatic-right website Parents Against Critical Theory (PACT), Polifko was called out as a racist by speakers during public comment after taking her seat. I don't know if this was true, but the poised, attractive face she put on after her election was a definite contrast to the fire-breathing lunatic she portrayed herself as during several pre-election public comment appearances before the school board.

As a board member, Polifko continually introduced motions that had no chance of passing. The strategy seemed to be to get other members to go "on the record" so their stances could be used against them in future elections.

My general take on this strategy was that it was worthless. Nobody cares about voting records in Congress, let alone the school board. Facing a brick wall regarding her agenda, Polifko decided not to seek election for a full term.

A good decision for everyone involved.

John Beatty was a very quiet man. He won the Catoctin District seat with 43.1 percent of the vote, beating two longtime school activists who ended up canceling each other out. Shortly after his election, Beatty offered this comment after a school board equity training: "It was worse for African Americans after Reconstruction because they did not have the patronage of a master." This comment cost him his seats on the equity and discipline committees.

Despite such missteps and his muted personality, Beatty declared his candidacy for the Tenth District Republican congressional nomination. At only thirty-two, with a thin political résumé, I had to wonder if he was delusional. His subsequent actions on the school board appeared to be made through the lens of a candidate for higher office as Beatty declared himself the "lone conservative on the Loudoun County School Board." In October 2021, he called for the superintendent's resignation.

The father of six children, Beatty withdrew his progeny from LCPS and enrolled them in a Montessori school during the pandemic. Despite a long campaign for the congressional nomination, Beatty didn't make it past the fourth of nine rounds of ranked balloting in the Republican primary. Technically, his voting percentage was recorded as zero. That didn't stop him from launching another run for Congress after his school board term ended.

PART II

The Incident

The Day That Changed My Life

You never know when one phone call, one conversation, one act you didn't instigate will change your life.

A Late-Afternoon Emergency

All that can be said with certainty about May 28, 2021, the Friday before Memorial Day, at Stone Bridge High School in Loudoun County, Virginia, is that a fifteen-year-old girl and fourteen-year-old boy made very bad personal decisions. These decisions were negatively compounded and distorted by adults who certainly knew better than the children involved.

For reasons of clarity, I will refer to "the boy" and "the girl" when describing this incident and its aftermath. The following includes information gleaned from official testimony from the special grand jury set up by the governor months after the incident occurred.

From a special grand jury report looking into this incident: "From 11:46 to 11:59 am on May 28, 2021, the assailant was chatting with a female student on Discord, a messaging application, about potentially 'call[ing] a pass' to 'Have some fun' (attachment 2). The students were using their LCPS-issued Chromebooks to have this conversation and at least one of them was in class. The two individuals had met in the bathroom two weeks before to have consensual sex but had never had sex outside of SBHS."

Attachment 2 details the conversation between the two:

> Boy [assailant]: We could call a pass and—
> Have some "fun"
> Girl: Maybe
> Maybe

Boy: What about the bathroom by the Tech Ed classroom?
Girl: Here I'll meet u but I'm not promises anything
Wait for me

Discord is a messaging platform used by gamers and, as the nation later learned, low-level Massachusetts Air National Guardsmen posting national secrets. To accommodate the school division's e-sports program, LCPS did not block it when students first began to use it. Once students began abusing it, however, the school division eventually blocked it.

Students immediately began creating work-arounds to access it. I observed that the ability of the "digital natives" in our student body to breach security measures was both frightening and a testament to their fortitude and ingenuity.

Loudoun County Sheriff's Office Detective Corrine Czekaj (pronounced check-eye) later detailed the messages the victim and the perpetrator sent each other over Discord for the special grand jury. These messages were cited in the public special grand jury report but were not attributed to the two people involved in this case. The special grand jury instead used them as "generic" examples of the kind of messages being sent over LCPS-issued computers. They were presented as unrelated examples of how the school division's technology was being misused.

On May 12, 2021, the boy sent this message at 1:40 p.m. (during school hours) using the screen name Zappers32: "Okay. Who here would you let fuck you until your mind breaks and who would you fuck until their mind breaks?"

Nine minutes later, Zappers32 sent another message: "I was told by [a second female Stone Bridge student] that her mind was pretty shaken by five minutes so an hour would break her mind." Testimony from another witness stated that the boy and the second student snuck off and had sex during a theater event.

The graphic Discord messages proved to be a thorny problem for Czekaj's investigation. "I will say, at the very beginning of this case . . . it was a little messy in that, if you read the Discord messages, they were highly sexualized, [the perpetrator], definitely. [The victim] also had some sexualized conversations in there. And [the victim] agreed to meet him.

"So I'm not saying he was OK in doing what he did, because he was absolutely not, but that, clearly in my view, clearly he needed some kind of help. That view clearly began to shift to we have—we have a more serious problem here; that he couldn't even go a couple of months without getting into some kind of physical and sexual trouble."

The special grand jury report continued, "At 12:00 pm [sic] the two students met in the handicap stall of a female bathroom at SBHS. The male student became 'handsy' and then more aggressive, which caused bruising on her chest. The female laid down on her stomach on the floor, and the male held her arms down as he penetrated her."

Which wasn't the whole story.

They weren't in the bathroom alone.

Reading through special grand jury transcripts on March 7, 2023, I came across the testimony of Ann Duffy, a teacher's assistant who had walked into the girls' bathroom on May 28, 2021. Duffy was succinct about her actions on that day. "I walked in, saw some feet, went to the bathroom, washed my hands, and left."

Duffy defended her actions. "Well, in my fifteen years at Stone Bridge, I've never, ever heard of anybody bringing two people from a stall to the admin . . . I've never heard anybody saying they found people together in a stall . . . I've been in stalls with my girlfriends."

Duffy wasn't the only one in the bathroom at the time the two students occupied it.

A report made by the Stone Bridge High School's SRO, Tavis Henry, a Loudoun County Sheriff's Office deputy, stated that a surveillance camera outside the bathroom (LCPS does not place such cameras inside bathrooms) detailed what went on during the time frame of the bathroom stall incident. "While they were in the bathroom you could see multiple students and a teacher walk into the bathroom. While others were walking out of the bathroom there were no signs observed of anything out of the ordinary happening. Both [the male student] and [the female student] were seen leaving the bathroom walking in the same direction with each other." The report later noted that they were in study hall together. The report placed their time in the bathroom between 11:57 a.m. and 12:24 p.m.

Henry's report noted that he had previously observed the interaction between these students. "During dismissal and arrival to school I always see the [male student] and [female student] wrestling, touching or around each other in ways that are deemed inappropriate behavior for school throughout the school year."

The report also stated: "[The female student] also disclosed she had consensual vaginal intercourse with [the male student] two weeks ago in the same bathroom stall. She did not disclose that during the interview because her father had told her to only talk about what happened today."

Then there was the matter of what the boy involved in the incident was wearing, which the right-wing media would later describe, ad nauseam, as a dress. Henry's description of what the boy's clothing looked like was a bit different when he testified before the special grand jury on August 23, 2022. "I(t) look(ed) feminine. It was a bunch of dark clothing that I've noticed he will wear. I'm going to say [the] kilt/skirt that he wore was kind of dark in color."

While the right-wing media reacted with horror at the thought of student sex at school, it really isn't all that uncommon. Stone Bridge Principal Tim Flynn touched on this during his special grand jury testimony. He said that he knew about the "Lumber Loft," an area backstage near the drama department, where students went to have sex. "Well, teenagers having sex at high school is not a new thing. And, you know, if you've been a principal at all, there are certain places where that would occur; and it's the bathrooms, behind the stage in fine arts, the locker room is a hot spot area."

Czekaj said something in passing that I took note of. She said that Heidi Hayes, who was then an assistant principal at Stone Bridge, immediately called in SRO Henry when she learned of the alleged nature of the assault on May 28, 2021—a fact that flew in the face of Glenn Youngkin's repeated assertion during his election and afterward that it took a gubernatorial order to get an investigation started.

A question from a special grand jury juror to Czekaj amplified this point. "To your knowledge, did Mrs. Hayes, when she was informed of the incident, did she follow the appropriate protocols to—did she shut the students down? Did she start contacting parents and authorities?" Czekaj answered, "So they did several things correct, in that they notified the SRO immediately."

The special grand jury report detailed the aftermath of the bathroom liaison gone wrong: "Around 2:15 pm the father of the victim arrived at SBHS. The school resource officer (SRO) initially denied the father entry into the school because he did not have identification. The father called his wife, who is inside the school with their daughter, asking for help to get in. She told the father that what they initially thought was an assault against their daughter was actually a sexual assault. This further infuriated the father, who caused a scene, and the SRO eventually escorted him inside the building. The father was escorted out of the building at 2:30 pm." As Tim Flynn related to me, the victim's father, Scott Smith—a plumber, whose company name is Plumb Crazy—went berserk in the main office. Smith, who is a large man, was physically threatening staff. Students and staff were hiding in adjacent offices because of this display of anger. Students and staff in the nearby library heard Smith's outburst and related that they were concerned about their safety.

Flynn told the special grand jury that, when he came back from checking on something in the physical education area, there was a chaotic scene in the main office. "Mr. Smith was enraged, very loud, vulgar, threatening behavior, was not following the directions of the administration. I got called in."

Flynn said that Smith exploded. Special Prosecutor Theo Stamos asked him to be explicit. "You know, 'Who the fuck are you?'" Flynn estimated that five additional security personnel were called in to deal with the situation.

Flynn also testified that Smith's daughter apologized for her father's behavior.

Scott Smith was unapologetic as he testified about his actions before the special grand jury. Smith gave this account of his arrival at Stone Bridge and his initial interaction with SRO Tavis Henry: "I basically said 'Bro, I'm coming through the door. You have a choice right now: Either escort me to the office to get my wife and child, you know, or all hell is about to break loose.'

"I was pissed off because I was really angry . . . So, yeah, I went into that school pissed. One, because I couldn't get to my daughter and my wife that needed me, you know, because law enforcement felt that they needed to stop me. How dare they?"

Smith said that he left Stone Bridge voluntarily after a confrontation in the office with law enforcement and staff. He told the special grand jury about a confrontation that followed in the school's parking lot. "At one point, I had to ask, 'OK, everybody who has guns and handcuffs, please stand over here. Everybody who works for LCPS and doesn't have handcuffs and guns, please stand over here.' Somebody asked me why I asked that. I said, 'Just so I know who I'm dealing with here.' I mean, you know, what the hell?"

Scott Smith's actions were why Tim Flynn called me later that afternoon.

Flynn detailed our relationship in such situations to the special grand jury.

"When there's a disruption at our school that a lot of people are aware of, we notify the community with Connect Ed messages, which did occur that day." Tim Flynn said that he called me when such messages were needed.

"So is that who you normally deal with for communications issues?" Theo Stamos asked.

"I have for years, but he's not—I have for many years," Flynn answered. "So yeah, I have a tendency to call him. But he's not in charge of that department anymore. There's somebody else in charge, Joan Sahlgren. But I'm pretty sure I talked to Wayde that day."

"But tell us what you said on the phone to Mr. Byard about the incident," Theo continued.

"He was aware of the whole situation," Flynn replied.

Theo pressed on, "And what does that mean? What did you tell him?"

"That there was an allegation of sexual assault, the dad came in and was very upset," Flynn replied. "It was a significant disruption, and we needed to notify the community of the disruption."

That alleged reference to the sexual assault was what led to my indictment. One sentence in testimony fourteen months after the fact.

That's it.

I truly don't remember if Flynn mentioned Scott Smith's name or the reason he was upset. I was concentrating on the multiple sheriff's office cruisers on the scene with student dismissal coming up. This would become a major point of contention in the legal proceedings against me. My final email communication with Flynn that Friday afternoon certainly didn't convey anything about a cover-up: "Take some time to de-stress, Mr. Flynn."

During his special grand jury testimony, Flynn remembered a much more detailed conversation between us than I did. I believed that he remembered various conversations that day, held in a state of emotional distress, and placed a level of surety into our communications that simply wasn't there. For instance, at 3:09 p.m., Flynn sent an email to Director of High School Education Nereida Gonzalez-Sales, Executive Principal Secondary Kirk Dolson, Director of School Administration Douglas "Doug" Fulton, and Director of Safety and Security John Clark. I would note that this email chain did not include me or my boss, Joan Sahlgren. The email: "While the officer was investigating the alleged sexual assault, the Father showed up and created a second incident. He is out of the building now but this was quite a show that scared and intimidated students and staff. I believe we are going to need to do a no trespass letter for the father. He probably should have been arrested. We did avoid that. We had to call for additional police."

While the situation of May 28, 2021, was unique, it was not outside of the range of services I've performed for principals through the years. My office helped principals in crisis by adapting messages from templates and getting these messages to the principal in a hurry. The principal would then distribute the message to the public via blast email. My office produced an average of five or six such messages a day, a number that climbed up to a dozen on busy days (usually Fridays). There wasn't a template for the unique situation Stone Bridge was facing. I worked through the details Flynn provided me, wrote a draft, and sent it up the administrative chain for possible alterations and approval.

Having followed this process, I sent Flynn the following message for distribution to the school community:

Incident at Stone Bridge Today

This is Stone Bridge Principal Tim Flynn. There was an incident in the main office area today that required the Loudoun County Sheriff's Office to dispatch deputies to Stone Bridge. The incident was confined to the main office area and entrance area to the school. There was no threat to the safety of the student body. The incident was witnessed by a small number of students who were meeting with staff adjacent to the main office. Counseling services and the services of our Unified Mental Health Team are available for any student who may need to talk about today's incident.

Students might have noticed Sheriff's Office personnel on campus and I wanted to let you know that something out of the ordinary happened at school today. The safety of our students and staff is the top priority of Loudoun County Public Schools. If you have any concerns, you may contact me at [redacted].

At least one Stone Bridge parent who received this message wasn't pleased. Principals are supposed to delete parents related to an incident from the mass notification. Tim Flynn didn't do this. I'll give him a pass on this considering the emotional state he was in.

Scott Smith told the special grand jury about his reaction to the May 28 email from Stone Bridge regarding the incident involving his daughter.

"I mean, 'Good evening Stone Bridge families. This is Stone Bridge Principal Tim Flynn. There was an incident in the main office area today that required the Loudoun County Sheriff's Office to dispatch deputies to Stone Bridge.' My question to you is: Why the hell weren't they already there?

"'The incident was confined to the main office and the entrance area to the school. There was no threat to the safety of the student body'—which is a lie. They didn't know where the sexual predator was. He was hiding in a bathroom, and they found him as he was trying to get on a school bus at the end of the day, OK?

"And that's one of the things that Flynn and I were arguing about is; where is the sexual predator? Do you have him in a room? Is he contained? They had no clue.

"'There was no threat to the safety of the student body.' That's not true. That is absolutely a lie.

"'The incident was witnessed by a small number of students who were meeting with staff adjacent to the main office.' Well, there were kids, actually, that were with my daughter that were helping to tell them what was going on.

"'Counseling services'—this is a good one. This really upset me, 'Counseling services and services of our Unified Mental Team are available for any student who may need to talk about today's incident.' I've yet to get services for my daughter. My daughter was the one that was raped, yet they're offering services to anyone who was upset by the outraged father. Really?

"'Students may have noticed Sheriff's Office personnel on campus and I wanted to let you know that something out of the ordinary happened at school.' Out of the ordinary? I think it was a little bit more than out of the ordinary . . ."

Smith said that he didn't know that the email had been drafted by administrative staff in the central office and not Flynn. Reading his testimony, it appeared to me that he had been coached. Smith hit too many talking points the prosecution used against me later for this to be spontaneous.

The Reason "Assault" Wasn't Mentioned in the May 28 Email

The special grand jury report noted: "This statement, drafted by the public information officer and edited and approved by the superintendent (attachment 10), deliberately makes no mention of the sexual assault that took place just hours earlier."

Theo Stamos hit upon this point during her special grand jury questioning of Tim Flynn. "When did it occur to you, or did it even occur to you, that this was deceptive?"

"I wouldn't use the word 'deceptive,'" Flynn replied. "For me, the Sheriff's Office was investigating the sexual assault. For me, it's very important not to compromise the investigation. And so to put information out to the community that may have compromised that . . ."

"Working with the Sheriff's Office, they make it very clear they don't want us to investigate or put information out." Part of Flynn's later testimony included the fact that the sheriff's office threatened Stone Bridge staff with arrest if they interfered with the legal investigation.

In retrospect, we told the truth as we then knew it and got crucified anyway. And, yes, we made no mention of a sexual assault because, at that time, law enforcement had not determined that that was what had happened, and no charges had been filed. In my mind, this was a critical element of this entire circus. It is a key reason why parents and school board members need to reflect before acting given that they don't have all of the details that those of us with the actual information and protocols have.

Standard operating procedure for announcing any arrests or alleged crimes at a school is to allow the Loudoun County Sheriff's Office or Leesburg Police Department, which has jurisdiction over some LCPS schools, to issue a media release on an incident, then we make sure the school community at the affected school sees this release. This is generally done through a blast email to students, parents, and staff.

Through an informal—this was a mistake, all such procedures should be codified in policy—practice between myself and my then-counterpart,

Kraig Troxell, the sheriff's office would draft a media release on an alleged crime at a school, then send it to me for review. I would review the message with my supervisor, Joan Sahlgren, who would sometimes send it on to the chief of staff or superintendent for their input. I would communicate with Kraig about any language we thought should be changed. Such changes were usually minor and were almost always accepted by the sheriff's office.

Our practice was to let the sheriff's office announce the alleged crime first, with the affected school sending out a blast email five minutes later incorporating the sheriff's office release.

Here's an example of what would have been sent on May 28, 2021, had such a sheriff's office release existed:

> ### Sheriff's Office Investigating Assault at Stone Bridge High School
> *To the Stone Bridge High School community,*
>
> *This is Principal Tim Flynn. The Loudoun County Sheriff's Office has issued a report about an incident today at Stone Bridge High School. I wanted you to be aware of this report. The safety and security of students and staff is Loudoun County Public Schools' highest priority.*

The following should have been the sheriff's office report:

> ### Sheriff's Office Investigating Assault at Stone Bridge High School
> *The Loudoun County Sheriff's Office arrested a male student today at Stone Bridge High School and charged him with assault as the result of an incident in a school bathroom.*
>
> *The male juvenile is being held at the Loudoun County Youth Detention Center without bond.*

This was what *should* have been sent out by law enforcement that day. However, the boy involved in this incident wasn't arrested and charged until more than a month later. I find it very odd that the sheriff's office did not put out a release at the time of the boy's arrest. Usually they'd put out a release if a teacher was arrested for disorderly conduct for farting in class. I'm exaggerating a bit. The most common release involving teachers involves a teacher being drunk in class. This usually happened two or three times a year.

The sheriff's office made no mention of the circumstances of the assault at Stone Bridge until October 7, 2021, when it issued this media release following a second incident involving the fourteen-year-old boy at an adjacent high school, Broad Run, to which he had been transferred. In its release, the sheriff's office stated why it hadn't reported the May 28 assault to the public: "The October 6 incident at Broad Run High School did not involve complex circumstances, the arrest was immediate, and the arrest was reported to the community as information released was unlikely to disclose the identity of the victim. However, the May 28, 2021, investigation was different in that the suspect and victim were familiar with each other, the investigation was complex, and a public announcement had the potential to identify a juvenile victim."

The investigation into what happened in a girls' bathroom at Stone Bridge High School on May 28, 2021, was indeed "complex." The fourteen-year-old boy was not arrested on two counts of forcible sodomy until July 8. It took that long for sheriff's office investigators to sort out what had allegedly happened.

Going back to May 28, LCPS couldn't say that an assault had occurred because that hadn't been established by the sheriff's office. To do so would have prejudiced any legal and school board discipline that followed. There are strict federal and state guidelines restricting the release of student records, including the records of student discipline. On the federal level, there is the Family Educational Rights and Privacy Act (FERPA). Code of Virginia Section 2.2-3705.4 (1) also governs the release of student records, including disciplinary records. It states that only parents and guardians of a student, or the student if they are older than eighteen, may authorize the release of such records.

In their testimony before the special grand jury, at least one school board member defended the message LCPS sent out on May 28. Carlton Davis pressed Atoosa Reaser about whether the school division should have said more about the assault at Stone Bridge at the time it happened.

"We don't decide (if) students are guilty before the Sheriff's Department finishes," Atoosa replied. Later she added, "What could we have done on May 28? It's just a question mark at that point. It happens all the time that there are accusations of, of altercations, and then we find out the facts are different than they were (initially presented). It would have been extremely prejudicial to the students involved for us to start making decisions until law enforcement finishes with their investigation. And they were very vocal at the school about telling the school division personnel 'You must stand down until we finish.' And our staff is not going against directives from law enforcement."

At this point, Davis started to lose control. "You want to defend the school system. You want to parse the Code [of Virginia] because you're a lawyer. I get all that."

Atoosa went on the offensive in reply to this statement. "You asked me to come here to tell you what I think happened. What I think happened was they were investigating. It was a complicated investigation that took time. They did not properly report it to the right person, so the information didn't get discussed. It didn't get to us. And maybe we could have done something."

"What's the narrative that isn't true?" Davis asked.

"The fact that people knew and didn't do anything about it," Atoosa answered. "That's, that's just not true."

The Beginning of the May 28 Investigation

On May 3, 2022, Detective Corrine Czekaj testified about her role in investigating the May 28, 2021, incident. I was impressed by the professionalism and candor of her testimony. Czekaj had been with the sheriff's office since 2009 and its special victims unit since 2014.

Carlton Davis began the questioning by asking about Czekaj's actions on the day of the assault. "And did you go to the school on the 28th?"

Czekaj answered, "I did not, due to the time, which was sometime in the afternoon. School had—I believe had already let out and, quite frankly, it sounded like there was a cluster going on at the school."

Czekaj continued, "So I decided to—the one person that was at the school that I needed to interview first is the victim . . . I advised the unit on scene to have her parents meet me at the Child Advocacy Center, which is . . . specifically for the interview of children."

It was there that the victim gave her version of the events to Czekaj. "They were in the stall. He was organizing apps on her phone. She describes him getting 'handsy' was the word that she used. She describes him kind of touching her breasts and becoming more aggressive. She stated that she laid down on the—on the floor of the bathroom, facedown, to prevent further touching.

"At that point he straddled her, pulled down her shorts and underwear, held her arms as he penetrated her with his penis. She said she clenched her anus, trying to prevent the insertion, but he was able to get in. She describes someone coming into the bathroom, at which point caused [the boy] to jump up, which caused her further pain."

At this point, I cursed the inaction of Ann Duffy. No matter whose version you believe about the events of May 28, 2021, this whole matter could have ended right then if she had simply knocked on the door.

Czekaj continued, "And when she was able to get off the floor, she was seated against the wall. He grabbed her shoulders—he pushed her shoulders down, grabbed her face, and he attempted to put his penis in her mouth. She talked about turning her head away, actively keeping her mouth closed to resist the penetration. She said that he attempted to do this three times, that his penis did penetrate her mouth, touch her teeth for a second."

Two things struck me as I read this.

One, if this account was true, I truly feel for this child. As a father of two daughters, this account was absolutely horrific and broke my heart.

Two, if all this was truly what went on in that bathroom stall, how could someone in that same room not notice and do something?

Davis then asked Czekaj "how they came to get in the bathroom in the first place?"

Czekaj answered that this information was disclosed in a subsequent interview. "She had further disclosed that they had had consensual sex in that same bathroom about two weeks prior, but she didn't disclose that because her dad told her just to talk about that day."

When Scott Smith screamed at school board meetings about what was being hidden, I wondered how he'd feel about making this public. Czekaj added that the bathroom wasn't processed by a forensics team because of the previous instance of consensual sex. I found this baffling. Then again, virtually everything about this case baffled me.

A Whirlwind of Messages

Were there signs that could have stopped this assault from happening? No one could have predicted the future; that's impossible. There were several messages that should have raised red flags, however, that seemed to go only into the circular file.

Unheeded Warning

An email I was shown during my special grand jury testimony involved a Stone Bridge teaching assistant telling another teacher and their department chair about the boy involved in the May 28 incident. This was written on May 12, 2021, more than two weeks before the bathroom incident. "Good afternoon! Even though he started the year very well, and though he gets along with his peers [the boy's name] seems to have a problem with listening and keeping his hands to himself. He has come into class more than once with his arm around a girl's neck. I have caught him sitting on other girls' laps several times. There doesn't need to be a global pandemic to say that this is unacceptable! His refusal and disregard to me and my assistant has us at our wits end. I understand the school year is quickly ending, and that students and staff alike are counting down the days but if this kind of reckless behavior persists, I wouldn't want to be held accountable if someone should get hurt."

One of the recipients of this email was a teacher who did not know the boy and assumed that they had received it in error. The teaching assistant's department chair also received the email. According to the special grand jury report, the department chair testified that she was confused by the message. She didn't know if the teaching assistant was complaining about the violation of COVID-19 protocols or something else. The department chair followed up with the student's case manager. The case manager called the student's mother. Nobody put up a huge red flag to the administration that someone perceived a major behavioral problem with a student that could escalate into some form of physical violence—as it eventually ended up doing. The special grand jury report also noted that none of this was recorded in the boy's case file.

The fact that this boy had a case worker told me that he was a special needs student. "Special needs" is a category that covers a plethora of physical and mental conditions. Among these are students who are "emotionally disturbed" or ED. This is a designation that would certainly seem to describe the boy in the May 28 incident. I can't confirm this because his records are sealed to me under state and federal confidentiality laws. However, according to the special grand jury report, the boy's grandmother had warned his probation officer that the boy was a "sociopath." When your grandma says you're a sociopath . . .

So how was such a person mingling with the general student population?

Through the past several decades, "inclusion" and "mainstreaming" have become sacred words where special needs students are concerned, even those who are emotionally disturbed. Elected officials who have never been in a classroom or filled an administrative role in a public school create well-intended legislation. This "feel good" legislation has tenets that cannot be practically fulfilled, especially in school districts facing funding and staffing shortages. "Unfunded mandates" are some of the biggest problems facing American public education today.

These unfunded mandates produce dire classroom situations. I don't think that these situations should be called "unintended consequences" because they are so numerous and well-documented that, by now, legislators are almost intentionally inflicting pain in the classroom with their far-reaching, underfunded efforts.

Several times a year, I had to construct an emergency message telling parents about an ED student destroying a classroom, threatening their peers, or running amok in the hallways while staff monitored them (the theory being that confronting the student would only escalate their behavior). Everyone in the school knows who these students are. Everyone lives in fear of an emotional explosion. But, there they are in the classroom in the name of "inclusion" and "mainstreaming." Federal law dictates that special needs students be educated in the "least restrictive environment." By placing them in general education classrooms that are not staffed to meet their needs, such students often place restrictions on others seeking an education.

I'm sorry, but this just shouldn't be.

LCPS has calm-down rooms for such students, which are only mildly effective. Special needs students regularly inflict physical harm on teachers through biting, scratching, punching, and kicking. At best, such students are a constant distraction for teachers and their fellow students. At worst, they cause physical harm. Special needs teachers usually last about five years in that role. I'm amazed they last that long, given some of what they have to put up with. They're aided by assistants, who are among the lowest-paid employees in the school division. Finding qualified substitutes for these positions is all but impossible.

The special needs culture extends beyond the classroom.

Special needs students constitute 11.6 percent of the LCPS student body. A much higher percentage of principals are former special needs teachers, especially at the elementary level. At that level, the assistant principal is dedicated mainly to special education. Many feel that it's sometimes better to know the intricacies of special education law than academics.

In the ideological warfare that surrounds public education, common sense is a spectator whose voice is rarely heard.

An Unexplored Email

I found something that was noted—and dismissed—in the special grand jury report interesting. At 1:28 p.m. on May 28, Tim Flynn sent an email to his supervisor, the director of high school education, that noted: "I have a female student who alleges another student attempted to rape her in the bathroom today. We are sending this to law enforcement. The girl is currently with the nurse. We will address this by the numbers. This was the same student who was transferred here from THS for a similar allegation."

The special grand jury report then noted: "It is unclear why the SBHS principal included that last sentence in his email or its relevance to the situation. The fact the SBHS principal included it at all, however, suggest [sic] he was skeptical of the veracity of the allegation from the outset."

As well he should have been.

The "THS" referred to in the email was Tuscarora High School, the fifteen-year-old female student's original school. Had those conducting the special grand jury probe bothered to ask, Scott and Jessica Smith could have waived the state and federal laws regarding the confidentiality of student records and revealed the reason for the transfer to the grand jurors. This could have explained the complex situation facing Stone Bridge's administration.

The Superintendent's Message of May 28

Superintendent Scott Ziegler sent a message to the school board through an email address, LCPS Confidential, about the May 28 incident on the day it happened. The subject line was: "CONFIDENTIAL, School Incident." I will note that I was not among the LCPS administrators copied on this message, which follows: "The purpose of this email is to provide you with information regarding an incident that occurred at Stone Bridge HS. This afternoon a female student alleged that a male student sexually assaulted her in the restroom. The LCSO is investigating the matter. Secondary to the assault investigation, the female student's parent responded to the school and caused a disruption by using threatening and profane language that was overheard by staff and students. Additional law enforcement units responded to the school to assist with the parent.

"The school's counseling team is providing services for students who witnessed the parent's behavior. The alleged victim is being tended to by LCSO.

"As LCSO is investigating both incidents, further updates may not be available."

The special grand jury asked the school board members if they should have asked for more information. "When you saw that email as school board chair, did you think anything of it at the time?" Carlton Davis asked Brenda Sheridan. "Did you go back to Scott and ask for more information? Can you talk to us about what you did or what conversation you had upon receiving the email?"

Sheridan replied, "So, of course, when I read the email—any time you read an email like this—your heart breaks for the students involved. And, of course, there are no student names. We don't know who is involved. We don't actually know what happened. We just know an allegation has been made." Later, she added, "When the Loudoun County Sheriff's Office was investigating the matter . . . we shouldn't be involved until after that was finished. That was standard."

Davis pressed her on this point. "But the question is, what did you do to find out more information? Sure, the Sheriff's Office may be involved, but people in the school certainly knew a lot about what was going on, because it occurred at the school. I mean, how often do you get emails that there was an alleged sexual assault? Those are very strong words."

Sheridan maintained the logical, factual course; a stream of thought that was not accepted by the prosecution. "Sure, so generally when we get any email like this, I wouldn't ask for more information until it was brought to us, because as the schools, School Board, we're the final adjudicator when it comes to expulsions or any student discipline. So if we were to ask for information that could sway me one way or the other, I would not be an impartial adjudicator when it comes time for, perhaps, the student appeal or an expulsion. So I wouldn't, while it was being investigated, the School Board would not be made privy to any details."

Davis stayed the course, even though he was not getting what he wanted. "But you can ask, as a School Board member, you can always ask for more details. Something, nothing . . ."

"As a long-standing School Board member, I wouldn't have gone back and asked for details. I would have known to wait until the, it was . . ."

Davis interrupted, "Well you should have known to wait because you've been on the board for 10 years."

"Right, correct." Sheridan sensed that she was finally getting through Davis's thick skull.

"Do you think, maybe, Dr. Ziegler knew more than he was letting on in that email?" Davis asked Atoosa Reaser. "I didn't think about whether he knew more or not, but it wouldn't surprise me if there were things that other people are required to keep confidential until investigations are complete, and that's common," she answered.

More Chaos at Stone Bridge

Tim Flynn encountered two crises at Stone Bridge the morning of June 1, 2021.

First, a student suffered a medical emergency during student arrival. The school called an ambulance to campus. Next, Scott Smith tried to forcibly enter the building after his violent behavior the previous Friday.

Corrine Czekaj's investigative notes set the scene for what happened. SRO Tavis Henry received a phone call from a sheriff's office lieutenant about the Smiths wanting to return to the high school to talk to administrators. Henry requested another deputy to escort the couple into the building with an expected arrival time of 11:00 a.m. In her notes, Czekaj detailed the need for immediate preparation given the chaos surrounding the previous incident with Scott and Jessica Smith. Despite the preparation, Czekaj noted that Scott Smith caused yet another disruption that "scared staff and students to the point of tears and fear."

Most LCPS schools have a security vestibule, an area between the main entrance to the school and the corridor leading to the interior of the building. A visitor shows an ID to a camera outside the main entrance and states their reason for wanting to enter the school through a device known as an aPhone. If everything checks out, the visitor is buzzed into the security vestibule. There they are identified again by the office staff before being buzzed into the building. Somehow, Scott Smith managed to get into the security vestibule but was denied entry into the building. He started a tirade that immediately caught the attention of students in the adjacent library.

The Loudoun County Sheriff's Office was called to Stone Bridge for the second time in two business days to deal with Scott Smith.

Scott Smith recounted his actions on June 1 for the special grand jury:

"We all march up to the front door and that's when I was told that there was a no-trespassing order, verbally, not by a sheriff, or whatever, that delivers them to your home, normally. I've had a few of them. No, verbal. What? Whatever." How often have you been served a no-trespass order? Had a few of them? There's more than a little to unpack here.

Later, Smith added, "I always wanted, like, 15 minutes of fame, but not this way."

After talking with Tim Flynn about the morning's events, I sent him the following message to distribute to the community:

Emergency Vehicles on Campus at Stone Bridge

This is Principal Tim Flynn,

Emergency vehicles were summoned to Stone Bridge twice today. At 9:00 a.m. during student arrival, a student suffered a medical emergency and the rescue squad was summoned. At 11:00 a.m., we had a non-student attempt to enter the building without authorization. This individual did not get past the vestibule area, although they did attempt to attract attention from students in the library. The individual was quickly escorted out of the building by Loudoun County Sheriff's Office deputies. Several sheriff's office cruisers remained on our campus until about 12:30.

This incident was witnessed by a large number of students, although student and staff safety was not compromised. Counseling services and the services of our Unified Mental Health Team are available for any student who may wish to talk about today's incident. The safety of our students and staff is the top priority of Loudoun County Public Schools. If you have any concerns, you may contact me at [redacted].

The Boy in the Skirt and His Mother

Meanwhile, Corrine Czekaj went to Stone Bridge on June 1 to interview students about the May 28 incident. One student wrote the following as part of the questioning: "[The boy] and [the girl] have a romantic past and so does [the boy] and [a second female Stone Bridge student]. This all started when [the boy] and [the second female Stone Bridge student] did, quote, 'it' at the school. I seen him grab people every day for a while."

Czekaj talked to the boy, with his mother present, during the June 1 interviews. The boy hinted that the girl in the May 28 incident had had sex with another student.

Czekaj said that after the alleged assault was reported, the boy said that he hid out in a bathroom—with his computer—until school was over. I wondered how school staff, who were looking for him, didn't find him in the bathroom given that he was a stationary target.

Czekaj detailed what the boy told her about the alleged assault. After the assault, he then hinted at doing something else, "which I later asked him what it was, and he said that he meant, quote, 'head.'

"I asked him if—about force being used. He did confirm that—let me see what his words were—that he held her arm behind her back."

A couple of things go through my head on reading this. First, I can't imagine having this conversation in front of my mother. Second, given the blunt language of Zappers32, I can't believe "hinting" was in his repertoire.

Czekaj recorded the reaction of the boy's mother to the alleged incident. The mother said that she was concerned about her son's lack of respect for personal space. She also revealed that he exposed himself in the sixth grade. Tim Flynn advised the mother that her son couldn't use the girls' bathroom because he identified as male. So much for the school giving permission for a biological male to use a girls' bathroom.

During special grand jury testimony, Carlton Davis broached the subject of the boy's sexual identity with Czekaj. "Are you aware of [the boy's] comfort with his male sexuality?"

Czekaj replied, "His mom advised me he came out to her as pansexual, which she openly accepted, and he was kind of angry that she didn't react and that then he became aggressive about it." For those unfamiliar with the term, someone who is pansexual is someone who is romantically attracted to people regardless of their sex or gender.

In a *New York Times* article, the boy's mother had this to say about her son's sexuality, "He had presented to me this desire to explore a different lifestyle." But the mother added that her son was "absolutely not" transgender. "He did not identify as fluid or anything like that."

The special grand jury testimony provided more insight into the situation.

Davis asked the question that would go on to inflame right-wing imaginations about this incident. "Do you know anything about [the boy] wearing skirts just so he can have easier access to the girls' bathroom?"

"I don't know for sure why he began wearing skirts or wore a skirt that day," Czekaj answered. "I do know that his mom said he—he won't be wearing skirts anymore. He'll be showing up to school in pants or shorts."

Mom also shared with Czekaj that her son was deleting things off his computer and that the school had given him a second computer. Two things slap me in the face about this statement: One, why was he allowed to keep his school-issued computer before being formally questioned? Two, why in God's name did LCPS give him another one?

Tavis Henry also interviewed the boy and his mother, whom I noted did not have the same last name. Mirroring what he had told Czekaj, the boy stated that the female student appeared to be stoned during their encounter and that the alleged sodomy consisted of ten seconds of him placing his penis in the wrong place.

Henry's report stated that the boy's mother compared her son to a movie character. "She compared him to Will in *Good Will Hunting* who sees psychologists as a chew toy." The mother went on to say that her son had yet to find his Robin Williams. What I found in other court documents later led me to believe that this boy was beyond help.

Court documents also stated that the boy had a long disciplinary history in middle school and had moved to New Jersey for a time before returning to LCPS.

A Son Only a Mother Could Love (Maybe)

In November of 2021, interviews began surfacing with the mother of the boy involved in the Stone Bridge incident. Right-wing media outlets like the *Daily Mail*, the *Daily Wire*, and the *New York Post* respected her request to protect her and her son's identity.

The mother said that her son was not transgender and did not wear a skirt to gain access to a girls' bathroom. She told the *Daily Mail* that he was "trying to find himself" and that this "involved all kinds of styles." The boy would "wear a skirt one day and then the next day he would wear jeans and a T-shirt, a Polo or a hoodie."

"I believe he was doing it because it gave him the attention he desperately needed and sought."

A photo that accompanied these stories was certainly attention-getting. It portrayed a young man, face blurred, in a black, female blouse with a plunging neckline and a black, plaid skirt. This outfit was accented by a black collar with the word "Kitten" in gold letters and a small charm hanging from it. The boy's hairstyle was flamboyant, shaved on the sides, long hair cascading from the top of his head. The photo depicted him standing in front of a rainbow Pride flag.

The mother didn't soft-pedal her son's reasons for being in the bathroom. "He's a 15-year-old that wanted to have sex in the bathroom with somebody that was willing." Her son accidentally performed anal sex on the girl, the mother said, after his watch got caught on his skirt.

Tuesday, June 22, 2021:
A Riotous School Board Meeting

On Tuesday, June 22, 2021, the shit hit the fan, and Loudoun County became international news.

For the first time in a long time, an audience was allowed in the school board meeting room while public comment was offered. In the days leading up to the meeting, rumors flew about who would be there. Republicans started a rumor that Antifa was busing in God knows who from Washington, DC. Fairfax County Republicans put out a call for people to attend, even though the meeting wasn't in Fairfax.

A ton of ultra-Right misinformation stoked the outrage, with Fox News the unquestioned leader of the misinformation. According to Media Matters, Fox aired seventy-eight segments about racial matters involving LCPS between March and June 2021. The Fox News demographic (fifty-five to dead) showed up in force for the June 22 Loudoun County School Board meeting, wearing matching red T-shirts with neatly printed red placards featuring white lettering (We The Parents Stand Up!). They were protesting against CRT, equity education, the transgender agenda, and anything else Tucker Carlson was spouting off on at the moment.

Foreshadowing what would happen at this meeting were incidents during the prior board meeting on June 8. At that time, the school board left the dais when, after being warned, speakers vitriolically assailed the board and staff.

Multiple TV crews and news outlets were in the room for the June 22 meeting, including, for the first time, the international news service Reuters. Broadcast cameras were wedged into two areas flanking the board dais at the front of the room, which gave them an up-close view of the action.

In the hours leading up to the meeting, people swarmed the parking lot in front of the Administration Building, attending dueling rallies, with the Right more represented by far. There were banners and flags, lawn signs railing against CRT and for and against trans rights, and a box truck with a large electronic signboard on its side. The digital image on the side of the truck flashed a photo of a haggard-looking school board member, Beth Barts, with wording calling for her recall. Heated rhetoric from portable sound systems filled the air with anger.

It was a hot, sunny day, which didn't help things as already-agitated people—more than six hundred—moved slowly through security and into the building. I was standing next to LCPS Director of Safety and Security John Clark, a former Secret Service agent, as people filed into the meeting room. Clark spotted a carton of eggs in a woman's purse. When questioned, the woman said that someone in the parking lot had given her the eggs. She didn't know why. Well, you damn well know it wasn't a farmer's market out there. The eggs were confiscated. Thanks to Clark's well-trained eyes, the school board was at least spared the indignity of being egged. By the time the meeting started, the school board meeting room was packed to capacity with people sitting shoulder-to-shoulder in cramped rows of chairs.

Chair Brenda Sheridan set the ground rules for public comment at the outset: no loud applause or heckling speakers or the school board, no waving of signs, no overt demonstrations. If the crowd was unruly, she would call a five-minute recess. If a second disturbance occurred, public comment would end.

Because of the number of speakers, each was allowed one minute to address the board. Comments that afternoon included railing against Critical Race Theory, which speakers likened to the indoctrination methods of communist China; the perils of letting transgender students into locker rooms and bathrooms; the government using schools to create an authoritarian state; and the fiery punishment God would inflict on the school board for their crimes against the children of Loudoun County.

Things went badly from the start. Every time someone spoke in favor of transgender rights or equity initiatives, there were snide comments, taunts, and collective groans from those wearing red. Brenda Sheridan made good on her promise and called a recess after the audience's behavior got out of hand. All nine school board members exited quickly off the dais for a break that lasted far longer than five minutes. Audience members screamed "Cowards!" and "Resign!" as the board members left. A Reuters' photographer captured one woman—long, curly, red hair, face contorted by anger—whose visage soon became the face of White, suburban rage in America.

When the meeting resumed, it was obvious we weren't going to make it to the end of the speakers' list.

The speaker that pushed the crowd over the edge was former Virginia State Senator Dick Black. Black had been a political outlier in the General Assembly ever since he served in the House of Delegates from 1998 to 2006. An ultra, ultra conservative, he crusaded against abortion, porn, and gay rights. Black was best known in Richmond for distributing plastic fetuses to emphasize his antiabortion stance. Defeated in his last House race, he entered the Senate in 2012 in the newly created Thirteenth District and served until retiring in 2020.

Black was speaker fifty-one of a scheduled 250.

The seventy-seven-year-old's oration before the school board was incendiary. He used his minute to recite the ultra-Right's greatest hits. "I am retired Senator Dick Black of Ashburn, Virginia. You retaliated against Tanner Cross by yanking him from teaching for addressing a public hearing of this board. The judge ordered you to reinstate Mr. Cross because, if his comments were not protected speech, then free speech does not exist at all.

"It's absurd and immoral for teachers to call boys girls and girls boys. You're making teachers lie to students, and even kids know that it's wrong.

"This board has a dark history of suppressing free speech. They caught you red-handed with an enemies list to punish opponents of Critical Race Theory. You're teaching children to hate others because of their skin color and you're forcing them to lie about other kids' gender. I am disgusted by your bigotry . . ."

At this point, Black's minute was up, and the mic went dead, although he could still be heard saying "and depravity." He kept yelling more invective, but his words were drowned out by the approving roar of the people who had been standing and waving placards throughout his oration.

Vice Chair Atoosa Reaser made a quick motion: "Madam Chair, I move to end public comment." Broad Run member Leslee King quickly seconded the motion, and the board voted 9 to 0 to end public comment, with Denise Corbo weighing in remotely. As promised, Brenda Sheridan called an end to public comment. "Public comment is now over and we will move on to our next agenda item." Wishful thinking. It quickly became obvious that the board would not be moving to its next agenda item as screaming insults rained down upon it from the audience. The school board exited from behind its bulletproof, reinforced dais at the front of the room.

Members of the crowd again began screaming "Resign!", "Shame on you!", and "Cowards!" at board members as they left. Senior school administration members were left to fend for themselves as the room dissolved into a three-ring circus.

A graphic appeared on the image broadcast from the meeting room: "The Loudoun County School Board Is In Recess And Will Return Shortly." After a few seconds, the background of the angry crowd was replaced by American and Virginia flags.

From my vantage point in the media box at the back of the room, three things grabbed my attention.

On my right, Elicia Leudemann, who goes by Elicia Brand, stood on top of a chair. Wearing a tank top featuring an American flag, she began to sing the national anthem. Many people joined in. (Leudemann/Brand later became the publicity advisor for Scott and Jessica Smith.)

At the center of the room, Jon Tigges—who later admitted he was not an LCPS parent—jumped on a chair and started speaking on a portable sound system. I didn't know where that system came from or how it had gotten through security into the room. Tigges said something to the effect that this was a public building and that the public was going to speak. He would moderate as public comment continued.

After what seemed like an eternity, Superintendent Scott Ziegler came into the room and declared an unlawful assembly. Under the Code of Virginia, a person who has the responsibility for maintaining a building has the right to do this. The declaration was followed by two dozen Loudoun County Sheriff's Office deputies entering the back of the room to sweep it clear. They confronted Jon Tigges at the front of the room and asked him to leave. When Tigges refused, they arrested him and cuffed his hands behind his back. Not willing to go down without a fight, Tigges struggled with multiple deputies and began making a break toward a locked door.

To my left, several deputies began wrestling with Scott Smith. As he wrestled, Smith's shirt flipped up and his pants fell down to the point that his genitals were almost exposed. His mouth was bright red. I couldn't tell if it was lipstick or blood. At first, I thought he might be a transgender man whom the mob had set upon. I later learned that the deputies had arrested Smith after a confrontation with a woman in the audience.

I learned more details about the confrontation from Scott Smith's testimony to the special grand jury on June 22, 2022.

Even his own father had warned him against going to the school board meeting. "So I, basically, you know, you know—my dad told me to stay away from the school board meeting because he said, you know, 'Scott, Loudoun County is going to chew you up and spit you out. You just need to focus, you know, on the family.' And I said, 'Yeah, OK.' That was a few days before that, or whatever, but I didn't understand. I didn't know what they were voting on. I didn't even know what the bathroom policy was. I was really confused, really." Policy 8040 was on the agenda that night, but for discussion, not a vote.

Smith said that his arrest on June 22, 2021, resulted from an LGBTQ activist confronting him and threatening to harm his business. Smith recounted the legal hearing that followed his arrest. "I told the magistrate to his face, 'You don't want to press these charges. This is not going to work out well for anyone.'"

Scott Smith was not an immediate concern of mine on June 22, 2021, however.

I went back to my office after the sheriff's office cleared the room and switched on the computer. The Internet was flooded with images from the school board meeting. People were posting images and videos from the meeting, and some had streamed the events live.

After the pandemonium ceased, the board decided to resume the meeting without the public present. Joan Sahlgren and I spent most of the remainder of the meeting polishing a statement that Chair Sheridan would read justifying the ending of public comment. "We will not back down from fighting for the rights of our students and continuing our focus on equity," she said at the meeting's end.

A Haunting Question

One thing that was said during the June 22 meeting—something that would return to haunt us all later—went almost unnoticed at the time. School board member Beth Barts asked the superintendent if there had been any assaults in LCPS bathrooms. "Do we have assaults in our bathrooms or in our locker rooms regularly? I would hope not, but I would like a clarification." Scott Ziegler replied: "To my knowledge, we don't have any record of assaults occurring in our restrooms."

This statement and the question that prompted it were, respectively, a stretching of the truth and—intentionally or not—a setup. When Barts asked the question she knew that the school board had been informed, confidentially, that there had been an alleged assault at Stone Bridge on May 28. Why she wanted this to be public—besides creating the kind of chaos she revels in—was beyond me.

Scott was technically correct in stating that there had not been an assault. No charges had yet been filed. He also claimed that he thought Barts was asking if there had been any bathroom assaults involving transgender students. Such legal technicalities, however, don't hold up in the court of public opinion.

Reading Barts's special grand jury testimony regarding this question more than eighteen months later, my mind was blown. Barts said that she was not referring to the Stone Bridge incident but, rather, a 2018 incident at Tuscarora High School that resulted in three football players being charged with sexual assault. It should be noted that this incident occurred long before LCPS hired Scott Ziegler. What follows is the word salad Barts offered as the rationale behind her question. "And it was very upsetting for our community, so I was surprised he didn't know about it, because that had been all over the news. But he completely looked oblivious. He really—I don't think he knew about it, because he wasn't even around then."

Barts then tried to explain her logic in asking the question, which did nothing to clarify her motivation. "And my point was, I guess—and I don't know if I had a point—I just found it interesting that the assault that I knew about and the community knew about in the bathroom—and this was a locker room, but there is [sic] bathrooms in the locker rooms—happened to be not at all, it was football players, like, sexually assaulting one of their own.

"And that was really the only—to me that was more concerning, bathroom safety from that point, than worrying about people going to the bathroom and using the identity they identify with."

Barts then told the special grand jury something I found especially stunning. "I had forgotten about the Stone Bridge incident. I didn't even think about that, honestly."

Barts added that she didn't particularly pay attention to Scott Ziegler's May 28 email to the school board about the alleged assault. "No, because that was just an alleged, and we got emails all the time about assaults that we never got any more information about."

A Tangible Effect of the June 22 School Board Riot

In the aftermath of the near-riot at the school board meeting, Superintendent Scott Ziegler requested extra security for the next school board meeting on August 11. In an August 6 email to Sheriff Chapman, Ziegler asked for a five-person quick reaction force, undercover sheriff's office personnel in the Administration Building, and a special operations team on standby.

In a reply email the same day, Chapman let the superintendent know that this would not be happening. "Your request is extraordinary and would likely constitute LCSO's commitment of a minimum of approximately 65 sworn deputies. Despite this, you fail to provide any justification for such a manpower intensive request."

Ziegler offered this reply: "I agree with you that LCSO is the expert on public safety and law enforcement, so the request and deployment of LCSO resources mirrored those of June 22—a plan developed by LCSO."

LCPS Chief Operations Officer Kevin Lewis, who then oversaw the school division's security department, had further conversations with Chapman on the subject. Lewis summed up the sheriff's feeling that the "School Board is firing people up and calling LCSO to clean it up." A note obtained by Fox News noted that Chapman felt that the "School board is being dismissive of people they don't agree with."

Protecting Loudoun's largest public building after a riot, and in the midst of continued large-scale demonstrations, was no longer on the agenda for the sheriff's office.

Once the sheriff's office withdrew its protection for school board meetings, LCPS hired a private security firm. Wanding and bag searches were instituted at the public entrance to the Administration Building. Two armed guards, sometimes three, were at the staff entrance guarding an empty parking lot as I left after midnight on meeting nights.

I felt like the most-protected person in Northern Virginia.

The truest statement made in the special grand jury report was buried on page eighteen: "Several witnesses (myself included) testified the sheriff and superintendent are not on speaking terms and tension exists between the leadership of LCPS and LCSO. The citizens of Loudoun County deserve better than two high-profile individuals publicly squabbling and refusing to put aside any petty differences . . . The safety of the students and community require it."

Later the report stated: "It is important to point out the lack of cooperation between LCPS and LCSO was an underlying issue throughout summer 2021. This unquestionably contributed to LCPS' delinquency in opening the Title IX investigation into the SBHS sexual assault. Though the charging of the SBHS assailant in early July should have been enough for the chief of staff, under his interpretation, to launch a Title IX investigation, LCSO refused to provide the actual charges to LCPS."

Petty squabbles between an elected official, the sheriff, and an appointed bureaucrat, the superintendent of schools, led to a communications breakdown that had unfortunate future consequences.

Carlton Davis brought this up during his special grand jury questioning of Brenda Sheridan. "So you're making it sound like it's a law-enforcement problem. That law enforcement didn't share with the school system what you believe they should have shared."

"I think there was a breakdown in communication," Sheridan answered, "and I think that the—according to the report that staff gave us—that we, we asked several times for a status on the student, and they were told, repeatedly, that it was under investigation."

There was no chance, however, that the special grand jury report (or the officials from the attorney general's office who wrote the report) was going to place equal blame on the sheriff's office. Loudoun County Sheriff Mike Chapman, a Republican, was at Virginia Attorney General Jason Miyares's left side during a press conference during which Miyares affirmed that he was starting an investigation of LCPS during a November 4, 2021, news conference. Objectivity and digging for the truth were never on the agenda for the special grand jury.

Possible Ramifications of the June 22 School Board Riot

Loudoun County Deputy Commonwealth's Attorney Barry Alan Zweig testified before the special grand jury on September 28, 2021, the day before I was secretly indicted.

What he said blew me away.

Zweig testified that it was his opinion that the boy involved in the May 28, 2021, incident was charged in reaction to the riot at the June 22, 2021, school board meeting. "They weren't going to arrest him. They weren't going to charge him. So he remained at liberty in the community from that day forward.

"Between May 28th of 2021 and July 1st of 2021, which I believe is the date they sought petitions, nothing changed. They didn't get any additional information to the best of my knowledge . . . And then, on July 1st, they choose to charge him."

Why didn't this make the special grand jury's report?

During the special grand jury testimony, Carlton Davis asked Detective Corrine Czekaj why, when the alleged offense took place on May 28, the boy involved wasn't taken into custody until July 8. "That's 41 days . . . Why did it take so long between the incident and when he was taken into custody?"

Czekaj's answer outlined the complexity of the case and why, again, LCPS couldn't have said it was an assault on May 28. "So for juveniles, once you take them into custody and they're held, there's a Virginia code that states they have—there's [sic] 21 days until you can bring them to adjudication, so basically a trial.

"With cases like—let's say like a robbery or a physical assault where there's, you know, video of it happening and there's not much else to collect, that's easy. Unfortunately, for cases involving sexual assault, generally, these incidents themselves are not on video. So there's DNA we have to collect. There's [sic] several people we have to interview. The lab takes several months to compare that kit and the DNA, and then there's electronic communication. I believe Discord [the app through which the boy and victim communicated] returned the messages to me in July."

While this sounds reasonable, I still think Barry Alan Zweig had a point.

Vox Populi

June 22, 2021, wasn't the first time public comment turned vile during a meeting of the Loudoun County School Board.

Most public bodies have a portion of their meeting set aside for public comment. The idea is that ordinary citizens provide important input about agenda items. In reality, such exercises are an opportunity for the angry, perpetually aggrieved, and just plain crazy to loudly vent their grievances.

Wise public bodies put a strict limit—thirty minutes is a popular choice—on how long this part of the meeting can last. Some limit the number of appearances a speaker can make in a designated time period (one appearance a month).

The Loudoun County School Board was not a wise public body.

There was no limit on how many speakers could sign up or a specific time dedicated to public comment. If fewer than sixty speakers signed up, they would be allotted two minutes each.

I would create a summary of each school board meeting, known as the résumé, summarizing board actions and noting speakers before the board along with the topics they addressed. I would note many of these topics as "various concerns," because speakers had the habit of spewing out disorganized ramblings that would touch on any number of things. At the behest of the then chief of staff in 2021, I went back over the roster of speakers for the past three years to identify repeat speakers. There were forty to sixty who would show up at virtually every meeting. This wasn't a significant part of the population in a county of more than 400,000, but they created the illusion of massive discontent and drew constant media attention. Such speakers were known as C.A.V.E. (Citizens Against Virtually Everything) dwellers.

While their faces remained the same, their speaking subjects would morph to reflect the predominant far-right hot topic de jour (distance learning, mask-wearing, vaccination, CRT, transgender matters).

In an August 2023 article in *The New York Times*, Ian Prior admitted how small the number of people voicing their opinions actually was. "Most parents aren't fully engaged in this. It's 10 percent here, 10 percent there." Ultimately, he added, the much-hyped culture war over schools was "a battle between those 10 percents."

Like most local political bodies, the meetings of the Loudoun County School Board are televised. Using grant funds, I upgraded the cameras in the board room to HD broadcast quality. This presented a clear picture of what was going on for the few lost souls—usually numbering around four hundred—who would entertain themselves watching hours of bureaucracy in action. It was also perfect for clipping small segments to create YouTube videos. Loudoun's public comments would often go viral, and some even inspired sketches on *Saturday Night Live*. Parody met reality.

Loudoun County School Board meetings became the perfect venue for political performance artists from other jurisdictions who would stop by to enhance their online presence. A particularly egregious example of this phenomenon was non-Loudoun resident and non-LCPS employee, Lilit Vanetsyan. Lilit spoke at a meeting giving the impression that she was an LCPS teacher who was offended by the school division's equity training. As she spoke, I searched the Outlook email directory to check if she was, indeed, one of our employees.

She was not.

Speakers were required to list their phone number on the speaker sign-up list. The next day, I called Lilit. "Are you a Loudoun County Public Schools teacher?"

"Depends who's asking," was the snotty reply.

"A senior administrator at Loudoun County Public Schools."

Despite a concerted effort, I could find no public school division claiming Lilit as an employee. This didn't stop "Brave Teacher Speaks Out Against Biased Race Training" from going viral. Lilit appeared in her "brave teacher" persona on Fox News. Clearing the fact-checking bar at Fox News appeared to be easy. Finally, through the Virginia Freedom of Information Act, I found out that Lilit was once employed by Fairfax County Schools as "a 0.60 Music Teacher." A part-time music teacher. I could certainly see how Critical Race Theory affected her work.

The one good thing about Lilit's chicanery was that it prompted the school board to enact a measure that the administration had been begging for. The school board decided that only Loudoun residents, those with businesses in Loudoun, current or former LCPS employees, and those with some other tenuous ties to Loudoun would be allowed to speak. It was also decided that—as many school districts do—public speaking would be shot from a wide view at the back of the room, rather than focusing on each speaker at the podium. The rationale? Speakers should be there to address the board, not to make YouTube videos.

One of the most famous Loudoun County School Board speakers was Brandon Michon. On January 26, 2021, he delivered a particularly unhinged diatribe that could be titled "Figure It Out!" The gist of Michon's ramblings was that he wanted children back in school for in-person learning. Some highlights of his impassioned oratory: "The garbage workers who pick up my freakin' trash risk their lives every day more than anyone in this school system." He referred to the school board as a "bunch of cowards" who were "hiding behind our children as an excuse for keeping schools closed." Michon then demanded the school board, "Figure it out, or get off the podium! Because, you know what? There are people like me and a lot of other people out there who will gladly take your seat and figure it out. It's not a high bar. Raise the freakin' bar!"

Michon was quickly booked for an appearance on Fox News with Tucker Carlson. Buoyed by his national media appearances, Michon decided to set his political sights much higher than the school board and ran for the

Republican nomination for the Tenth District congressional seat. "Let's Go Brandon" signs soon appeared along Route 7 in western Loudoun County, which was a bit confusing. Were these signs meant to insult President Biden or boost the candidacy of Loudoun's "Mad Dad"?

In the end, it didn't matter.

Michon got only 13.9 percent of the vote in the Republican primary.

Finding the optimum spot to speak at a Loudoun County School Board meeting was akin to getting a good seat at a restaurant. Some citizens tried to sign up so that they could speak back-to-back. This was a tactic used by those reading documents too long for the time constraints, such as a Parents Bill of Rights.

Ian Prior of Fight for Schools was a regular in the hallway outside the school board meeting room. He edited the scripts that various "concerned parents" would use, making sure to cover all of his organization's talking points. There was not much genuine or original sentiment expressed by the speakers—everything was very stage-managed for maximum media effectiveness.

The speakers that bothered me the most were the teachers who disparaged the superintendent and school board during public comment. If this was such an evil organization, why would you work for it? On a practical level, it showed a stunning ignorance of the real world. If an employee went before the CEO and board of directors of a corporation, called them idiots and worse, and said they wouldn't obey company policy, security would remove them mid-speech. The contents of their office would be on the sidewalk within an hour.

Sometimes, a "celebrity" speaker would show up. Conservative political commentator Matt Walsh announced that he was moving to Loudoun County after the school board imposed the residency requirement on speakers. He rented a basement from a sympathetic resident for one dollar and was part of a rally in the parking lot before the meeting. I don't remember his comments being anything exceptional, and he only turned up once.

Ah, the parking lot . . .

Every second and fourth Tuesday, bright and early, small orange cones were placed around the main parking lot in front of the Administration Building to designate a protest area. The "cones of invincibility" I called them. As the months wore on from the June 22, 2021, riot, the protests became smaller and less volatile. Sometimes a stage was set up in a corner where speakers let forth some pre-meeting venom and sang patriotic songs.

Most of these rallies were set up for a crowd of hundreds and drew fifty or so attendees. On one sad occasion, a giant TV screen was set up in the protest zone so that a throng of people could view the meeting inside. It played in high-definition grandeur to a crowd of no one.

The Keyboard Warrior Brigade and Other Complainants Weigh In

The most-infamous online presence in Loudoun County—and this is really saying something—was Scott Mineo, who ran PACT. This group vehemently opposed the teaching of Critical Race Theory in public schools—something that no public school system does—among a list of other grievances. Media watchers drew links between PACT and QAnon and One America News Network (OANN).

Mineo was a regular speaker at school board meetings and the protests outside them. At one point, he announced that he would be forming a group of young PACT supporters, dubbed PACT Rats. As far as I know, this organization never took off.

I know from his Freedom of Information Act requests that Mineo was always looking for connections—monetary or philosophical—between LCPS and the National Association for the Advancement of Colored People (NAACP). However, he denied that this obsession had any racial overtones. "Being against Critical Race Theory doesn't mean that someone holds the position of a white supremacist."

Mineo had a standard for determining who was a White supremacist: "If you're going to call me a white supremacist, you better have some pictures of me walking around with a freaking hood. Because I'm not. I'm not. I know what I am."

Mineo admitted to the media that he posted to social media platforms using the name Vito Malara. Vito Malara seemed to tow Mineo's own line for White supremacy. A Vito Malara offering from 2017 regarding a crime in Baltimore: "Pack of savages. Is this just another example of black youth's [sic] being frustrated and expressing themselves? Nope. Just another day for many inner city blacks and innocent white victims."

Vito also had a nasty side, posting his fair share of racially motivated tweets. "The NAACP has got to go. They are not legitimate. They are nothing more than a radical group of racists, troublemakers, and victim creators."

Asked about his racist-strewn postings in May 2021, Mineo defended his alter ego. "When you're talking about a fatherless environment, maybe it was a hit-and-run. Those aren't my stats. I stand by my (or Vito's) words. You can't tie me to white supremacy."

Mineo had the uncanny habit of showing up at student walkouts and parental rallies whenever the media needed the perspective of a "concerned parent."

In 2021, Mineo/Malara said that leading PACT had made him more diplomatic. "I know I have to be more careful with my words. It's not a bad thing. It forces you to think."

Before I started the drive to my lawyer's office in Fairfax on March 7, 2023, I read a post Mineo had placed on the PACT Facebook page the night before. (I made it a habit to scroll through the opposition's social media postings each morning.) It was a pathetic, whining rant from a victimizer playing victim as he announced that he would no longer run PACT. It read, in part:

My intentions have always been noble, even though occasionally gone awry. I hope that some individuals have found value in the information I have provided despite their disagreement with my standpoint or approach. These past three years have been a turbulent and time-consuming ride, which has resulted in me taking numerous blows and sacrificing a lot for what purposes you might ask? Good question. Our daughter will be graduating in June, and it is high time others become involved. While individuals do not have to resort to toxicity to maintain the flow of information and message, I do hope that someone or some people will recognize the gravity of the situation and get involved in some capacity. Going forward, the "PACT" that you may have developed strong feelings towards in the last three years will cease to engage in derogatory and highly objectionable statements or positions. While I will still disseminate information, I will no longer act as the "hitman" for Loudoun County, and I hope someone else will be willing to take on this role.

The next day, the PACT Facebook page was gone, along with Vito Malara's.

Mineo later whined about his lot in life during a sympathetic interview on WJLA-TV. "They went after my job. That happened in early February. The *[sic]* referred me to the FBI, the IRS and DHS, all because they don't like my opinions.

"They're probably going to sit back and celebrate the fact that I'm unemployed. I'm having a hard time finding a job. And who knows what's next with the IRS and FBI? But they've done more than just put me out of a job. It's impacting my family, my kids."

Who knew that actions would have consequences?

Reporting of the doings of Loudoun County's school board by right-wing media set up a deluge of online activity. Every time Loudoun was featured on Fox News, conservative talk radio, or outlets like the *Daily Caller*, hundreds of emails would flood in.

The following are emails that typified what school board members received:

"Don't be surprised when you low-IQ, poorly educated, and morally bankrupt pinko traitors are dragged from your beds in the middle of the night and hanged by the neck until dead by the righteously angry parents of your community. I will be cheering them on. White men built all the best things in the world. Every other civilization is inferior."

"You fucking disgusting piece of shit. YOU ARE A TRAITOR TO THE USA!"

"A public hanging is in order . . . Should only take a few seconds."

Some messages went beyond the laziness of frustrated keyboard warriors. This handwritten note showed up at the home of Loudoun County School Board Chair Brenda Sheridan addressed to her adult children: "It is too bad your mother is an ugly communist whore. If she doesn't quit or resign before the end of the year, we will kill her, but first, we will kill you."

Sometimes, LCPS's detractors got personal, calling my office to express outrage about something they had seen on Fox.

Occasionally, curiosity would get the better of me, and I would return the call of someone who asked for a follow-up conversation.

One such conversation that I particularly remember was with an older gentleman from Naperville, Illinois. Knowing this part of the state, I asked him if he was a Cubs or Cardinals fan as an ice-breaker.

Cards.

So we spoke a few minutes about the good old days of Ken Boyer, Lou Brock, Bob Gibson, and the 1964 and 1967 World Champions. A rapport established, I asked him why he was so upset by Loudoun County Public Schools. He said that Loudoun's issues reflected those he saw in Naperville, where they'd experienced Black Lives Matter protests and a general shift in what had been the established norms of decent society. About the only thing he still liked about his hometown was the parks system, which he said was excellent. After talking for fifteen minutes or so, we parted on friendly terms. He was just a lonely old man who watched too much Fox News.

I vowed to check out the parks system if I ever passed through Naperville.

Legally, communications staff can't block comments made on the official LCPS Facebook page. This policy has led to thousands of ugly comments swamping the page. The uglier comments were reported to Facebook, which, after a huge number of comments concerning a single user, would temporarily ban the user. These users would always reemerge, however, like a turd that won't flush.

What Happened after the Riot?

The vitriol spewed by extremists at the school board meeting in person and online became fuel for local and national players that didn't seem to be intent on addressing the actual communication breakdown that occurred on May 28, but rather focused on moving forward individual political agendas.

The Future Governor/Governor Versus the Loudoun County School Board

Axiom Strategies founder Jeff Roe, Glenn Youngkin's campaign consultant, summed up Youngkin's appeal to parents for *The New York Times*. "Glenn became a vessel for their anger."

Empty vessels make the most noise.

And the Youngkin campaign made plenty of noise in Loudoun.

Youngkin, with the help of the ever-present Ian Prior, painted the Loudoun County School Board as the primary practitioner of the "woke" ideology plaguing the public schools of Virginia. (Even though the board was only enacting policy dictated by Virginia's General Assembly.)

Youngkin staged rallies outside the LCPS Administration Building. His campaign set up a stage to the left of the imposing, five-story structure. It gave the illusion that this latter-day David was standing in front of a monolithic institutional Goliath and readying his stone for release. One of the few Black people attending the rally was always seated just behind his right shoulder so that they were in all the televised and photographic coverage of the event. (Thus demonstrating, I suppose, the diverse support the candidate enjoyed.)

Youngkin held his first rally outside the Administration Building on June 30, 2021, a little more than a week after the riotous school board meeting. Ian Prior was the kickoff speaker at the event. During the rally, Youngkin said that Loudoun County was "absolutely ground zero for the fight to return our schools to a curriculum that prepares our students for the future . . . Our children should not be the victims of the left-liberal progressives' culture war."

Youngkin's attacks on the school board didn't end with his election. It quickly became evident that Youngkin didn't know the difference between being a CEO and a steward of democracy.

Youngkin introduced an amendment that would move the Loudoun County School Board election up a year to November 2022. This would force board members into a very fast election cycle and potentially shorten their term by one year. The governor offered this rationale for his action: "The last few years just absolutely signified some real challenges with the Loudoun County School Board. And so, in the spirit of transparency and accountability, my amendment gives parents the ability to elect their School Board. This election can reflect the will of the parents."

Neglecting, of course, the fact that parents elected the current board, many by healthy margins, which certainly already reflected "the will of the parents."

The Washington Post noted that the amendment "stunned many state political observers as an intrusion into local election integrity without modern precedent in Virginia."

Nonetheless, the Republican House of Delegates passed the amendment. It was narrowly defeated in the Democratic-controlled State Senate, with one

Republican, David R. Suetterlein of Roanoke, voting against it. His rationale was the first common-sense utterance I'd heard come out of a Republican mouth in a very long time. "We can't just get to a place where, because we so oppose someone, we're going to unilaterally shorten their term."

Jennifer Victor, a political scientist at George Mason University, succinctly summed up this failed legislative maneuver. "From a democracy standpoint, it's just bad. For governors to be getting involved in changing the rules in a local election—it just runs counter to all of the goals we have for how elections and democracies are supposed to run."

The Passage of Policy 8040

The Loudoun County School Board adopted Policy 8040, Rights of Transgender and Gender-Expansive Students, on a 7-to-2 vote (Jeff Morse and John Beatty voted "No") on August 11, 2021. It was based on model policy set forth by the Virginia Department of Education. Of the several models available, the one adopted by the board was the most liberal, mandating the conversion of bathrooms and locker rooms for transgender use. This went way beyond the dictate to address students by their preferred names and pronouns. It was later revealed that only 10 percent of Virginia's school boards adopted new policies to meet the General Assembly's legislation. Other school divisions maintained that they had existing policies that met the requirements of the legislation.

In retrospect, I believe those divisions chose the proper course.

At the close of 2022, LCPS had 82,534 students. Of these students, 40,115 (48.6 percent) listed their gender as female, and 42,352 (51.3 percent) listed their gender as male. One-tenth of 1 percent (67) listed themselves as non-binary. Granted, there were probably many more non-binary students who did not wish to identify themselves on an official transcript. I don't blame them. Even if the number of non-binary students was ten times higher, it would still be only 1 percent of the total student population. With a public frustrated and angry with distance learning during the pandemic, focusing undue attention on a minute fraction of the student body was a huge strategic mistake.

It was mosquito hunting with a bazooka.

And it really might not have been what students wanted. During the fall of 2022, LGBTQ students and their allies walked out of school to protest the Youngkin administration's proposed policies regarding transgender students. I arranged for student spokesmen for the media that inevitably gathered. Speaking with them gave me insight into what the students—the people actually affected by such policies—wanted. First and foremost, they wanted to be recognized by their chosen identity and not to be harassed. Bathrooms and locker rooms were not on their agenda. Such places were usually uncomfortable for any student. Being singled out in special areas only made it worse.

The most visible sign of the bathroom conversions following the adoption of 8040 was the designation sign next to the door of single-stall bathrooms. Traditionally, these signs featured a male stick figure and a female stick figure wearing a dress. The new signage featured a male stick figure, a female stick figure, and a figure that was half-and-half. I have to ask if the third figure was really necessary. It appeared to be a slap in the face to any conservative person who entered the school, especially an elementary school. Parents accosted more than one principal about the new signs. School administrators really shouldn't have had to deal with such nonsense.

During the special grand jury, Carlton Davis questioned Brenda Sheridan about the relationship between the Stone Bridge incident and Policy 8040. "Well, here's my question to you: Did Scott Ziegler at any time, at any time ever, mention to you that the incident at Stone Bridge High School had anything to do with Policy 8040?"

Sheridan didn't bite. "I don't think so."

Davis asked Atoosa Reaser about Policy 8040 and the horrifying image of a boy in a dress following a girl into the girls' bathroom. Atoosa pointed

out that the boy was wearing a kilt, not a dress. "I think there's a big difference in the impression that people have [about] a kilt versus a dress."

Oh, Atoosa, in the court of public opinion, such differences didn't matter.

A Boy's Busy Summer

While Loudoun County was being thrown into the political bonfire, the boy
involved in the Stone Bridge incident was having an eventful summer. The
following was set forth in special grand jury testimony.

The way Deputy Commonwealth's Attorney Barry Zweig described what
happened after the boy was arrested on July 8, 2021, and arraigned the next
day, truly freaked me out.

First, the boy's mother told the court that she was going on a two-week
vacation, so some arrangements would have to be made as to where her son
would be staying. Another complication was that you can't hold a juvenile
prisoner for more than twenty-one days unless their case has gone forward.
The boy's next hearing was scheduled for September 29. It was decided that
the boy would be sent to stay with his grandmother on a farm in Pennsylvania, partially because she didn't have Internet service. Staying off the Internet
was a stipulation of the boy's release. Because the GPS ankle monitor he was
required to wear wouldn't operate at this distance, it was decided that he
would check in by phone every day and assure everyone that he was being
a good boy.

Jason Bickmore had been a Loudoun County juvenile probation officer
since 2007. During the June 28, 2022, special grand jury, he reported on his
notes. His first meeting with the boy was a videoconference on July 19, 2021,
while the boy was being held at the Loudoun County Juvenile Detention
Center. Theo Stamos read from Bickmore's notes about the meeting. The
probation officer was struck by something about the prisoner's demeanor.
"[The boy] has adjusted a little too easily to his experience and doesn't appear

to have any real concerns at the moment."

"Can you explain what motivated you to include that entry?" Theo asked. Bickmore replied, "He just seemed overly relaxed; that I would expect somebody to be a little more nervous about their situation, but he didn't present that way."

Bickmore related a discussion he had with the boy's mother at a July 26, 2021, court hearing. "He had ongoing behavioral problems since he was a young child, and she was concerned it was escalating at this point. She wasn't concerned for her own safety, but she was concerned about where things were headed for him if we didn't conduct an appropriate intervention at this time."

Bickmore then discussed the particulars of the case and why it was so difficult to prosecute. "So when you have a 'He said, she said' situation and you have cases where you don't normally prosecute and have, also, a victim who at this point we knew had some other behavioral problems and some mental health issues—we weren't sure if she would be good to testify. We don't want to, sometimes, put a victim on the stand and retraumatize them. There's a lot of complications."

A judge decided that the boy could not attend Stone Bridge High School. On August 5, 2021, Bickmore said that the school situation was still in flux. It was up to the boy's mother to find her son a new school to attend. Theo asked, "I mean, you don't have the authority to ask where this kid goes to school, do you, or place him in a different school?"

"I mean, I could," Bickmore replied. "But it's certainly a parent's obligation to find out what's going on with their kid's schooling situation, though . . . I thought that is definitely something mom could handle . . . or at least start."

Earth to Jason, mom took off on a two-week vacation as far away from her problem as she could get. I'm sorry, if the schools took the blame for this, some of it should have been spread to Court Services. Some heads, starting with Jason Bickmore's, should have rolled.

Bickmore finally phoned Stone Bridge Assistant Principal Fernando

Montanez, the first time Court Services had reached out to the schools, only two days before the start of the new school year.

Bickmore also testified that he had a phone conversation with the boy's mother on August 24. "Mom is frustrated by her son for not following the rules." According to Bickmore, Mom also said that her son was looking over his younger brother's shoulder to watch YouTube, a violation of the "no computer" stipulation of his probation. Mom was also upset that the boy left the charger for his ankle monitor in Pennsylvania so that his ankle monitor would not work, something she thought he did deliberately, Bickmore noted.

Mom set out her frustrations in an email to Bickmore. "[The boy continues] to break simple rules and guidelines of my house with little or no regard for the purpose of consequences, no matter the severity or length . . .As discussed, [he] does not recognize consequences, nor does he consider them a threat, because there's always an end to them. He can manipulate situations and people to bend to his will."

On August 26, Bickmore received a call from the boy's grandmother stating that her grandson was a sociopath and did not care about consequences. In addition, the boy was wetting and soiling his pants on purpose.

Theo's reaction to this litany of insanity was to draw attention back to her primary target. "Were you particularly frustrated with the Loudoun County Public Schools at this point?"

To Bickmore's credit, he didn't entirely take the bait. "I was frustrated with the situation, yes. I would have looked for the schools to contact me prior to that, but I also know that it's the beginning of the school year and it's not easy to get ahold of school representatives at that point . . . My assessment is that he is a young man who is greatly in need of structure and services, and he has not been able to get any of those at this point."

It was especially hard when school officials didn't know that the student had been charged with a crime because the sheriff's office and court services hadn't told them. Theo pressed on with her original line of questioning. "And whose fault is that?"

Bickmore gave an honest answer: "I don't know. I don't know how I would place blame. I mean there's—I don't know how to answer that question."

At this point, Bickmore offered the first information I'd heard about the boy's father. The father lived in New Jersey and had a new family.

Theo pressed on with the school's line of questioning. Bickmore offered some reasonable answers. "We tend not to communicate with the schools [sic] pre-adjudication in most cases, if we can avoid it, depending on the situation. But in this . . ."

Theo interrupted, "Excuse me. What is the reason for that?"

Bickmore replied, "Just because the young man is presumed innocent and sometimes schools can make decisions based on stuff that they shouldn't know at that point . . . Normally, that release of information is not done until post-adjudication when I start to do my investigation and write for the court."

Theo changed the direction of her cross-examination.

"Did you take forensic criminology? Did you have cases involving, like, what the background of Jack the Ripper was like?"

"Sure," Bickmore replied.

"And Ted Bundy?"

"Right."

Jack the Ripper and Ted Bundy might have been a stretch, but the boy was a troublesome mix of intelligence and dysfunction. According to Bickmore, the boy's IQ was 118—smart, but not Lex Luthor. He had a record of trouble at multiple schools at both the elementary and middle school levels. "I think he's bisexual, but I also think, you know, when speaking with his mother he likes to be provocative," said Bickmore.

During his evaluation, the boy said that he had multiple personalities. On May 28, 2021, he said a personality he called "Lust" was in control and basically admitted to committing rape. "I'm really not sure what it (was)," Bickmore said of this assertion. "If it was real, it was a problem; and if it wasn't and it was an attempt to manipulate my evaluation. That was a problem as well."

Bickmore also offered that the boy sometimes had "homicidal ideation." "It means that he sometimes feels homicidal towards people, that he feels violent towards people." Bickmore added that the boy said that he would sometimes hear voices and get into physical confrontations at his treatment facility.

A juror asked Bickmore if the boy showed any signs of remorse.

"There are certain times when he did, but for the most part, not so much. That's not unusual for kids with his level of disturbance, but it's certainly an issue and something we're working on in treatment."

A juror asked Bickmore if he had seen another juvenile like the boy.

"He is unique, but I will tell you that, unfortunately, I have had several young men who are just as equally disturbing. It doesn't happen very often. I think it's important for people to understand that in the juvenile world, in sex offenses, recidivism rates are extremely low. We're talking about somewhere between 4 and 6 percent."

Those words don't comfort me. What comforted me even less was when Bickmore related that, while the boy was on probation until he turned eighteen, he could be released from the residential treatment facility sooner "if he works through his program."

Bickmore offered this parting summation on the whole situation.

"So it was a very difficult position, and I wouldn't have wanted to be in it. Obviously, the outcomes in this situation are terrible, but I don't—I don't know that anybody could have prevented the situation from occurring."

What Went Wrong (as Far as I Knew)

It's popular in certain quarters of the media to blame all of America's ills on the Trump administration. However, a part of the institutional failures that riddled LCPS's investigation of the Stone Bridge incident were triggered by

Trump's secretary of education, Betsy DeVos. DeVos issued a new interpretation of Title IX investigations involving how allegations of sexual misconduct in school should be handled. Title IX governs how schools taking federal funding must handle sexual misconduct cases involving America's 56 million K through twelve and twenty million college students. In what she heralded as the signature achievement of her tenure, DeVos restricted schools' investigative powers and gave students accused of a sexual offense more avenues to defend themselves. "Too many students have lost access to their education because their school inadequately responded when a student filed a complaint of sexual harassment or sexual assault," according to DeVos as quoted in a 2020 Department of Education release. As it was understood by LCPS and the sheriff's office, this meant that the school division could begin its investigation only after law enforcement had concluded its investigation.

LCPS Chief of Staff Dr. Mark Smith said this before the special grand jury: "In this case, the student reported that someone tried to rape her, and law enforcement immediately took over at that point. We did not—the school didn't—to my understanding, did not question the individual, did not question anyone else.

"And I heard a report that law enforcement informed the school that, if they interfered in any way, they could be arrested for obstruction of justice."

LCPS Director of School Administration Dr. Doug Fulton testified that he received pushback from Mark Smith about opening a Title IX investigation into the May 28 incident. Ultimately, Doug said that Scott Ziegler told him to stand down when Doug brought his concerns to the superintendent. Doug also noted that the boy involved in the May 28 incident had thirteen disciplinary incidents going back to grade school.

At one point, Theo Stamos asked Doug about a conversation with the boy's mother, "But she told you that he was charged with two sexual assaults, is that correct?"

Doug answered with more tact than I would have been able to exhibit on the stand. "No, she did not say that. She said he was charged with an incident with a young lady and that she was frustrated with him. But she was also frustrated with the other person involved. And she went back and forth between defending him and accusing him."

Compounding the lack of coordination between LCPS and the sheriff's office was the bureaucratic ineptitude of the court system. Loudoun County's Juvenile Intake Office was required to notify the school division when a student was served a juvenile petition, the equivalent of an arrest warrant for an adult. Juvenile Intake didn't phone, email, or snail mail the superintendent the information about the arrest of the boy involved in the incident at Stone Bridge. Instead, they mailed it to David "Dave" Spage, the current principal of Broad Run, through an interoffice system. The envelope was sent to Dave Spage using a central administration title he hadn't held since 2014. (The rationale for sending it through the interoffice system was student privacy.) It should be noted that my office prints a guide and directory each year in which every administrator's name and title are listed. Hundreds of these booklets are distributed to Loudoun County's government each year. In addition, up-to-date staff lists are available on the LCPS website, and job titles are included on the Outlook email system that LCPS shares with the county government. To send a letter containing important information to an address that was seven years out of date was inexcusable.

The special grand jury report further noted that Juvenile Intake had sent thirty-nine such messages to LCPS in 2021, and it was unknown how many the superintendent had seen.

County Administrator Tim Hemstreet later said that LCPS secretaries should have known who the Juvenile Intake letter was intended for and gotten it to the correct party. This was bureaucratic ass-covering at its worst.

A Fall Season of Escalating Discontent

After a behind-the-scenes summer of turmoil, Loudoun catapulted to the center of the national stage. The factors that pushed Loudoun into the spotlight were a tight gubernatorial race, well-organized right-wing groups looking for an issue to exploit, the federal Justice Department seeking to protect school boards, and another terrible decision by a fourteen-year-old that would give the national media the story that it was looking for.

When the Free to Learn Coalition Joined the Fray

I got a shock channel-surfing through NFL games on September 12, 2021. An ad during the second half of the then-Washington Football Team's 20-16 loss to the Chargers directly attacked LCPS. The ad included incendiary dialogue such as, "Loudoun County, Virginia, spent nearly half-a-million to develop a divisive curriculum promoted by political activists. When parents spoke up, officials threatened to silence them."

The Loudoun ad was part of a $1 million campaign by the Free to Learn Coalition, which had other ads airing in Arizona and New York.

"Loudoun County Public School leadership has prioritized political activism above all else," Free to Learn President Alleigh Marré said in a statement regarding the ad. "We have seen targeted efforts to silence dissenting parents and push teachers into reporting their colleagues. This activist behavior by Loudoun County leaders will not be tolerated."

The Free to Learn Coalition bills itself as a nonpartisan organization. It's actually backed by the right-wing Judicial Crisis Network. Its main business is creating illegitimate school board candidate websites filled with partisan "facts" about the candidate, many of which are incorrect.

The Loudoun ad really didn't have much impact. The Washington Football Team (now called the Washington Commanders), plays in front of a half-empty stadium most weeks and a declining TV audience. The generic political attack generated about as much enthusiasm as the generic football team.

Snowflakes to the Right of Me

On October 4, 2021, United States Attorney General Merrick Garland issued a memo aimed at combating threats against school officials and school boards nationwide. The memo came out less than a week after the National School Boards Association (NSBA) wrote to the Biden administration about threats being made to its members and asked for help. The NSBA labeled the disturbances at school board meetings and threats against its members "domestic terrorism." Appearing to later regret its actions, the NSBA said, "we regret and apologize" for the letter.

But the damage had been done.

Right-wing media fueled delusions about government agents hauling off people who were merely vocal about wanting to take back their children's education.

Domestic terrorism aside, the NSBA had very good reason to ask for federal support. Its letter asked the FBI, the Department of Homeland Security, and the Secret Service to investigate cases where federal laws protecting the civil rights of school board members may have been violated. The letter cited more than twenty cases of violence aimed at school officials in California, New Jersey, Georgia, and Florida. Of course, attention regarding the memo turned to Loudoun County. Conservative commentators asked if Scott Smith—pants pulled down past his midsection—was an example of a "domestic terrorist." Smith ended up adopting this label as evidence of his persecution.

Second Assault, Same Suspect

The boy involved in the May 28 incident at Stone Bridge was involved in another incident at Broad Run High School, to which he had been transferred. It was unclear whether the Juvenile and Domestic Relations District Court had ordered the boy to attend a public high school as a condition of his pretrial release, though such a condition is common for juveniles pending resolution of their charges. Broad Run Principal Dave Spage and the school resource officer were aware of the boy's presence and that he was wearing an ankle monitor. Before the special grand jury, probation officer Jason Bickmore offered that Spage knew nothing about the conversations with the boy's mother and grandmother concerning the boy's incredibly odd behavior. That certainly would have been good information for the principal to have.

On October 6, 2021, the boy was walking down a hallway with a female student he knew between classes. After the bell rang, the girl teased the boy about being late to class, which angered him. He forced her into an empty classroom and put his arm around her neck and his hand over her mouth. At the boy's trial, the Loudoun County deputy commonwealth's attorney noted that the boy wasn't choking her. The classmates then took seats on desks and began talking to each other. At some point, the boy put his hand under the girl's bra and touched her breast. The boy admitted to touching the girl's breast, but said that it was over her shirt.

Detective Corrine Czekaj testified before the special grand jury about the October 6 assault at Broad Run High School, which catapulted the May 28 incident into national prominence. Czekaj said this was a case of a very naive girl meeting a sexual predator, with the predator taking full advantage of the situation. The victim on October 6 told investigators that she felt sorry that the boy had no friends at school and that she would talk to him. The boy showed the victim the ankle monitor he was wearing but didn't say why he was wearing it.

Sometime after the incident, a girlfriend took the victim to Broad Run SRO Brandon Hayes. Hayes testified that the boy was followed for an hour after the first report of the October 6, 2021, incident at Broad Run before being arrested. Eyes were on him at all times while witness statements were gathered in an orderly manner, according to Hayes. Hayes also testified that Broad Run's administration was asked to hold off on its investigation until the completion of the sheriff's office probe.

Hayes praised Principal Dave Spage and his administrative team for being visible and for using mobile, miniature desks so that they could work while being present in the hallways. Keeping an eye on individual students among a student population of 1,200 is difficult, Hayes added. "I will say that I know (Spage) was trying his best to keep an eye on [the boy], without making it too obvious so the rest of the student body didn't figure out that we were watching a certain kid, if that makes sense.

"Because once that gets out, then it starts with the text messages and then, the next thing you know, you have everybody showing up at the school like 'Why is this kid in our school?'

"I will say the administrative staff is always in the hallways and they're always out trying to stop kids from doing stuff. But they've got 1,200 kids in a school."

During the special grand jury, Carlton Davis asked Atoosa Reaser if she had been alarmed to learn about the October 6, 2021, incident at Broad Run from the media. "Probably in a different way than you think . . .," Atoosa answered. "Yes, it was embarrassing to me that law enforcement had spoken with the press before coming to us."

October 7, 2021: First Official Notification of an Arrest

The sheriff's office released a statement about the alleged sexual assaults at Stone Bridge and Broad Run high schools on October 7, 2021.

It read: "There has been misinformation regarding an investigation into a reported sexual assault that occurred on May 28, 2021, at Stone Bridge

High School in Ashburn, VA. Due to exclusions under the Virginia Code regarding disclosure of juvenile reports and the fact the case is pending court proceedings, the Loudoun County Sheriff's Office (LCSO) is limited as to what information can be released.

"On May 28, 2021, an LCSO School Resource Officer was notified by Stone Bridge High School staff of a possible sexual assault. A thorough investigation and evidentiary analysis was conducted over the course of several weeks by the Loudoun County Sheriff's Office Special Victims Unit.

"Once the elements of the crime were determined, on July 8, 2021, a 14-year-old was arrested in the case with two counts of forcible sodomy.

"Following the arrest on July 8, 2021, the judicial process was turned over to the Loudoun County Commonwealth Attorney's Office to determine bail, or in the case of a juvenile, the continuance of detention or other legal restrictions set forth as part of court proceedings in the Loudoun County Juvenile and Domestic Relations District Court.

"As stated in both the current and former Memorandum of Understanding between the LCSO and Loudoun County Public Schools (LCPS), the Loudoun County Sheriff's Office is not involved in school discipline (nor the placement of students). Nevertheless, the LCSO works closely with school officials throughout all criminal investigations.

"The October 6, 2021, incident at Broad Run High School did not involve complex circumstances, the arrest was immediate, and the arrest was reported to the community as information released was unlikely to disclose the identity of the victim. However, the May 28, 2021, investigation was different in that the suspect and victim were familiar with each other, the investigation was complex, and the public announcement had the potential to identify a juvenile victim.

"The Loudoun County Sheriff's Office remains committed to the safety of all students and will investigate all incidents reported by Loudoun County Public Schools to the fullest extent of the law."

This was the first time that I learned—hand on Bible—that an arrest had been made for the assault at Stone Bridge. I may have heard rumor, innuendo, and hearsay about an assault, but this was the actual proof. In my dealings with the sheriff's office throughout the years, I have always released their arrest information regarding offenses at school. I would have announced the occurrence of assault earlier had the LCSO announced it.

This would become a key element of my defense.

Explosion on the Right

On October 11, 2021, Luke Rosiak of the *Daily Wire* published a story, including an interview with Scott Smith, that ignited a media frenzy.

While the full story is only available behind a paywall, Rosiak's tweets provided the gist of the story, which relied heavily on the words of Scott Smith. "The person who attacked our daughter is apparently bisexual and occasionally wears dresses because he likes them."

At another point, Smith blamed Policy 8040, which I remind you was still more than two months from being passed after his daughter's assault, as the genesis of his daughter's woes. "The point is kids are using it as an advantage to get into the bathrooms."

Rosiak described Smith thusly: "The father of the victim is a man you've seen: The bald man being dragged by police."

Rosiak then spun a narrative about the June 22 meeting that the right wing accepted and promoted as the truth. "The county's top elected prosecutor personally tried to put him in jail, keeping him from telling his story at the meeting where the trans policy passed."

This series of events was offered by Rosiak for Smith's arrest: "Scott was arrested after an argument with the Anti-Racist Parents of Loudoun Facebook group (which threatened to 'hack' and 'expose' parents who questioned school policies) who approached him at the meeting. Chardonnay Antifa was apparently not only behind keyboards."

National forces, according to Rosiak, seized upon Smith for their own evil ends. "The National School Board[s] Association included Scott Smith in its list used to deem parents 'domestic terrorists.'"

Presenting both sides of the story was something Rosiak said he tried to do, sadly failing in this effort. "I thought this might be an opportunity for both sides to understand each other. It did not happen. Instead, we just have pain, fear and strife in Loudoun County—the richest county in the country— as courts and schools are converted to political machines."

A Reasoned Reply

After the Rosiak article, I helped compose the following statement released to the LCPS community via blast email on October 13, 2021: "Loudoun County Public Schools is aware of the media and social media reports concerning alleged sexual assaults at two of our high school campuses. While LCPS takes student privacy seriously and cannot reveal details concerning the actions of any specific student, we want to clarify our investigative process. Principals are legally required to report to the local law enforcement agency any act, including sexual assault, that may constitute a felony offense under Va. Code 22.1-279.3.1. That process was followed with respect to these allegations. Loudoun County Sheriff's Office was contacted within minutes of receiving the initial report on May 28. Once a matter has been reported to law enforcement, LCPS does not begin its investigation until law enforcement advises LCPS that it has completed the criminal investigation. To maintain the integrity of the criminal investigation, law enforcement requested that LCPS not interview students until their investigation is concluded. LCPS has cooperated, and continues to cooperate, with law enforcement. Furthermore, LCPS is prohibited from disciplining any student without following the Title IX grievance process, which includes investigating complaints of sexual harassment and sexual assault. LCPS does impose interim measures to protect the safety of students involved in the original incident, deter retaliation, and preserve [the] integrity of investigation and resolution process. LCPS has complied and continues to comply with its obligations under Title IX. School Board members are typically not given details of disciplinary matters. The board may be obligated to consider long-term suspensions or expulsions and must ensure that students have not been deprived of due process. Consequently, members of the Loudoun County School Board were not aware of the specific details of this incident until it was reported by media outlets earlier this week. We are unable to locate any records that indicate Scott Smith had registered in advance to speak at the June 22, 2021, board meeting."

A False Narrative

In the weeks following Rosiak's initial story, a false narrative concerning the sexual assault at Stone Bridge and Scott Smith gained a foothold on the Right. Media Matters recorded eighty-eight segments on the Stone Bridge assault by Fox News between October 11 and November 4.

Luke Rosiak appeared on *Tucker Carlson Tonight* to kick off the festival of lying. "This story is one of the most disturbing I've ever worked on. It raises the possibility that the Loudoun County Public Schools covered up the rape of a 14-year-old girl at the hands of a boy wearing a skirt in order to pass a school policy that Democrats were adamant about passing." Then the conspiracy theory involving Smith kicked in, "and to prevent this coming out potentially, they arrested the father of the victim."

To be clear, LCPS doesn't have the power to arrest anyone. Scott Smith was arrested by the Loudoun County Sheriff's Office because he was swearing profusely at a woman while leaning toward her with a clenched fist. He was convicted of disorderly conduct and resisting arrest for his actions involving the Loudoun County Sheriff's Office and given a ten-day suspended sentence. Notice Rosiak's use of the word "potentially"—the equivalent of saying "I can't prove this at all, but it exists in my fevered imagination."

The *Daily Signal*, an outlet for the Heritage Foundation, quoted anti-trans activist Lauren Adams, "Assaults like these are the natural result of transgender bathroom policies, which allow boys to freely enter girls' spaces and erode boundaries."

By October 27, 2021, this line of lying had reached the United States Senate. Senator Tom Cotton assailed Attorney General Merrick Garland with this, "(a girl) was raped in a bathroom by a boy wearing girls' clothes and the Loudoun County School Board covered it up because it would interfere with their transgender policy during Pride Month." The Pride Month reference was a nice rhetorical embellishment.

The Media

As someone who has devoted more than twenty years to local journalism, I'm dismayed by the state of local journalism. Sometimes I sound like the cranky old man extolling the imagined virtues of bygone days. But I was fortunate to catch the last golden wave of local journalism in America.

Today's local journalism is anything but golden.

Understaffed and overexcited, today's local media relies heavily on social media tips to ignite a story. Once ignited, a story takes on its most incendiary form to make it stand out and compete with social media.

Attending Loudoun County School Board meetings became the default setting for some Washington TV stations. News directors and reporters would misread the agenda, confusing information items (subjects to be discussed by board members) and action items (those to be voted on). Reporters and cameramen would be deployed in anticipation of seeing heated debate and dramatic voting only to be treated to mundane discussions and agenda house-keeping. Most of the reporters confessed that they didn't know why the news director had sent them to the meeting, only that they needed something to tease for the late news and a live segment chronicling all the "controversial" things that had been done. A saving grace for these reporters was that someone would always say something batshit crazy during public comment, so a fake piece on fake outrage could almost always be constructed.

A common scene after school board meetings was reporters standing in front of the darkened Administration Building bathed in the light of a camera spotlight trying their best to make it look as though something newsworthy had happened during the meeting.

Sometimes, I would call news directors to ask why they would continually send crews to Ashburn when our school board was doing nothing different than virtually every other school board in Virginia. The reply was always "because Loudoun is the hot spot." I would argue that we were the hot spot because the media kept coming out. Wasn't this a self-fulfilling prophecy?

I never got anywhere with that one.

Few reporters have any real idea about what they are seeing at school board meetings. The American education system is one of the most-highly regulated, complex institutions in the nation. That's why editors invariably assign the youngest, most-inexperienced reporters to cover it. By the time they have any idea about what's going on, they've moved on to more prominent stories or another market.

Individual reports are introduced and summed up afterward by authoritative news anchors who appear to have an in-depth knowledge of the facts behind the story. Nothing could be further from the truth. This is especially true of morning anchors who go on-air at four thirty in the morning. An overnight staffer (usually a new one willing to work the night shift) prepares their script and loads it on the teleprompter. Much of what goes into the script is pulled from past stories. These stories often include information that is outdated or flat-out wrong. The morning anchor, who is basically what the British call a "news reader," confidently reads the teleprompter à la Ron Burgundy saying anything, accurate or not, that has been loaded into the machine.

Local news is a cheap way to fill air time during the day. Most local stations have about eight hours of daily news programming. I'm fascinated that while the number of hours of local news has grown, the audience for this product has shrunk dramatically with the advent of streaming and social media. Young people, especially, stay away in droves when it comes to local news.

The most unpleasant part of my late tenure as public information officer was dealing with WJLA-TV, Channel 7, Washington. WJLA is owned by Sinclair Broadcast Group, basically Fox News lite. In many ways, Sinclair is much cleverer than Fox, buying local affiliates and injecting its right-wing views into supposedly objective local news coverage. News anchors are given "editorials" from the main office to read that purport to be heartfelt reflections of their beliefs.

A staple at Sinclair stations—again purporting to be a local investigative segment—is "Crisis in the Classroom." The "crises" being covered can range from a school shooting to students not being informed of a minor testing honor. The underlying concept is that something dire is happening to the children of the metropolitan Washington area and that the schools are at fault. Constant fuel for the outrage machine.

WJLA's most infamous reporter is Nick Minock. Nick came to Washington from Michigan via the Trump administration.

Nick earned a degree of journalistic infamy when he tweeted his gratitude to then-President Donald Trump for an interview while he was the political correspondent for WWMT-TV Grand Rapids/Kalamazoo. "Now that the 2016 award season is upon us, we'll find out if our coverage of Mr. Trump will win an Emmy and other awards! If we win, I will be sending a thank you card to 1600 Pennsylvania Avenue."

I don't know if he won an Emmy for this work, but Nick landed a spot as deputy spokesman for the US Department of Transportation from 2018 to 2021. The journalism website FTVLive noted that the Trump interviews Nick touted as "exclusives" were, in fact, not the result of any real journalistic effort. Sinclair had cut a corporate deal with Trump for "exclusive" access. It quickly became evident that Nick had a similar deal with the Youngkin administration. The governor always seemed to be available to give Nick a lengthy interview that would be "seen only on 7." Nick would then go on to attack interview subjects using Youngkin's talking points. A biased journalist pretending to be unbiased only added fuel to the community fire when it came to the reporting around the May 28 incident and the school board riot—a far cry from the duty of local journalism to dispassionately inform community members.

Keith Sanders, a professor at the University of Missouri School of Journalism in my day, taught a class about analyzing the media and polling. I thought it fairly dry stuff at the time but, in retrospect, a study Sanders shared with my class stuck in my mind. This poll found that 37 percent of people thought everything they saw on TV was real. George and Weezy lived in a "dee-lux apartment in the sky," and Archie Bunker was a real guy in Queens. Years later, I saw a poll stating that 37 percent (there must be some cosmic significance associated with this number) of the public believe everything they see on the Internet. The inevitable conclusion: A little more than one-third of our fellow Americans lack the mental acuity to see past the wonders of technology to evaluate content.

Sadly, many members of the media also fall into this category.

While broadcast news has its quirks and formulas, local print journalism is disorganized and almost dead.

There are exceptions to the rule when it comes to the general incompetence of local reporters. Rosalind "Roz" Helderman, of *The Washington Post*, began her career covering the Loudoun County School Board and went on to win the Pulitzer Prize. I joked with Roz that she owed me at least a mention in her Pulitzer speech since I had trained her so well. WTOP Radio's Neal Augenstein is another of my favorites. I always tried to get him background on an important story first because I knew he would do a thorough job of researching and presenting the information fairly. It was always my hope that others would emulate—if not outright steal—Neal's work when they did their reporting. A local fixture since 1997, Neal also had a voice people would often imitate in public.

I could relate.

Verdict Reached

The boy involved in the sexual assaults at Stone Bridge and Broad Run was found guilty of one count of forcible sodomy and one count of forcible fellatio in the Stone Bridge case during an adjudicatory hearing in Loudoun County Juvenile and Domestic Relations District Court on October 25, 2021. I was amazed that these proceedings were held in open court. In my experience as a journalist, the attorney for the victim usually asks for closed proceedings to protect the identity of the victim. Because juvenile proceedings are almost never open to the media, I was astounded that Scott and Jessica Smith did not request a closed proceeding.

The prosecution was handled by Loudoun County Commonwealth's Attorney Buta Biberaj. Biberaj handled this personally rather than let a subordinate prosecute what was, essentially, a minor case because, she told *The New York Times,* there was likely to be "animosity toward the attorney who tried it. I didn't want to subject our attorneys to that."

Biberaj was a first-term "progressive" commonwealth's attorney whose competence was questioned by fellow Democrats and Republicans alike. She became a lightning rod for those who decried that "wokeness" was invading the courtroom. That didn't stop her from fending off a primary challenge and seeking a second term. (A race that she lost in November 2023.)

The Many Missteps of an
Independent Investigation

An independent investigation handled properly could have shed light on actual missteps that happened. Even then, I have my doubts about how useful they actually are. Unfortunately, the investigation that followed was handled anything but properly.

Commissioning a Huge Mistake

In his zeal to put the Stone Bridge-Broad Run debacle behind the school division, Scott Ziegler made a key strategic mistake.

On a Friday morning, three days after Glenn Youngkin was elected governor in November 2021, the superintendent decided that he would announce the commissioning of an "independent review" by the law firm of Blankingship & Keith to delve into the particulars of the events at Stone Bridge and Broad Run high schools and their administrative aftermath. The Public Information Office was caught off-guard by this move. Joan was at her son's wedding and tried to conference in with our communications consultant.

Working with our communications consultant, my colleague, Calvin Parson Jr., and I tried to put together a media release that was not too aggressive and that did not set unreasonably high expectations. I recruited Calvin from the Washington Redskins (a time from before the Commanders) Charitable Foundation. He is an extremely talented and earnest young man who is an expert at working the media. He quickly set up a midday news conference in front of the Administration Building, drawing all the usual media suspects.

With Deputy Superintendent Dr. Ashley Ellis and school board Chair

Brenda Sheridan in the background, Ziegler made the following announcement: "Please know that this independent review is only one step in moving forward to help heal our school community. We will keep you up-to-date about the steps we take and the progress we make. Together, we believe we can make our schools a safer, more-nurturing environment for every student."

After this announcement, Calvin and I surmised that a report would be compiled and eventually shared with the public, much like an investigative report compiled by the US Government Accountability Office at the behest of a congressional committee. This did not turn out to be the case.

When the report was finished, Division Counsel Bob Falconi decided that the best course of action was not to publicly disclose its contents under the umbrella of attorney-client privilege and personnel records. He reasoned that any publicity beating LCPS would take was better than making the details of the report public. The report was given to the school board during an executive session.

Announcing an investigation and not revealing its results was a huge public relations blunder.

In February 2023, during a review of court documents, I found a letter to Ziegler from Loudoun County Sheriff Mike Chapman regarding the commissioning of the independent review: "I noticed that you commissioned an 'independent' review, which I assume will be paid for by LCPS using Loudoun County taxpayer dollars. You announced this a day after incoming Attorney General Jason Miyares stated publicly that he intends to investigate this incident. While I believe an independent review would be helpful, I have concerns of the legitimacy of such a review conducted at your direction. As the attorney general is accountable to the citizens of Virginia, I feel an Attorney General review is the most objective way to move forward on this issue."

Mike Chapman, the impartial, nonpartisan arbiter of the law.

The commissioning of an "independent review" is a standard move by school districts when faced with a crisis, and it shouldn't be. When considering commissioning an "independent review," I'd like school district leadership to ask the following questions: Who is your target audience? Whose minds do you think this report will change? For the vast majority of your stakeholders, the crisis has passed. Why create a mechanism through which the crisis can continually be revived?

Because such a report contains confidential personnel, and identifiable student, information, it has very little chance of ever being released. It has now become a "secret" report.

When a report is not released under Freedom of Information Act exemptions, news media and others will FOIA the cost of the report, which is not exempt. The story then becomes the cost of the "secret" report.

If a redacted report is released, opponents will cherry-pick information out of context and turn your words against you. "Even the school district's own report found huge flaws in the system."

The school district can't announce what direct action was taken as a result of the report. You can't say, "because of this report, the superintendent was fired."

A rogue school board member or school district employee could release the report, thus negating any privacy measures.

School law is a very small legal community. This means a law firm with close ties to the school district will probably be hired to compile the independent review. This opens the school district to charges of collusion and whitewashing.

You might uncover information that law enforcement or a grand jury didn't, leading to more legal entanglements.

The bottom line on commissioning an "independent review"—don't.

The Blankingship & Keith report haunted the school board for nearly two years. School board members said publicly that they would release it, then didn't.

As I drove through southern Loudoun County on the late afternoon of February 14, 2023, I had to admit that, as trying as my situation was, at least I didn't have to sit through the school board meeting going on a few miles to my north.

In December, five school board members—Tiffany Polifko, John Beatty, Jeff Morse, Atoosa Reaser, and Erika Ogedegbe—stated that they would be in favor of releasing the Blankingship & Keith independent review. During the February 14 meeting, Polifko made a motion to release the report. Stepping into yet another unforced political faux pas, the school board voted 6 to 3 not to release the report. Polifko, Beatty, and Denise Corbo were the three board members who voted in favor. Jeff Morse, Atoosa Reaser, and Erika Ogedegbe did a bipartisan waffle, which was justifiably criticized. At this point, I don't know what could be in the report that already wasn't known. Hiding it served no purpose.

Polifko wrapped her highly partisan motivation in some noble-sounding rhetoric. "Given the choice between advocating for children and families or advocating for the system, I will always choose children and families."

Ian Serotkin, now the Board's recently elected chair, summed up the position of the majority. "Being open and transparent is incredibly important, but so is [sic]the rights of our students and staff being able to communicate with legal counsel without it being made public."

Scott Smith, who was, as always, present at such events, yelled some choice words at the school board as he left the meeting. "You should [inaudible] you fucking scumbags. Fucking liars! What are you covering up? What?" I have to admit, I was curious myself on his last point.

Smith went on: "I'm the father of the first sexual assault student. What are they hiding in there? What are they hiding? They are hiding something big."

This was the public persona Smith had chosen to adopt. He exposed the identity of his child, which the legal system had tried to shield.

Finally, on the Tuesday following Memorial Day, May 30, 2023, Judge James P. Fisher ruled that the report be turned over to the attorney general's office within seven days. This didn't mean, though, that the Blankingship & Keith's analysis would be exposed to public scrutiny any time soon. Under the rules of the court, documents must be sealed and available only to the parties involved in the case.

In March of 2023, the attorney general's spokeswoman, Victoria LaCivita, said that the report's findings were potential evidence for "ongoing prosecutions" and that ethics rules could prevent their release.

The "ongoing prosecutions" bit gave me chills.

As expected, politicians weighed in on Fisher's ruling.

"I firmly believe the only way to rebuild trust between the community and LCPS is through transparency and communication, and that is why I have consistently advocated for the release of the Blankingship & Keith report," Denise Corbo said in a written statement. "Releasing the report to the Attorney General's office is the next step towards resolving the situation and holding the right parties responsible for what transpired. It is my hope the end goal of these proceedings will be continued change in policy, transparency, and communication in order to prevent situations like this from occurring in the future in our schools."

Media reports noted that Corbo actually showed up—in person—for court hearings concerning the Blankingship & Keith report on April 6 and May 30 (albeit wearing a mask). I guess her health concerns took a back seat when the opportunity for political grandstanding presented itself. Her talk about communication did raise some concerns on my part, however.

Surprisingly, Scott Ziegler said that the report should be released. The attorney general's request for the report was a part of his own upcoming case. "I am perplexed why the LCSB voted on multiple occasions to keep the release secret," Scott said in his own release. "As I have maintained, releasing the report was never my decision. I look forward to the full release of the report in a way that maintains the confidentiality and dignity of the students involved and brings much needed transparency to our community."

There's a lot to unpack here.

Supposedly, Scott had a private copy of the report and had definitely read it. Did this mean that he knew that there were no damaging assertions in it?

Pawning the decision not to release the report off on the school board was disingenuous, to say the least. As I remember, Scott's administration advocated keeping it under wraps under the umbrella of attorney-client privilege.

Jeff Morse issued a statement that I found to be truly disappointing. He said that it was a relief to have the report released and that a burden had been lifted. You could have lifted this burden a long time ago, Jeff.

John Beatty said the school board got bad legal advice. I can't argue with that.

Board members, current and former, who had voted for the report's release were at the May 30, 2023, hearing as potential witnesses, although none were called to the stand. That didn't keep Tom Marshall from being used by Nick Minock. "Who were they really protecting with not releasing it?" Marshall told Nick. "I didn't think it was the students."

Another former member, Andrew Hoyler, weighed in on Facebook. He was upset about Scott Ziegler having a private copy of the report. "This was shocking to me, as he was apparently deemed more trustworthy than the very individuals in office to represent the citizens of Loudoun."

On August 10, 2023, Theo Stamos said that she would request that the thirty-two-page Blankingship & Keith report be unsealed. Unsealing the report would make it easier for prosecutors to question witnesses who testified before the special grand jury and were quoted in the report. I was not interviewed by Blankingship & Keith and had been assured that my name was not mentioned in the report.

Release it, already. I didn't care.

A redacted version of the thirty-two-page report was finally released on September 14, 2023.

It was a big nothing.

The Only Tangible Effect of the Blankingship & Keith Report

After reading the Blankingship & Keith report, the school board fired Chief of Staff Dr. Mark Smith, though this was never disclosed officially because of the confidentiality of personnel records under the law.

During the pandemic, LCPS's administration became far too enamored with online communication and working from home. The Administration Building was basically empty for eighteen months, save for the Public Information staff, some brave souls in the Department of Instruction, and a few technology support staff. There were days when there were only a half-dozen cars in the massive parking lots that usually held hundreds. Supposedly, people were diligently monitoring phone calls from home using various apps. But almost every day, I would walk through the superintendent's office and hear the phones endlessly ringing off the hook. I feared that important calls weren't being answered. I also feared that school staff resented the empty Administration Building as vaccinations became available and they returned, in person, to school.

Mark Smith took full advantage of working remotely. I want to state, up front, that I like Mark a great deal and always found him to be responsive when I reached out to him online. I can understand why he would prefer to work at home. Mark had an incredibly long commute, and he and his wife had just welcomed their first child. But when you hold a key administrative position, you have to be available for in-person meetings. There is an urgency when someone comes into your office and tells you there's a situation that has to be addressed immediately. Emails revealed by the special grand jury investigation showed that people at lower levels in central administration saw the potential dangers in LCPS not pursuing its own investigation of the May 28 incident, and that it was justified in doing so. If these people had sat down in a room with the chief of staff and the superintendent and hashed things out, a lot of the grief that followed could have been avoided.

Regardless of what Mark should or shouldn't have done, he was definitely made the LCPS scapegoat in this affair.

Contrary to Beth Barts's testimony during the special grand jury, Mark said that the school board initiated his firing. "I was entered into an agreement to be placed on administrative leave, with pay, and not have any duties or job responsibilities. This was a result of action coming out of the School Board, where I was put in a position where I was made to either resign or be fired."

Mark said that Scott Ziegler briefed him on the reasons behind the school board's actions. "What was explained to me at the time was that the school board had recently reviewed the independent investigation that was conducted by an outside law firm into the sexual assaults that had happened in the school division.

"The school board felt that I exercised poor judgement in an email that I shared, and they determined that I needed to be removed . . . I felt I had no choice but to resign and try to find a way to salvage, you know, my finances and compensation."

As they did with the later firing of Scott Ziegler, board members refused to speak with Mark directly. They also let it be known that the infamous Blankingship & Keith report was off-limits. "I did ask to see the report. That was denied. I did ask to speak to the board. That was denied. And so, you know, at that point, I felt that really I had no way. Dr. Ziegler did not feel like he could advocate for me at that point or say anything to the board.

"He said it was a raw deal. He said he didn't have any political capital—I believe I recall—anything to really stand for me. He said he advocated for me in the closed session, but he said there was really nothing he could do."

Mark said that he signed a nondisclosure agreement (NDA) with the school board. The NDA stipulated that Mark would hold the school division and school board harmless and would not discuss the events surrounding the sexual assaults. "But it also stipulated there was no admission of wrong-doing on either party, and that I would have positive references both from the school division and the superintendent moving forward."

Mark testified that he was stunned when WJLA's Nick Minock tweeted that he had been fired. "This blew my mind. I mean—I mean that—entering into this agreement with Dr. Ziegler to find the best way for me and my family, and then to see this, this really—it damaged what I was looking to do to try to part ways in the best way and the most respectful way, with integrity, knowing that I felt I was done wrong, and the circumstances were beyond my control." As I read these words, I knew exactly how Mark felt. He said that the tweet derailed job negotiations with two other school divisions. Mark added that he knew that Tom Marshall was Nick Minock's source and that the only time he'd interacted with Marshall was when he helped Marshall silence his cell phone during a hearing.

"Did you feel completely thrown under the bus by this?" Carlton Davis asked Mark during the special grand jury.

"Completely."

I felt a twinge of pain as Mark spoke about his wife's reaction to Nick's tweet. "She's a bit more emotional than I, and she was devastated."

Again, I totally empathized.

One thing about Tom Marshall's special grand jury testimony truly disappointed me. He admitted to being Nick's source. "I was just repeating information I had heard, that was common knowledge. So nothing I said had not been already known previously." First, discussing a personnel matter is strictly prohibited by law. Next, it was never firmly established whether Mark Smith was fired or had resigned. Finally, Marshall made this rather startling admission: "First of all, I didn't know who Mark Smith was, because I had not met him. I was never introduced to him." Marshall couldn't help ending this section of his testimony by noting that Dr. Daniel Smith replaced Dr. Mark Smith as chief of staff. "I was kind of amused at the fact that Dr. Smith was replaced by Dr. Smith."

Very funny, Tom.

Mark summed up my credo throughout my ordeal in response to a question from a juror. "So I'm trying to stay strong and stay on my feet. And so we'll see what comes of this, because your name is all you have. So we'll see where we go from here."

Pleading No Contest and the Results

The trials of the boy involved in the Stone Bridge and Broad Run incidents were both climactic and anticlimactic. On the one hand, his attorney didn't put up much of a fight in court. On the other, his proceedings were held publicly, very rare for a juvenile case, and drew intense media attention. The boy involved in the sexual assaults at Stone Bridge and Broad Run pleaded "no contest" in the Broad Run case, accepting the conviction without admitting guilt.

The Sentencing

On January 12, 2022, the boy was sentenced to a "locked residential program" and supervised probation until he turned eighteen. In a first for a minor, Juvenile and Domestic Relations District Court Chief Judge Pamela Brooks ordered the boy to be entered into Virginia's sex offender registry. Brooks said that she imposed this part of the sentence after reading the results of his psychosexual and psychological reports. "Yours scares me," Brooks said of the boy's reports. "I don't know how else to put it. They scared me for yourself. They scared me for your family. They scared me for society."

This sex offender part of the sentence was later rescinded.

After the boy was convicted, prosecutor Barry Zweig said that the victim's family wanted the boy placed on the sex-offender registry. The commonwealth's attorney's office also believed that the boy should be on the registry. The dissenting voice on this action: Court Services Probation Officer Jason Bickmore. Zweig testified that Bickmore "believed it would be detrimental to his future success, both on probation and in life for him to be placed on the registry."

At the time of the sentencing, I thought that the sex offender designation for crimes committed by a fourteen-year-old was over the top. After reading the reports on the boy in the special grand jury transcripts, I think it might have been justified. One name kept coming to mind as I read the boy's sexual text messages and the way he liked to choke girls and hold his hand over their mouths: Ted Bundy. Like Bundy, the boy had a higher-than-average IQ (118) and showed an escalating pattern of violence.

At the conclusion of his sentencing hearing, the boy said, "I will never hurt anyone like this again."

I only hoped this was true.

Corrine Czekaj's testimony shed light on the proposed boy's sentencing before the October 6 assault. She said that Zweig was satisfied with reducing the two sodomy charges to sexual battery. The boy would then plead guilty, and the court would order a social history. "I am a bit partial to the step-down approach to cases with this seriousness," Czekaj added. "That stepdown approach would be that the finding was deferred for two years. After the first year, if he were compliant, the charge would be amended to misdemeanor sexual battery, and he would be continued on probation. And the finding on sexual battery would be deferred for the remaining one year of probation.

"If he remained fully compliant after the second year, the charge would be dismissed. This is something we used to do a lot in Prince William County, but that this jurisdiction does not do often or at all."

When she testified before the special grand jury, Czekaj seemed to have changed her mind on this point. The boy was about to turn sixteen when she offered this: "In a little more than two years, he'll be free and released upon an unsuspecting world. God help us and any female he encounters."

I later learned that this boy only spent about a month in the rehabilitation center before being released. To quote Corrine Czekaj, "God help us and any female he encounters."

PART III

*The Creation
of the Special Grand Jury*

First Day of the Administration

Glenn Youngkin was one of the only politicians to make good on a promise to get things done "on Day 1 of my administration."

I'll give him that.

On his first day in office, January 15, 2022, Youngkin issued a series of eleven executive orders. Three of them involved public education.

The first order forbade teaching "inherently divisive concepts, including Critical Race Theory." This was not a particularly tough one to execute because no Virginia kindergarten through twelfth-grade public schools teach CRT.

The second allowed parents to decide if their children should have to wear a mask in school. This order sparked immediate chaos, which I tend to believe was its intent. The Loudoun County School Board voted 8 to 1 to keep its masking mandate despite the gubernatorial order. Several large school divisions filed suit to maintain local sovereignty over this decision.

In Loudoun, there was a smattering of school protests that drew more than a smattering of media coverage.

At most schools, there were three or four mask-less students who were kept in isolated classrooms where teachers sent them work to do. Most expressed the feeling that they would like to put on their mask and go to class, but their parents wouldn't let them. Some of these parents referred to their students as "Freedom Fighters."

Rumors spread that LCPS was having students arrested for not wearing masks. This was the result of wild extrapolation of school policy. If a student repeatedly refused to wear their mask, there was a chance, *a chance*, they would be suspended. If they were suspended and set foot on school property without permission, there was a chance, *a chance*, they would be issued a no-trespass order. If they disobeyed the no-trespass order, there was a chance, *a very small chance*, they could be arrested.

The right-wing echo chamber interpreted this to mean that students were being arrested in Loudoun County for not wearing masks.

Superintendent Scott Ziegler was forced to release a statement. "I want to emphasize that, despite some unverified reports in the media, no students have been arrested for trespassing. Media accounts stating that LCPS is arresting students are not accurate and create fear and potential harm for our students."

Not content with stoking discontent around masks, under Executive Order Number Four (EO4), Youngkin authorized the investigation of the Loudoun County School Board. I will go into the details of this order later.

A week later, Youngkin went beyond issuing executive orders.

On January 21, 2022, the governor announced an email tip line to receive parental reports of "divisive practices" in Virginia's public schools. He sold this as "a customary constituent service." I suppose this is true . . . if you were living in the Soviet Bloc circa 1978. That was the year I visited what was then Czechoslovakia. An official tour guide, speaking very unofficially, told us that there was at least one government informant living on each city block in Prague. It was their duty to turn over fellow citizens having improper thoughts regarding state philosophy.

The tip line was soon flooded with messages, most supporting teachers and telling Youngkin what he could do with this authoritarian mechanism.

In the aftermath of this debacle, the Youngkin administration denied Freedom of Information Act requests seeking messages sent to the tip line. The governor denied access under the guise that the tips were among his "working papers and correspondence."

So much for the government transparency Youngkin berated others, including LCPS, for avoiding.

Youngkin's Creation of the Special Grand Jury

When Youngkin signed EO4 on January 15, 2022, which created the special grand jury, it stated: "By virtue of the authority vested in me as Governor, I hereby issue this Executive Order requesting the Attorney General conduct a full investigation into Loudoun County Public Schools.

"Importance of the Issue: In the Spring of 2021, the Loudoun County School Board and the Administration of Loudoun County Public Schools were made aware of a sexual assault that occurred in a Loudoun County High School. A decision was made to transfer the assailant to another Loudoun County high school, where the student was able to commit a second sexual assault. The Loudoun County School Board and school administrators with-held key details and knowingly lied to parents about the assaults. Neither the Loudoun County School Board, nor the administrators of the Loudoun County school system, have been held accountable for deceiving the very Virginians they serve. Virginia parents deserve answers and assurances that the safety of their children will never be compromised."

The charge given to the special grand jury had ominous overtones: "The special grand jury shall be impaneled and empowered to inquire and report on conditions involving or tending to promote criminal activity related to Loudoun County Public Schools and Loudoun County School Board."

Dr. Mark Smith's Testimony

The testimony of Dr. Mark Smith, LCPS's former chief of staff, on May 24, 2022, showed that I had been a target of this special grand jury investigation from the beginning.

Carlton Davis brought up the message that I drafted on May 28, 2021, presenting Mark with a copy of the email Tim Flynn sent out that afternoon.

Davis: "Does that ring a bell at all?"

Mark: "No. I believe we send out a lot of these in response to issues that happen in the school. I don't recall this one specifically."

Davis: "That statement was—I don't know if it was drafted—but it was certainly approved by Wayde Byard. Is that how you pronounce his name?"

Mark: "Byard."

Davis: "Byard. Would that surprise you that that came or was approved by Wayde?"

Mark: "Would it surprise me?"

Davis: "Yeah."

Mark: "I mean, typically, it would not surprise me. These are typically information emails that would go out to the community when there's something that's visible that there may be questions about."

Mark's testimony was clear, coherent, eloquent, and on point. Davis returned again and again to the assertion that something should have gone out about the alleged sexual assault. Mark never took the bait. At one point in his testimony, Mark talked about why allegations against students aren't broadcast publicly. "These types of investigations are very serious for egregious type [sic] of allegations. The concern I had was due process. And, you know, all of our students are entitled to due process, innocent until proven guilty."

Davis then changed tack in his questioning.

"Do you know if there was [a] concerted effort by Dr. Ziegler and/or the Communications Office to not share anything?"

Mark: "I do not know."

Davis: "Would it surprise you to know there was a concerted effort?"

Mark: "That would surprise me."

Heading into the Grand Jury

Between February and April 2023, I traveled to my attorney's office in Fairfax every Tuesday to read the special grand jury testimony. I wanted to familiarize myself with everything involved with my case. I also highlighted testimony I thought was critical with sticky red arrows, going through four boxes of these materials. What I read revealed details I hadn't known. I also gained insights into the other major players in this drama—and myself.

The World According to Scott Smith

Scott Smith's special grand jury testimony from June 14, 2022, revealed a man who knew his own faults, accepted them, and was totally oblivious to how others might be affected by them. His testimony was, at times, the howl of the alpha male, the anguish of a parent with a problem child, someone who parroted the right-wing media echo chamber, and the crying of a victim.

Scott Smith was cliché on many levels. I think there might have been a genuine person in there, but I doubt Scott Smith ever saw him or was even looking for him.

Smith gave the jurors a long description of himself that emphasized his humble roots.

"You know, I'm not some dude that just came out of college and moved here because there's IT jobs and 150, 200,000 dollars to make. No, I started here with a goddam shovel, a tractor, and then built a 20-year successful business. I didn't do anything to hurt Loudoun County. If anything, I made jobs. I supported people. I fixed their plumbing. And this is what Loudoun County does to me, my family? And then turns me into a domestic terrorist?"

Smith gave his opinion of the boy involved in the two sexual assaults. I did not disagree with his assessment. "We sent a psychopath sexual predator to a residential [*sic*] that's just going to toy with them, con them and you will read about him in the newspaper again. I guarantee it."

Smith also touched on the things being taught in schools. I have no clue why he was allowed to ramble on in this way, other than that it fit the attorney general's agenda. "And the stuff that's going on right now in schools across the country, if it doesn't stop, we're not going to have a country, because these children are going to be in charge."

Jessica Smith was also on the stand on June 22, 2022. Only one thing really stood out to me regarding her testimony. Carlton Davis asked, "And who's Wayde Byard?" Jessica Smith answered, "Wayde Byard is the public information officer for Loudoun County Public Schools."

Why was this question asked out of the blue?

My paranoia radar went on red alert.

This sense was heightened when I read how the June 14, 2022, session ended.

Theo Stamos took over and said, "So that's the presentation of evidence on the record, and now we will go off the record."

Off the record?

Why?

My Subpoena

I was surprised when I got a subpoena from Carlton Davis regarding the special grand jury on July 19, 2022. I had received subpoenas before and made note only of the date I was to appear, August 2. I didn't read the legal fine print. It contained these sentences: "An untruthful answer to any question may be the basis for prosecuting you for perjury. Anything you say may be used against you by the special grand jury or may later be used against you in court."

While I will maintain to my dying day that I told the truth, and told nothing but the truth before the special grand jury, I ruminated on these words as I read them months later.

My First Grand Jury Appearance

I made my first appearance before the special grand jury late in the afternoon session following testimony by at-large school board member Denise Corbo on August 2, 2022. There was only about a half hour left in the session. As Corbo left the courtroom with her attorney, she offered that "I may have said too much."

She was clearly giddy.

Not a good omen.

When my turn came, I entered the room with an attorney hired by the school division, Tim McEvoy. I was sworn in and took the stand. Through the years, I have covered many trials as a reporter and taken part in a few more as a witness. The first thing I noticed was that there was no judge in the room. The atmosphere was very informal, with grand jurors sitting around the room in no discernible order. The thing I noticed most about the grand jurors was a woman with bright blue hair sitting at a table directly in front of the witness stand.

I met McEvoy a few minutes before the afternoon session began. He had trouble finding parking in downtown Leesburg, and we texted several times as the 1:00 p.m. start time for the hearing approached. McEvoy waved to me from his car on Market Street to let me know he was nearby. I sat on a bench in front of the old Loudoun County Courthouse. I had gotten there very early. I killed some time by talking with an old friend, Loudoun County Circuit Court Clerk Gary Clemens, near the spot where the Confederate monument once stood. McEvoy caught up to me just as I was about to enter the court complex. We spent the time during Corbo's testimony getting to know one another.

On the way into my testimony, Theo Stamos said a very courteous hello. Inside the courtroom she underwent an almost schizophrenic transformation. She began shoving emails and documents in front of me concerning the sexual assault of the female student at Stone Bridge High School on May 28, 2021. There were documents concerning meetings that I had not attended, involving members of the superintendent's cabinet.

Honestly, my two appearances before the special grand jury are blurred in my mind. They were emotionally intense, and my primary objective was not to say anything wrong. On February 14 and 21, 2023, I went back through the transcripts to sort through what I had said before the special grand jury on each date. One thing that cut through the fog of memory was the way Theo Stamos behaved during these sessions. She was sarcastic, condescending, and demeaning toward witnesses. She took full advantage of the fact that no judge was present in the courtroom.

One thing Theo was absolutely obsessed with was why no mention of a sexual assault was made in the May 28, 2021, message to the community from Stone Bridge Principal Tim Flynn. By my count, Theo mentioned this forty-eight times during my brief initial appearance before the special grand jury.

Examples:

Theo: "So are we to understand that the drafting of this email had nothing to do with the sexual assault that Mr. Flynn alerted the—his superiors about."

Me: "I can only speculate. I know in retrospect, from what we have found out since, that there was a sexual assault. At that point in time, Mr. Flynn was very concerned because he had a disruptive parent who was being very loud, who was startling students and staff. That was the primary problem at the moment."

Theo: "OK. So at 4:36 on Friday, May 28th, as far as you know now, that was after—that was the time after the sexual assault in the bathroom of Stone Bridge High School.

"Are you aware of that?"

Me: "Yes, ma'am. At that time I don't think the principal had categorized it as an assault. The assistant principals had gone down to see what had happened.

"As I said, as we later found out, this was a boyfriend-girlfriend situation. They were trying to sort out what exactly had happened. But his primary concern was the unruly parent."

Theo: "So are we to understand that Mr. Flynn was not concerned about the allegation of a sexual assault in the girls' bathroom by a boy when you helped draft this alert to the school community?"

Me: "I would not say that. I would say at this point we really didn't know what happened, and I really couldn't speak to what Mr. Flynn's state of mind was. But he was very concerned he had a disruptive parent in the school."

Theo: "When you say here that there was no threat to the student body, I take it that you're—it didn't include the young girl who was raped and sexually assaulted in the bathroom?"

Me: "At this point I didn't know there was an assault in the bathroom. What I did know is we had an unruly (parent) who was confined to the central office who did not attack student body members."

As was her tactic, Theo used increasingly long and complex questions in an effort to trip me up or put words in my mouth.

At the end of this session, the court determined that I would return for more testimony on August 23.

McEvoy and I walked back to the former LCPS headquarters at North Street, where I had parked. He assured me that my testimony was fine and that I had said nothing wrong. As it turned out, that didn't matter. I would be indicted for what I said on this day, even though I considered my second special grand jury appearance much more contentious.

Second Grand Jury Appearance

My boss, Joan Sahlgren, was the first person on the stand on August 23, 2022. Her testimony took up the entire morning. While she and Tim McEvoy, who was also her attorney, were in the courtroom, I sat on a hard oak chair in the lobby reading the latest in the Lisbeth Salander series, *The Girl Who Takes an Eye for an Eye*.

It wasn't until the following year, while I was sitting in the reflective calm of my attorney Jennifer Leffler's conference room in February of 2023, that Jennifer and I agreed that my perjury charge was probably the result of differences in Joan's testimony on August 23, 2022, and mine. Reading the special grand jury transcripts in February, I saw that Theo Stamos was trying to put Joan at ease as Joan's testimony began. "So it's fairly informal. So if you need to take a break or get some water, please let us know."

Pleasantries out of the way, Theo hammered Joan, concentrating on what I told Joan on May 28, 2021. By my count, Theo asked Joan about the messaging or my role in it approximately thirty times. Again, Theo asked long questions and tried to put words in Joan's mouth. I want to say, up front, that I don't blame Joan for my indictment. My attitude during my special grand jury appearances, as I will document later, probably had something to do with that. Joan was an inexperienced witness being hammered by a very experienced prosecutor on a mission.

The following will give you just a bit of the flavor of the circuitous questions Theo asked and the answers Joan gave:

Theo: "OK. And if you could think back to that afternoon, May 28, apparently Mr. Byard, who is your public information officer, is the person you said informed you about this incident at Stone Bridge High School.

"What was it that you were learning about the incident at Stone Bridge High School from Mr. Byard?"

Joan: "It was a busy day. I don't—I know at the time what I was learning that the principal had had a situation with students and law enforcement had been called. And in addition a person, who turned out to be a parent, had shown up and caused a disruption at the front office. So there was a lot of law enforcement presence."

Theo: "OK, but there was a discussion about a report of a sexual assault in the bathroom. Whether or not it was characterized by anyone as a crime, were you aware there was a report of a sexual assault?"

Joan: "Yes."

Theo: "And when were you made aware of that?"

Joan: "That day. That day."

Theo: "OK, so you were made aware of it that day?"

Joan: "Not—I was—what did you just say? You said a report of a sexual assault?"

Theo: "Yes. That information came to light after that initial notification. But not as you stated previously that it was a crime, that it was a done deal at that point. So the way you said it the second time was more accurate, yes.

"Obviously, I'm not asking you to guess, there's a process in place. You're the Director of Communications, would it have been your public information officer, Mr. Byard, saying to you this is, you know, unfolding information. We now have more information."

Joan: "Yes, something like that. I can't tell you exactly how I found out, but yes."

Theo: "And you do know further that Mr. Flynn told Wayde Byard about the incident in the bathroom and also the fact that the father had appeared at the school?"

Joan: "I don't know what he told Wayde. I know what I knew."

Theo: "And now, because you are the Director of Communication, are you thinking, you know, let's just be proactive, do we need to do any messaging? Are you having any kind of conversations with Mr. Byard or Dr. Ziegler about let's figure out what we have here? Or is this like, 'Oh, well, so what?'"

Joan: "So at this point it would have been a law-enforcement matter. So once he was taken away, removed—once he was removed, that was a law-enforcement matter.

"So the Sheriff's Office would have reported on that arrest, charge, whatever they call it."

When Joan was questioned by members of the special grand jury at the end of her testimony, it was clear that they had picked up on Theo's plan of attack, and amplified it.

Juror: "So it's possible—I know you don't remember—but it's possible that he told you about the sexual assault aspect." ("He" being me.)

Joan: "It's possible."

Juror: "And then why was the alleged sexual assault not addressed in any way to the public at that time? Why was it chosen only to be the disturbance with the parent and not the actual reason for why the police were present at the school? Why was that decision made to your knowledge?"

Joan: "To my knowledge, well I wasn't there. But I will say, and I've said earlier today, that information we had was that two students had been involved in something. It was not known whether it was an assault or whether it was consensual. We didn't know anything at that time, other than something had happened."

My Testimony

In retrospect, I have to admit that I exhibited the attitude of my native New Jersey during my exchanges with Theo during my second special grand jury session.

If this session had been a boxing match, it would have begun with Theo throwing a barrage of punches trying to find a hole in my defenses. In short order she asked me:

- About my role in the November 5, 2021, news conference announcing the independent report and how it came about. (Other than writing an original draft of the superintendent's statement, which was then heavily edited, and rounding up the media, not much.)
- Did I know that LCPS Division Counsel Bob Falconi had previously worked for Blankingship & Keith? (I did not.)
- What did I know about Mark Smith's resignation? (Nothing.)
- What did I know about the LCPS transfer process? (I knew about different types of transfers—voluntary and involuntary—but, beyond that, not much.)

Theo then returned to her obsession, the message of May 28, 2021. "You don't have any recollection as to whether or not you said, 'Hey, Joan, you know, we're concerned because' or 'I'm concerned that this investigation is going to . . .'"

At this point, my mind and manners took a trip back to the Garden State. "I think at this point you are trying to put words in my mouth."

To which Theo replied: "No. I'm not."

Me: "Yes, you are, counsel."

Theo: "I asked you a question."

Me: "I am not—you are not asking questions. You are making a statement counsel."

Theo: "Listen and I will get to a question, sir."

As I read this on February 21, 2023, I flashed back to third grade at Commodore Perry Elementary School. I was part of a class of more than thirty students overseen by a first-year teacher who wasn't up to the task. Given this lapse in leadership I, immaturely, committed my fair share of mayhem. On the last day of school, she lined us up and predicted what we would do in the future. She told the boys they would be doctors, lawyers, policemen, firemen, astronauts, ballplayers, saving me for last. "And you're going to prison."

In 2023, I felt like tracking her down and saying, "You know what you said fifty-six years ago . . ."

The August 23 session also contained what I dub the "CNN incident."

Theo shoved an email in front of me from fourteen months before. "You indicate here that it was soon after she signed off on this statement that you are communicating with Ms. Sahlgren and you say, 'We've had all our friends calling in as well as a long talk with CNN.' Do you remember writing that?"

Me: "Yes."

Theo: "Who are your friends calling in?"

Me: "Usually the DC-area media, the four network affiliates, newspapers, *Washington Post*."

After a brief interlude, Theo returned to this line of questioning. "When you say here, 'as well as a long talk with CNN.' Who did you communicate with there?"

Me: "It was a producer, I believe. Don Lemon." (Don Lemon's producer, not Don Lemon personally.)

Theo: "And do you know the producer's name?"

Me: "I can't recall at the moment." (This was the absolute truth. I worked with at least a half dozen producers at CNN.)

Theo: "It was—you indicate to your boss that it was a long talk. What was long about it? What did you guys talk about?"

Me: "We talked about shop, we talked about various aspects—off the record—of things that are going on."

Theo: "Was it about the impaneling of the Special Grand Jury?"

Me: "I don't speak about 'off the record' with anybody who I speak with 'off the record' about." (I apologize for this twisted bit of grammar.)

Theo: "Well, that's convenient, but you're under oath here and you have to answer the question. This is not privileged."

Me: "I don't break the trust. I'm sorry."

Theo: "Excuse me?"

Me: "I don't break a trust with a reporter."

Theo: "Well, this is a confidential proceeding and you are required to answer the question. What conversation did you have with this reporter when you indicated it was a long talk with CNN? You are not privileged in that."

Me: "I don't know. It was about scheduling, about he [Don Lemon] has an interest in talking to Chair Sheridan and various subjects. I really can't recall exactly what was discussed."

Theo: "What was discussed off the record?"

Me: "I don't talk about off the record."

Theo: "Well, you're going to have to talk about it, Mr. Byard."

Me: "It's a trust I don't break." (Now we were definitely back in third grade. "You're gonna make me? I don't think so.")

Theo: "Isn't it the reporter's trust that doesn't—I mean, you're the source."

Me: "It's both ends of the equation."

Theo: "Well, we're going to have to ask Mr. Plowman, Judge Plowman, to come back and order you to answer because you don't have a right not to answer."

So now we're going to the principal's office? Fine. Let's go to the principal's office. Seriously, a couple of points stick out to me here. One: What does what I may or may not have said to CNN have anything to do with the investigation of the events of May 28, 2021, at Stone Bridge High School? Two: Since when can a court in the United States of America compel you to say anything? Just because this was a special grand jury doesn't mean there's a special provision to waive your constitutional rights. I can see compelling someone to testify about the identity of a murderer or the whereabouts of a kidnapped child. What I said to a producer at CNN certainly didn't rise to that level.

At this point a cooler head—that of my then attorney, Tim McEvoy—entered this unpleasant interaction. After a brief discussion between McEvoy and Theo in the vestibule just outside the courtroom, they decided that I would testify that I couldn't remember what, exactly, it was I said to CNN, which, by the way, was the truth.

After I said this, Theo shot back a response dripping with sarcasm: "Sure, OK."

A member of the general public might ask, "How could you forget a conversation with CNN?" During 2021 and 2022, I engaged in hundreds of conversations with journalists from around the world as Loudoun became the epicenter of culture war controversy. Of these, only one really stood out: a conversation with a producer for Fox News's Martha MacCallum. I talked to Fox News, in its many incarnations, more than any other news outlet. In this instance, Ian Prior had made a false claim that LCPS was spending $3 million on "equity." A quick call to LCPS Chief Financial Officer Sharon

Willoughby showed that this figure included additional English learner teachers and additional staff for Title I schools. This figure was given to the Board of Supervisors as part of a budget presentation. I called the producer back and explained the basis of the figures and that this amount of money was not being spent on equity training. To her credit, MacCallum did not pursue this outrageous claim on-air.

At the conclusion of my testimony, the grand jurors asked a few questions. None of them struck me as controversial, with most centering on minor points of clarification. There were no deep queries or contentious exchanges. My overall impression of the grand jurors was that they were indifferent and somewhat bored.

Based on their reaction, I thought I had nothing to fear.

This was reinforced by Tim McEvoy. Walking back to North Street, he told me that, while the CNN exchange was contentious, it wasn't particularly damaging. McEvoy thought I could be called back before the special grand jury, but probably not.

The Unsealing of the Special Grand Jury Report

The special grand jury report on its eight-month investigation into LCPS was unsealed on Monday, December 5, 2022. The actual "report" section of the document was twenty-four pages long. It was clear to me from reading the report that the grand jurors didn't write it. It was studded with legal jargon and relatively elegant turns of phrase. My guess was that Theo Stamos and her cohort, Carlton Davis, wrote it and the foreperson signed off.

The media quickly labeled the report as "scathing" based on the following oft-quoted section: "We believe throughout this ordeal LCPS administrators were looking out for their own interests instead of the best interests of LCPS."

The next paragraph seemed to shoot down the cover-up controversy: "We conclude there was not a coordinated cover-up between LCPS administrators and the members of the Loudoun County School Board." Reading this, I was somewhat relieved. I was hoping that the cover-up theory had been put to rest.

The special grand jury report included eight recommendations for LCPS, noting that they were "in no particular order." I will list these along with my reaction to them.

- **One:** To increase transparency and foster better communication, LCPS should include as much information as reasonably possible when informing parents, staff, students, and the community about significant incidents occurring on school property, on a school bus, or at a school-sponsored event.
  Reaction: Done. LCPS puts out hundreds of emails each year informing the school community about unusual events; even those on school buses or at school-sponsored events. We offer all the details we can, given the restrictions of FERPA and the Code of Virginia. In the coming weeks, many people would point out to me that the attorney general's team seemed to have a basic lack of knowledge of school law.

- **Two:** LCPS should take steps to reexamine its transfer process.
  Reaction: Done. Scott Ziegler made good on his promise to overhaul the transfer process made at the November 5 media conference. He reported to the school board on the progress made concerning this issue.

- **Three:** The LCPS director of security needs to be more involved in situations that threaten the safety and security of students, faculty, and staff.
  Reaction: The LCPS director of safety and security, John Clark, is a former Secret Service agent. His office monitors all manner of online threats and reports them to law enforcement. His office, however, is not a law-enforcement agency. The safety and security office was often told to back off by

the sheriff's office whenever it pushed for information on the sheriff's investigations of school incidents.

- **Four:** LCSB [Loudoun County School Board] should tighten policies regarding the type of apps available to students to download on their school-issued devices and should review their Google alerts administrations and law enforcement about possible threats to students, faculty, and staff. *Reaction:* A valid, naïve point. LCPS's technical staff was constantly blocking apps. Students constantly found ways around blocking using proxies or other methods at which digital natives are adept. This was, and is, an ongoing technical war being fought by virtually every sector of society.

- **Five:** The elected members of LCSB should limit the degree to which legitimate matters and information of public concern are shielded from the public under the cloak of maintaining attorney-client privilege. *Reaction:* Most of the information discussed under attorney-client privilege involves personnel and student disciplinary matters. Such information is protected, as previously noted, by state and federal confidentiality laws.

- **Six:** Communications, cooperation, and coordination across agencies must be improved when addressing issues of criminal conduct by students, faculty, and staff. *Reaction:* This is what's known in the news business as "burying the lede" (to begin a story with details of secondary importance). This is why the special grand jury's recommendations had been presented "in no particular order." Inter-agency communication failed on a massive scale regarding the 2021 sexual assaults at Loudoun County high schools. Some of this failure was the result of clashing egos. Some of the failure was pure bureaucratic incompetence. To me, this was the most important and valid sentence in the entire special grand jury report.

- **Seven:** Strengthen avenues of support for faculty and staff confronted with challenging scenarios that could pose a danger and/or impede learning.
  Reaction: Fair enough. If people had listened to staff concerns being raised about the assailant in the May 28, 2021, incident, a lot of grief could have been avoided.
- **Eight:** The superintendent's recommendation for the nonrenewal of a teacher's contract should be the subject of a separate agenda item and not placed on the LCSB consent agenda.
  Reaction: In a school division the size of LCPS, there are literally hundreds of personnel actions—non-renewals, hirings, resignations, retirements—that occur every year. Most of the non-renewals are for poor performance, not legal wrongdoing. Even if non-renewals are all considered one at a time by the school board, the reasons for nonrenewal can't be discussed because of confidentiality laws. Going through non-renewals one by one could publicly expose the teacher's identity and ruin any chance for their future employment.

After the twenty-four-page section, there was a sixty-seven-page section of documents. "Key documents are attached to this report so that the public can have faith our conclusions rest on solid evidence." The documents in this section were cherry-picked from thousands of documents and were largely taken out of context. I, for one, had no faith they represented "solid evidence." (Then again, I admit to being biased.)

Division Counsel Bob Falconi put together a reaction statement to the special grand jury report that both Joan and I found to be too combative. We went back and forth on Microsoft Teams and Google Docs, eventually coming up with a statement that school board Chair Jeff Morse and future

Chair Ian Serotkin endorsed. I got it out to numerous media organizations before the evening newscasts.

In retrospect, it was still too combative and was later condemned as "tone deaf."

The statement: "In spite of the recent allegations, we are pleased that the special grand jury's extensive investigation found no evidence of criminal conduct on the part of anyone within LCPS, and not a single indictment was filed as a result of this lengthy process."

After the special grand jury issued its final report, Virginia Attorney General Jason Miyares stated that it was not being dismissed, an ominous statement that might have meant that indictments were coming.

On *The Ingraham Angle*, Ian Prior let slip some insider information about what was coming, "I suspect we could see more down the road in the very near future."

The Lead-Up to Indictment

A midnight firing, a celebration of a life well-lived, a sudden death, and fractured nerves marked the beginning of December 2022.

What the Attorney General Really Wanted

The report issued by the special grand jury stated what I believed the attorney general and/or Theo Stamos was really upset about.

The report stated: "The statement drafted by the public information officer and edited and approved by the superintendent, deliberately makes no mention of the sexual assault that took place just hours earlier. Nor does it mention the fact that the assailant had gone missing in SBHS for hours after he committed the sexual assault, jeopardizing the safety of all students."

Let's address these assertions one at a time:

One: Yes, we deliberately did not mention the sexual assault because the sheriff's office had not yet determined one had occurred. All we knew was that two students had sex in a bathroom after having sex there before.

Two: The assailant, sensing the trouble he was in, was hiding in the bathroom. I doubt a terrified fourteen-year-old boy in a skirt was jeopardizing the safety of the entire Stone Bridge student body. In addition, he was not a crazed predator stalking random girls. He and the victim in this incident knew one another and had met consensually.

The Firing of the Superintendent

About 10:00 p.m. on December 6, 2022, I turned off my cell phone and took an Advil PM, something I almost never do. At 10:55 the phone rang. It was Allison Papson, the senior assignment editor at WTTG-TV, Fox 5. Allison asked me to confirm a report that the superintendent, Dr. Scott Ziegler, had been fired by the school board. I answered something to the effect that I couldn't confirm that and hung up. (The school board had held a routine hearing that I wasn't required to attend.) I turned on my cell phone, called Joan Sahlgren, and asked her if she knew anything about this. She replied that division counsel had just told the superintendent's cabinet that this was the case. Nobody at the upper echelon of LCPS's administrative team had been told in advance that this was happening.

I called Denver Peschken, who televised school board meetings, and asked if this was true. Denver said that it was. The school board had come out of executive session, voted to fire the superintendent "without cause," adjourned quickly, and disappeared into the night. Firing without cause was an important wrinkle in this decision because it meant that Scott could collect a year's salary per the terms of his contract. This also would get him near the thirty-year mark necessary for a full pension.

Having confirmed the firing with two sources, I began answering the twenty or so media inquiries I had in my email with the sparse amount of information I had. I finally got to bed around midnight.

Later, I learned that Scott was not in the room when he was fired. He was in his second-floor office when the news came. This news hadn't come from a school board member. Scott was ordered to turn over his phone and computer and was escorted out of the building by three armed security guards. He did not deserve this impersonal treatment. A board member should have had the courage to look Scott in the eye and tell him the news. Scott made mistakes as superintendent. I believe most of these were honest. Given the amount of abuse he took on a national scale during his brief tenure, he deserved more than a cold, corporate dismissal.

At 6:00 a.m. the next morning, Scott's executive assistant, as good and loyal a person as you will ever meet, packed up Scott's office and took the contents to a neutral location.

Scott was no longer allowed in the Administration Building.

Later, I learned that the board of supervisors meeting, which was held at the same time as the school board's, featured several supervisors calling for Scott's immediate firing. This was a coordinated attack.

A very cowardly, coordinated attack.

Satiating the Media/Shooting Down Vito Malara

The school board fled the dais the night of Scott's firing without naming an interim superintendent. This was more than a minor problem, since state law requires that every school division have a superintendent. An emergency meeting was called on December 7, 2022, to name Chief of Staff Daniel Smith as interim superintendent. Daniel had only been on the job since April and was untainted by the Stone Bridge-Broad Run scandal. A boyish forty-three, he came to Loudoun from a principal's post at a major high school in Fairfax.

More than a few people in the Administration Building wondered if he would be up to the job.

During the afternoon, a school board member told Daniel that they wouldn't vote for him—even though there was no backup plan—if he didn't fire several more senior administrators. Daniel told the school board member that he was not their hit man.

My esteem for Daniel skyrocketed. I told those questioning his ability that he would be all right.

As the emergency meeting was convened, Daniel's appointment was confirmed 6-1-2, with the school member who vowed to oppose him keeping their word and two members absent. The two absences struck me as a particularly egregious act of political cowardice. A school board's primary job is to select a superintendent. What in the hell could have been more important? If you opposed Daniel, say so from the start and say why.

Before the media started their post-appointment questioning, I set some ground rules: each media member would get one question, with follow-up questions coming only after everyone had the opportunity to ask a question. I only had to enforce this rule a few times, politely. Daniel, Jeff Morse, and Ian Serotkin answered the media's questions firmly, admitting some points that the special grand jury made were correct and stating that they now wanted to concentrate on the future and on regaining the community's trust.

One person I did not allow to ask questions was PACT leader Scott Mineo.

I told Mineo that we were taking questions only from accredited media.

"Who determines who is accredited?"

"I do."

Mineo didn't get to ask a question but appeared as a "concerned" parent on several TV news broadcasts later in the evening.

Afterward, I met three school board members in the school board conference room adjacent to the meeting venue. They said that they were impressed by how I ran "linebacker" with the media.

If this was the last news conference I conducted for LCPS, at least it was a good one.

The LCPS Family Reunion

During a Rock & Roll Hall of Fame induction ceremony, Carly Simon mentioned that Mick Jagger sang backup on "You're So Vain," something I hadn't known before. Once you hear Mick, you really can't hear anything else in the song. I was playing this song on my car's CD player as I drove to work on Friday, December 9, 2022—yes, I still have a CD player—and Carly was just getting to the part where the song's protagonist is flying his Learjet up to Nova Scotia, when the phone cut in. Broad Run Principal Dave Spage informed me that a beloved teacher and coach, John Costello, had been killed in a car accident while vacationing in Hawaii. I diverted to Broad Run to help Dave with a very difficult community message.

John Costello was one of Dave's best friends. Costello was vacationing to use up some accumulated sick leave before retiring at the end of the school year. He and his wife had returned to the site of their honeymoon. A teenage driver T-boned their car at an intersection, killing John instantly and leaving his wife, who sustained only minor injuries, witnessing everything.

Tragic.

Earlier in the week, the special grand jury report unfairly portrayed Dave as a cold, unfeeling bureaucrat who callously disregarded a sexual assault. Dave is stoic, but far from unemotional or uncaring. Besides the report and John Costello's death, other things were straining him to an emotional breaking point that morning. Dave's mother-in-law, a retired secretary at Sterling Middle School viewed as a community treasure, was in the last stages of terminal cancer.

Movie-star good-looking, Dave is a former Marine reservist known for his calm in tough situations, of which I've helped him work through a few. As we crafted the community message, I asked Dave how he was doing.

"Not good."

I've known Dave and his family a long time. When someone like Dave Spage says he's not doing well, it cuts you to the core.

Dave and I composed the message, and Dave recorded it in a halting voice. Afterward, I walked the halls at Broad Run. They were silent as a tomb as students and staff processed their grief. I mentioned to others at the central office that Dave needed emotional support. They agreed. I was proud of my professional family as they rallied around a colleague.

At six o'clock that evening, we held a celebration of life for former Assistant Superintendent for Instruction Sharon Ackerman at the Administration Building.

The story that best defined Sharon's devotion to LCPS was told often. She once worked until her appendix exploded to complete a budget presentation. Organ failure was no excuse to turn in your work late. She also worked through chemotherapy treatments after being diagnosed with breast cancer.

Sharon died at seventy-seven after a third bout with breast cancer. On her deathbed, Sharon told her husband, Irv, that she was worried about not being able to get back a deposit they'd made on a vacation at Sandals.

That was Sharon.

I asked Irv about the most appropriate venue for Sharon's celebration. "The office, that's where she lived."

The office it was.

The December 9, 2022, celebration was scheduled to last two hours but lasted almost three. No one wanted to leave. It had the feeling of a large family reunion—about two hundred people attended—with some traveling from New Mexico, North Carolina, and Florida to pay tribute to an extraordinary woman. After the ceremony, some of us retired to the nearby Clyde's restaurant to continue our reminiscence and renew friendships.

Driving home, I felt a sense of mourning for the school division we once were.

The alternate date offered by Irv for this celebration was Monday, December 12.

For reasons that will soon become obvious, I'm glad we managed to gather on the ninth.

Tim Flynn

The other principal in the sad special grand jury saga, Tim Flynn, is full of shit.

That's why I liked him.

Flynn is a prototypical Irishman, a leprechaun on steroids. A former Army National Guard sergeant, he is boisterous and opinionated. Sometimes you just have to stand back and let Flynn get his blarney out before getting a word in edgewise.

Flynn is a Red Sox fan, which I maintain is a form of mental illness. I also liked reminding him that his beloved Patriots would have had two more Super Bowl trophies if it hadn't been for Eli Manning and my Giants.

Flynn was LCPS's Principal of the Year at Belmont Ridge Middle School before coming to Stone Bridge. He had endured a lot as a principal. At one point, a violent student with deep psychological problems stalked Flynn, his wife, and their two young daughters. There are so many pressures on public-school principals that the public never sees.

I want principals to know that I see them as people and care about their lives. I don't want to be the faceless bureaucrat on the other end of the phone. When a principal calls me, I want them to know they're talking to someone who cares about them.

When someone like Glenn Youngkin—a second-rate political opportunist—throws people like Dave Spage and Tim Flynn to the wolves, my blood boils.

Prepping for Indictments

Joan and I had minor freak-outs on consecutive days: December 10 and 11, 2022.

On Saturday, Joan called saying she was worried about the messaging we would have to prepare in case the special grand jury issued indictments Monday or Tuesday. We decided to work on messaging Monday morning and run it by our communications consultant so that we would be prepared.

On Sunday morning, as I often did, I turned on my spare computer on the kitchen table to work on Freedom of Information Act requests. I began communication with Division Counsel Bob Falconi on Teams. Before long, Bob, Joan, and I were in a videoconference. Bob, who was clearly agitated and upset, said that he expected special grand jury indictments Monday or Tuesday. He was guessing Tuesday because that was a school board meeting day and would cause maximum embarrassment.

PART IV

Indictment

Down the Indictment Rabbit Hole

I had been involved with Our Health, one of the most successful nonprofits in Northern Virginia, since its inception in 1996. By 2023, Our Health had redeveloped 70,000 square feet of old buildings in downtown Winchester, Virginia, into Class A office space. The organization currently has twenty-one nonprofit agencies on campus and is affiliated with seventy-one others. Through the years, I served Our Health in a variety of leadership positions and as a major fundraiser, generating $181,000 in donations.

As I faced my legal problems during the first half of 2023, I would often drive by Our Health to remind myself that I was capable of doing generous and important things.

You have to do that every once in a while.

During a Zoom meeting with the Our Health board shortly after noon on December 12, 2022, LCPS Division Counsel Bob Falconi came into my office and told me to shut off everything immediately. Bob looked absolutely stricken. He told me that myself and former Superintendent Dr. Scott Ziegler were the only two people indicted by the special grand jury. Scott was indicted on three misdemeanors, which were detailed in the information the attorney general's office released. I was charged with felony perjury. The charges against me were not detailed. (I later discovered that I had been "secretly" indicted by the Special Grand Jury on September 28. It was never explained why it took almost three months for this indictment to be revealed. Merry Christmas.)

I quickly met in the division counsel's office with Interim Superintendent Dr. Daniel Smith; my boss, Joan Sahlgren; Chief Human Resources Officer Lisa Boland; and Bob Falconi. During the weekend, Joan had said that she wanted me in the office on Monday, instead of in Winchester at the Our Health meeting, because we needed to be prepared with draft talking points and a media release if LCPS staff were indicted. I'd been working on this language before hopping on my Zoom meeting, never thinking that this statement would be released regarding me. Daniel, Lisa, Bob, and Joan were clearly shaken. I put on my best spokesperson face and told them I was OK. I was glad that some other people who were supposed targets of an indictment had been spared.

Bob told me that my status would be "suspended, leave without pay." The Code of Virginia states that school employees charged with a felony must be put on "leave without pay." I didn't protest and tried not to appear distressed by the devastating news. The Code states the suspended employee's salary will be held in an interest-bearing escrow account pending resolution of the case. If the employee is found not guilty, they collect this amount—a ray of hope for a gloomy day. If the employee is found guilty and exhausts their appeals, this money is returned to the school division. This was another reason—besides the fact that I wasn't guilty—that I would never agree to a plea agreement. As I prepared my retirement documents in November 2023, I discovered that I would have lost my Virginia pension had I been found guilty. I'm glad I didn't know this on December 12, 2022. It would have added a whole new level of anxiety to the coming months.

After a short time, Daniel decided it would be best if I left the building immediately so the media didn't get a "perp walk" shot of me leaving the premises. I turned in my phone and computer and detached my badge, which got me through the building's locked doors, from my New York Giants' lanyard. (I alternated between Yankees' and Giants' lanyards depending on the season.) I'll admit a big mistake here: I used my business phone for all my work and personal calls and texts. I should have used separate private and business phones like most people do. When my phone went, a huge chunk of my resources went with it.

Lisa Boland walked me out a side door to the parking lot. As I looked back, the last thing I saw was Joan, tears welling in her eyes, waving goodbye and clutching her heart. Once outside, I had trouble finding my car, an anonymous black 2016 Subaru Legacy. Hitting the key fob, I located it. Once I sat in the driver's seat, Lisa remembered that I had to turn in my parking pass. I handed it over.

Lisa was starting to cry as she said it was an "honor" to walk me out of the building.

I've driven the fifty-one miles between my house and the Administration Building thousands of times at all hours of the day and night. I grew up a hundred feet from the Erie Lackawanna Railway tracks in Mahwah, New Jersey. When I drive, I usually pretend I'm following a train schedule. You have to do something to break the monotony. I have time markers for Hamilton, Purcellville, the Shenandoah River, Berryville, and the Frederick County-Clarke County line. Sometimes I play CDs. Like most members of my generation, I play the music very loud. The Beatles, Billy Joel, AC/DC, Tina Turner, and Rod Stewart are often on the playlist.

On this day, I rode in silence; feeling numb, but oddly calm.

The next challenge was telling my wife what had happened. I thought about the George Thorogood song "One Bourbon, One Scotch, One Beer."

"Had to tell the landlady I'da lost my job . . ."

And, by the way, I had been indicted for a felony.

One of the first people to contact me after I got home was Bill Collins, whom I have known for more than thirty years. I got to know Bill when he was executive director of the Shenandoah Apple Blossom Festival, Winchester's premier social event. Bill also owned the Valley Baseball League's Winchester Royals, which I covered for years, and we participated in the same fantasy baseball league. Bill reminded me that I had stood by him when he was unjustly fired by the Apple Blossom Festival Board of Directors, and now he would be there for me.

Another fantasy baseball friend who reached out was Billy Grubbs, who sent me regular emails inquiring about my health, mental and otherwise. Billy set up a lunch meeting with Bill Collins and Bent Ferrell, a former chair of the Clarke County School Board whom I worked with for ten years at LCPS. We met once a month at an authentic Mexican restaurant south of Winchester and had some authentic conversation.

This kind of support proved vital to keeping my sanity.

Julia Judkins and Why I Was Indicted

A good friend who helped me get past the crisis of being indicted was attorney Julia Judkins. She was the first person I emailed when I got home on December 12.

Julia formerly served as an outside counsel for LCPS, a hired gun brought in to handle complex legal matters. She is someone you don't want to face in a courtroom. Super smart, composed, and logical to a fault, Julia is the person you want sitting next to you at the defendant's table. We became professional friends during a series of court cases involving a local gadfly.

We conferred about finding suitable legal counsel. Julia was semiretired at the time and working for Fairfax County Public Schools, thus ineligible to represent me. She would have been my first choice as my attorney.

Julia was the first person to tell me why I had been indicted: They were trying to get me to flip and implicate others' wrongdoing so that they could seek further indictments.

I'll now extrapolate on Julia's observation and tell you why I think it was correct.

Because they put me on suspension *without* pay, they were going to delay a trial any way they could—ruin me financially—then extend a plea deal in return for some damning testimony against others.

Even though the special grand jury had issued its *final* report, the attorney general had not dismissed it on the basis that more indictments might be forthcoming. Jason Miyares and Glenn Youngkin had said as much.

Despite its inflammatory report, the special grand jury had essentially come up dry. It needed the heads of more senior LCPS administrators in order to be called a success.

The events of the following months proved Julia's initial analysis to be spot-on. These months were long and exhausting, and I was buoyed by my family and friends, the pillars standing firm in the swirling eddies I found myself trapped in after the indictment.

My Wife

Brenda Kay Fertig is the oldest child of a family that put the "d" in dysfunction.

Her father, career Army, shipped off to Vietnam a functional alcoholic and came back a raging one with a case of gonorrhea. He abandoned his family shortly thereafter for a girl a year older than Brenda. Brenda's mother was a dirt-poor hillbilly who had Brenda at seventeen and two more children by the time she was twenty. Mentally unstable, Brenda's mom had a fourth child, born with a congenital condition that would kill him in his early teens.

Brenda started working at fifteen and was managing her family's finances soon thereafter. Brenda's mom took off after emptying the family bank account when Brenda was seventeen, leading to the family's eviction from their home. Brenda lived without electricity and water while hoping for a financial miracle. After the eviction, neighbors looted the family's belongings, which had been put out in the street, and the landlord confiscated the family's furniture. Three photos were all that remained of Brenda's childhood; two of them were Polaroids.

Briefly homeless, Brenda was taken in by foster parents Janet and Ronnie Smith, who through the decades, along with their four children, became Brenda's true family. At this point, Brenda's career goal was to become a beautician. Urged on by the Smiths, she decided to become a teacher. Brenda worked her way through community college, college, and two master's degrees, the second of which she obtained while helping to raise our toddler. In 2023, Brenda was presented with the Gold Medallion, an honor that the Laurel Ridge Community College Board awards to distinguished staff. It was one of only three such awards presented during a ceremony in the college's conference center.

We met totally by accident in February 1981. Brenda called *The Winchester Star* newsroom, where I was in my second month as a general assignment reporter. I picked up the call. Brenda wanted someone to do a story about her Future Business Leaders of America (FBLA) chapter, which she served as an advisor. To that point, my social life in Winchester had been a complete dud. I tried singles volleyball. All I got was sweaty. A divorcee at work let me know that she was very interested, but the thing she was obviously interested in was a father for her small child. No thank you.

In future years, I would joke that Brenda and I met through a wrong number—a perfect metaphor for our relationship. Turns out, nothing could have been further from the truth. That was the luckiest call of my life.

The young woman I met in the office of James Wood High School had strawberry blond hair and a stunning pair of beautiful blue eyes. Her most charming feature was a glowing natural smile that burst forth spontaneously. Considering all that Brenda had been through by the time she was twenty-three, I considered her ability to smile at all amazing. During the interview that followed, I smoothly asked Brenda for her phone number, "In case I had any more questions." After I left, Brenda's students excitedly speculated that Miss Fertig was about to get asked on a date.

She was.

We went out two days later, were engaged by June, and married on December 19, 1981, in Keyser, West Virginia. Brenda is four months older than I am, which has led to tired jokes about me being married to an "older woman."

I was initially a lousy husband.

I was immature and self-centered.

I was fixated on work and brought way too much of it home. I was named sports editor at twenty-six and assistant managing editor at thirty-two. The pressure of my work led to the development of a massive esophageal ulcer—at first misdiagnosed as a fatal form of cancer—also at thirty-two.

I socialized too much.

It was a small miracle that Brenda didn't divorce me during our first five years of marriage.

We had my first daughter in 1986 and a second in 1990. In 1994, Brenda suffered a near-fatal miscarriage. A devout Catholic, she refused to terminate the pregnancy—even when it appeared that the baby was dead—and suffered massive internal bleeding. It came down to me to make the decision on the pregnancy when Brenda passed the point of coherency. I chose my wife over a child who was most probably dead. Afterward, the doctor consoled me with the facts that the child was dead, probably was never viable, and that this was not an abortion (he doesn't perform them). He asked me if I wanted to name the child. I numbly answered, "No."

That decision haunts me to this day.

A business teacher by training, Brenda has an incredible grasp of finances. She managed to pay off two college educations and two fairly impressive weddings without incurring long-term debt. We live in a modest brick rambler we purchased for $125,700 in 1989. In 2008, we augmented our property by buying a derelict house next door and tearing it down. Altogether, we have about three acres that we keep well-manicured.

When we were twenty-five, Brenda scheduled the first of years of meetings with several financial advisors. The first advisor, an older insurance agent, advised that by the time we retired in forty years, we'd need an average annual income of $100,000 to maintain a middle-class lifestyle. We about shit ourselves in the car afterward; a natural reaction considering we made $25,000 per annum between us at the time.

But we—and by "we" I mean Brenda—developed a long-term financial plan and stuck to it. This proved a saving grace on the afternoon of December 12, 2022, when we sat down to take stock of where we were financially.

Brenda had just retired from her job at Laurel Ridge Community College and would receive a retirement salary of more than $5,000 a month starting January 1. The Virginia Retirement System offered a limited plop—large one-time payments—to reduce future monthly retirement payments. Her first plop, also due in January, was more than $30,000. HGTV addict that she was, Brenda had saved $30,000 to build a back porch on our house. Supply chain issues, construction costs, blah, blah, blah, and any number of added complications meant that this project had never come to fruition. I had just received a large—at least for me—royalty payment on my latest book, *Spottswood Poles: A Baseball and American Legend*. I was going to spend this on an elaborate Christmas present for my wife (that's my story, and I'm sticking to it). Brenda wisely used the royalty money to wipe out a small debt before it became a troublesome one.

Work-related costs, such as gas and car repairs for commuting, were now off the table.

Through Brenda's diligent money management, we had obtained a perfect credit score of 850. We had a potentially large line of credit through Visa. Doing some quick business math, we figured that we could last six months easily without touching our mid-six-figure retirement accounts.

Not long after my indictment, Brenda showed me a video Laurel Ridge had made to honor her retirement. In almost every photo, I saw the incredible smile that I fell in love with in February 1981. It had been a long time since that smile had been directed at me.

I don't deserve Brenda Kay Fertig Byard.

My Family

One of the first people to call me after my indictment was announced was my sister Dale. We had been estranged for the better part of a decade and rarely, if ever, talked. She is six years younger than me. We live five miles apart, but never visit one another. Dale teaches at an LCPS middle school. Our lack of communication showed that while the Byards view themselves as a normal family, we have our share of dysfunction.

Dale told me that no one at school believed I was guilty. She offered to sit with my wife at my initial court hearing the next day. Brenda and I decided it was best I went alone. After a brief talk, Dale and I agreed to get our extended family together sometime during the holidays. This event happened at the Fairfax home of my niece. Seeing everyone together was great. It also left me with a sense of loss for the bitterness that had seeped into my familial relations.

My brother Kyle was born on November 1, 1959, one day short of my second birthday. Family planning at its finest. He is a much smarter, more skilled version of me. I am the beta test of the Byard brothers, the failed prototype.

Labeled as gifted at a very early age, Kyle was senior class president, valedictorian, and a track and cross-country star in high school before graduating from the US Air Force Academy. He was labeled a potential government asset while still in grade school and became a glider pilot at fifteen through a "special" program. He received a pair of nominations to the US Air Force Academy. After twenty years in the military, he became an executive with an environmental clean-up company and very wealthy.

Kyle was the primary caretaker for my eighty-eight-year-old mother, who resided in an assisted-living facility near his home outside Sacramento. Brenda and I took care of my mother and father until dad's death from dementia in 2016. Kyle said that it was his turn to step up and take care of our surviving parent.

Kyle and I usually spoke after Tuesday school board meetings. I always stopped at the 7-Eleven in Berryville, Virginia, twenty-three miles from my house to purchase a cup of "I can't believe it's almost coffee" from the dispensers in the back of the store. I would then call Kyle—taking advantage of the time difference between us—and we would talk about any number of topics (politics, international affairs, the Yankees, and family were the favorites) before I hit the remote on the garage door sometime after midnight.

My last visit to my brother and mother in Sacramento began on Thursday, September 29, 2022. I didn't know at that time that I'd been secretly indicted the day before. This was a perfect visit.

Kyle and I hiked around what was left of Folsom Lake. Climate change and water demand have shrunk the lake to the point that you can see the town that was flooded to create it. Of particular interest was a century-old bridge that looked as though you could drive across it today. I met my new ten-month-old grandniece at Golden Gate Park in San Francisco during a bluegrass festival. She was an incredibly happy baby, which I hoped wasn't the result of people smoking marijuana around us. When I held her, I held her close and whispered that she shouldn't breathe in too deeply.

I spent an hour each day with mom at the care facility that served as her home, which was about as much as she could sustain as her dementia advanced. I bought her a large cup of black coffee from Starbucks and listened as she talked about things long past, mashing different memories together while we sat in the facility's courtyard. Our last talk was a good one. She was fairly lucid and shared a lot of memories from childhood. The effort clearly exhausted her. After we talked for ninety minutes, an attendant wheeled her back into a common area where a documentary on the British royal family was playing on TV. I looked back as I exited the memory care area and saw her head slump down as she fell asleep. As I drove away from the care facility, I determined that if this was the last time we met face-to-face, this was as good a memory as I would ever have.

I have two married adult daughters and a four-year-old grandson. I will reference them in this story. Because their last names are different from mine, I will not name them.

Consider that "witness protection."

Little Man/The Greatest Joy of My Life

The brightest spot about my indictment/suspension was that it gave me more time to spend with my grandson at a formative and exciting time in his life.

You don't get to choose what your grandchildren call you. My grandson dubbed me "Pappy," "Pap" for short. Every grandparent says their grandchild is brilliant/exceptional. Mine actually is.

At three, he knew the sequencing that started his dad's industrial-strength tractor and four-wheeler. I know that once my grandson's legs reach the clutch and gas pedals, we'll be making several trips to the emergency room. He knows the special function of each of the huge saws and sanders my son-in-law uses in his contracting business and how to turn them on. Thank God there's a master electrical kill switch in the workshop.

I pray my grandson makes it to adulthood with ten fingers.

The boy emulates his craftsman father. We bought him a miniature tool kit that he carries around the house as he looks for things to fix. When he's in the mood to fix something, he says his name is "Mike" (not his real name) and that he does "big work." When the work is really big, he tries to call in his helper, "Bill." "Mike" will pick up a toy phone and call his helper, only to get a frustrated look on his face and hang up abruptly. "Bill doesn't work on Tuesdays."

That Bill . . .

The one power tool that I allowed my grandson to use was the leaf blower, which he employed to sweep the garage floor. This setup worked just fine until he hit a bag of potting soil with the blower turned up full throttle.

Everybody in my family, with the exception of me, is a big country music fan. That meant when we would pick my grandson up, country music would be on the radio. I noted to my wife that country music lyrics rely heavily on the consumption of alcohol. While he didn't fully comprehend this, my grandson knew the words to every song that came on and cheerfully sang along. Thus, there was a lot of singing about tequila and beer coming from the child seat behind us. "Half of me wants a cold beer, and the other half does too." He recognized the album covers on the car's display screen and demanded the radio be turned up whenever he spotted a favorite.

Skeletons are one of my grandson's obsessions. Two stores on Winchester's walking mall had skeletons in their display windows. We always paid these skeletons a visit because they represented free fun. So was dropping in on one of the area's playgrounds. Having an extended time off allowed me to watch as he accomplished increasingly difficult physical tasks.

The best thing about my grandson is his laugh; unaffected and spontaneous. It sounds like angels singing.

Physically, he resembles me a great deal. He also has my sentimental and sometimes-naive nature. Part of the prayers I say every day is that God makes him less vulnerable and sensitive than I am.

It will make his life much easier.

My grandson's other grandfather, as good and decent a man who's ever lived, died on June 25, 2022. It's a true shame my grandson won't really remember him. I promised my son-in-law I would be twice the grandfather to make up for this loss.

I also promised myself if there was any settlement money after this ordeal, I would put some of it into a trust for my grandson. Money equals armor against situations such as the one I found myself in.

What prayer can't do, money can.

Some Dark Voices

After my indictment, I got a small dose of what the school board was going through in terms of harassment from the general public.

It was December 19, 2022, my forty-first wedding anniversary. At 5:15 a.m. someone called on the landline phone. My wife said that I should answer because it could be my brother calling about mom. As had become my habit, I answered in my best "Lurch" voice from the Addams Family. "Hello." (Why not freak this person out a little? Unfortunately, I've also freaked out some people I know. Sorry.)

The person on the other end didn't speak. Not even heavy breathing.

I Star 69ed the call and called back. Private number blocked.

Another brave American's voice in the dark.

This was the second call of this nature we'd received. The first guy mumbled something incoherent and hung up. Rage and stupidity don't often have trouble finding their voice. My guess? This guy thought he'd be talking to an answering machine. Making your thoughts known when there is actually someone on the other end of the line takes balls.

Keyboard warriors and anonymous phone-callers lack balls.

There were several Facebook messages from people who commented on my old posts. After my indictment, I stopped posting. I did, however, keep my Facebook page up. Facebook was a lifeline to my friends—my real friends, not the Facebook variety—during this ordeal.

Here are some of my fake Facebook "friends" who decided to contact me:

Danny Gonzalez wrote: "Can't wait for the civil suit that will be filed against you. Maybe the trans community who you so hard trying to please will help you with the legal cost."

When I clicked on the Facebook link to Danny's Facebook page, it said that this content was available only to a small group of people. Danny Gonzalez, another brave keyboard warrior.

Tim Gilbert: "Too bad you and Scotty won't got handcuffs put on both of you. Like you had on that concerned parent."

Tim's Facebook profile is a blank icon. (Reference previous analysis of Danny Gonzalez.)

I found John Kokaska's message while sifting through the other Facebook hate mail. It was dated January 19, 2022. I first saw it on December 21. I guess Kokaska's message didn't have the immediate impact he had intended. The message read, "You are a sick piece of trash defending pedophiles."

John Kokaska is from Ashville, Alabama. He loves Debbie Kokaska and the beach and has several iterations of "Back the Blue" on his page. Facebook noted: "You're not friends on Facebook."

I reported the comments to Facebook. It did not have a category for harassing comments, so I pressed the tab for "Hate Speech." Facebook wrote back that these comments did not meet its standards for Hate Speech. It advised that I could delete the comments and block the senders.

I blocked the senders and kept the comments.

Sometimes you need a reminder of just how stupid people can be.

Through years of reading hateful messages, I have been able to pinpoint the precise time at which such messages are sent: 1:39 a.m. Apparently, this is the moment of some galactic convergence that compels sleep-deprived people to air their stupidity publicly.

As a card-carrying member of the "legacy media," I'm flabbergasted that libel laws don't apply to the most-used and most-destructive of social media. In my time, there were definite rules about what could be written, what could be photographed, and what could be said on the airwaves. There were monetary consequences, through lawsuits, when these rules were broken. Social media needs to feel the sting of financial consequences before it cleans up its act.

Personal Insights

To know how I weathered the events that the events of May 28, 2021, ultimately thrust me into, it would be good to know a little about me.

4A Player

I am what baseball executives refer to as a "4A player;" too good to play at the top level of the minor leagues (Class AAA), but not good enough to be on a major-league roster.

I always seemed a step behind my contemporaries. I really didn't know why I struggled in school until I read Malcolm Gladwell's *Outliers* on the flight to California in 2022. Gladwell showed that athletes who succeed are most often the oldest in their youth sports leagues. It wasn't that they were inherently better, they were just bigger, stronger, and more coordinated than their peers at an age when such attributes are very different in players just a few months apart in age. I started school two months shy of my fifth birthday. A test coordinator told my mother that I, passing for a bright four-year-old, would be "bored" in school if she waited for me to be five before starting kindergarten. I may not have been bored in school, but I was always panicked by my immaturity and lagging physical and emotional development. These factors brought me a lot of grief, a great deal of which I inflicted on myself. Throw into this mix that I was a very sensitive kid, and it's a small miracle I made it to adulthood, or something like it.

I have a tendency to be one beat behind when catching on to social cues. I also have the annoying habit of blurting out unfocused answers in an attempt to be the first to answer and impress the teacher. This trait led to a blistering, but honest, yearbook inscription my sophomore year. "To the dumbest bright kid I've ever known," wrote my English teacher Louise Lynch.

She hit that nail on the head.

Today, they have a designation for students like me: "learns differently."

I definitely fit into that category.

My mom was an elementary school teacher hooked on phonics. Rainy weekend afternoons found my brother and me scrambling around the house to avoid sitting down with a phonics workbook. Mom's instruction, however reluctantly accepted, proved effective. I was reading on a college level in sixth grade.

Math was an entirely different story.

I had no interest in math despite the fact that my dad, before becoming a school administrator, was an advanced math teacher; a very good advanced math teacher. Students would come to our house for my father to tutor them. They certainly seemed to understand as he explained various mathematical concepts. When dad tutored me, I would nod my head, showing that I understood, and then would promptly forget everything and bomb tests.

While I didn't inherit my dad's mathematical ability, I definitely inherited his impetuous nature. Dad would make an impulsive decision, then stick to it when things would go totally south. Once committed, he would be completely engaged until reaching a conclusion, a conclusion that would often negatively impact his career.

I made such a decision shortly after coming to *The Winchester Star*.

During a city council meeting, there was a debate on whether city workers deserved improvements to their insurance benefits. The employees packed the gallery in the city hall courtroom where the meeting took place. They sat silently when the council called for public comment. Finally, I stood up and gave an impassioned—if somewhat disorganized—speech on behalf of the employees. In retrospect, I should have been fired. Instead, I was reassigned. Being fired might have resulted in me controlling my impulsivity at a younger age. Instead, this incident merely delayed my promotions at *The Star*.

One winter's morning when I was sports editor of *The Winchester Star*, there was a tremendous ice storm. Feeling obligated to give *The Star's* readers the best sports coverage possible, I set off down Apple Pie Ridge toward Winchester in the semidarkness. I held my breath as I made my way down the long, steep hill at the end of the ridge. Confident that I had navigated the worst stretch of my commute, I drove confidently onto a flat area.

That's when I learned about the concept of "black ice."

My car started skidding, and I did what they taught us in driver's ed.: steered into the skid.

Instead of going straight, my car, a Chevrolet Celebrity, started inching sideways, right toward a steep embankment.

I should mention at this point that I was listening to my "happy music."

We all have some music stashed away—like ABBA or Slim Whitman—that we wouldn't want the world to know is on our playlist.

My happy music includes Herman's Hermits. Thus, as my car went sideways over the embankment, flipping upside down, I was listening to Peter Noone mournfully extolling the virtues of Mrs. Brown's lovely daughter. The car hit the ground roof-first; the roof flattened to within a couple inches of my head, while happy ukulele music poured from the cassette player. I undid my seat belt, pushed open the door, and rolled out onto the ground. The only evidence of my mishap, other than the totaled car, was a grass stain on the right shoulder of my jacket.

The state police drove me home. Rather than take the time to process a traumatic life experience, I jumped into our second car, also a Celebrity, and started driving to work. I drove past the wreck site, made it to *The Star*, and went about the day's work as if nothing had happened.

Why do I perform such stupid, impulsive acts? I've analyzed this question over and over through the years. Did my impulsive behavior guide me in my combative interactions with Theo Stamos?

Maybe.

The "B" in Wayde B. Byard stands for "Belmont," the name of my paternal grandfather. He died when I was two, but I've always felt his presence in my life. (A psychic once described him as my guardian angel.)

There are times I have asked him to make himself known. When my father and I were cleaning out my grandparents' home for the final time, my dad went out to get something and left me alone in the home's musty attic. Dad had just wiped away the chalk writings he and his friends made on the rafters. He didn't want someone else musing on his childhood memories.

Seeing as this was a time of transition, I asked my grandfather if he'd like to come out and have a talk. I hoped his spirit might still be attached to the house. He had suffered a fatal heart attack while chipping ice on the sidewalk out front.

Nothing.

But, at critical junctures in my life when I could have suffered physical harm, I have felt like he has stepped in and guided me to safety.

You can call this irrational. I call it "extra help."

We all need as much of that as we can get.

Tom Rickman and The World's Greatest Failed Screenwriter

In 2008, I attended the screenwriting workshop for the Squaw Valley Community of Writers on the advice of my buddy Khris Baxter. You can qualify to attend this distinguished gathering by winning some regional writing contest or by being sponsored by a studio, such as Fox Searchlight Pictures. I won state screenwriting competitions for Virginia and Maryland and finished second in Francis Ford Coppola's American Zoetrope contest. My screenplay *An American Legend* was inspired by the life of Negro League great, Spottswood Poles. I first discovered Poles in the archives room of Winchester's Handley Regional Library and decided to give him the fictional life he deserved. His actual life should have been good enough to have landed him in the Baseball Hall of Fame. I didn't feel bad about doing a little heroic embellishing on Spottswood's behalf.

The Squaw Valley Community of Writers holds its summer workshops in the Sierra Nevada mountains next to Lake Tahoe. When I got to the lodge, which was all that was left of the 1960 Olympic Village, Diana Fuller, the program director, looked at me like a dog that had peed on the carpet. "You're supposed to be Black." Because of the subject matter of my screenplay, and the fact that I wrote from the Black perspective fairly convincingly, it was assumed—at least by the Squaw Valley selection committee—that I was Black. On the basis of being a minority, I had been assigned the best mentor in the program, Tom Rickman.

Nominated for a screenwriting Oscar for *Coal Miner's Daughter*, Tom Rickman was the coolest guy you'll ever meet, times ten. The top screenwriting teacher at the American Film Institute, Tom gave me a master's-degree course in screenwriting in three intense sessions. Tom's watchword was "organic." He said that you should be able to look back at the end of the movie and see how all the elements of a script led to a satisfying, organic conclusion to the film. This viewpoint has allowed me to analyze where incidents in my life—especially the failures—have led me to where I am now. This exercise gave me a great deal of confidence and comfort. Screenplays are divided into seventy scenes, or beats. At sixty-six, I acknowledge that I'm in the third act of my own movie. I just hope my life is the extended, director's version and contains scenes not a part of the original release.

The Fighter Pilot Method

It's amazing what you can learn on the New Jersey Turnpike. A lesson I learned there helped me conceive a survival strategy in the immediate aftermath of my indictment.

In December 1980, my brother and I were driving from Washington to my parents' home at West Point in his MG. My brother was then in his senior year training to be a fighter pilot at the US Air Force Academy. Looking to my right from the passenger seat of this low-slung vehicle, I could clearly see the lug nuts on the wheel of a huge truck as it made a heedless lane change and headed straight for us.

Panicking, I started screaming incomprehensibly.

My brother quickly navigated to the next lane over and gave me a lecture I have never forgotten. He said when a fighter pilot has a mechanical issue or is struck by enemy fire, they have twenty seconds to take actions that can save his/her life. Panicking, as I did, had eaten up valuable time on a clock that was already running. He then gave me a list of things you have to do when your aircraft is disabled. I've adapted these rules to handle crises experienced by the more earthbound.

Make a Realistic Assessment of the Situation. In short, don't bullshit your-self. The fighter pilot has to admit to himself/herself that a probable outcome of what is happening is that they will hit the ground nose-first at an incredible rate of speed and be vaporized. In my case, Brenda and I laid out the worst-case scenario for what could happen to us in the hours after my indictment. If the court proceedings stretched out to the maximum of nine months and I was found guilty, we could lose $150,000 in pay and legal fees. My future employment in a job in education or at any level of high responsibility would be finished. A sixty-five-year-old convicted felon was not going to rise to the top of the applicant pool. We might have to take Social Security and other retirement benefits early, which would incur thousands of dollars of lost income. Admitting the worst-case scenario meant you could start exploring options in fact-based reality. Not admitting the worst up front meant it would lurk in the back of your mind as an unacknowledged dread that would color your decisions whether you acknowledged this scenario or not.

Take Immediate, Decisive Action. I once met a former submarine officer who served in World War II. This gentleman said that there was an admiral who gave the same advice to all of his vessels as they headed into combat. "I don't care if you fire torpedoes. I don't care if you shit yourself. Just do something. Don't get sunk without taking some kind of action." I know I'm mixing military metaphors, but this is important advice. Going back to the aviator facing disaster; you have to follow your instinct and training and immediately take the action you think will have the most positive effect on your situation. In my case, this action was finding a competent attorney. Sad fact of life; you can serve an institution honorably, but when you are in trouble—like the metaphorical fighter pilot—you are on your own. The institution and its resources will be used to protect itself from further damage. If you're going to save yourself, you will have to chart your own course.

Take Stock of Your Remaining Assets and How You Might Use Them. The endangered pilot asks themselves, "Do I still have navigational control of my aircraft?" "How bad is the structural damage?" "How much fuel do I have?" "Where can I land—safely or otherwise—with the resources I have?" Brenda figured out that, based on her net monthly retirement income, we would be $35 short of covering our basic living expenses (house and car payments, medical insurance, utilities, taxes, and food). Through the years, with conservative investing, we had amassed more than $400,000 in various retirement accounts. Although we didn't want to start withdrawing these funds until the mandatory withdrawal age of seventy-two, they were there. We had a reliable financial advisor, a longtime accountant, and an insurance agent who knew Virginia's retirement system inside out to advise us—the equivalent of having someone in the control tower to offer you expert advice.

Know When to Eject. I have to admit, I really haven't gotten to this part in my story.

A Winter of Courts, Discontent, and Moments of Peace

The second half of December 2022 was a time of searching for me—searching for a reason for why I was being prosecuted, searching for an attorney, searching for some normalcy in my life, searching for a bit of peace during what was supposed to be the most peaceful time of the year.

Striding Up to the Defense

I started the trip to my indictment hearing early on Tuesday, December 13, 2022. I wore a semiformal black coat with shiny lapels; every other jacket I owned was hanging in my office, to which I no longer had access. As was my custom, I parked at North Street, the former LCPS headquarters, and walked the couple of blocks to the courthouse. When I arrived, three media members were outside the main entrance. One ran up like he was covering a Mafia Don making a court appearance. I wondered if I had ever been so enthusiastic as a young reporter.

Inside the courthouse, I made my way to the clerk's office to see where my hearing would be: Courtroom 2B. I couldn't have Tim McEvoy as my attorney. He was also representing Stone Bridge High School Principal Tim Flynn and thus had a conflict of interest. The night before the hearing, Tim McEvoy advised me to plead not guilty and tell the judge, James Plowman, that my attorney of record, Tim McEvoy, was not available because he was busy with another trial. I was worried about having Plowman as my judge. He was a former commonwealth's attorney elected as a Republican. Plowman still had strong ties to the Republican Party and had ruled adversely in everything involving the school division that had come before his court.

I have to note here that even though Tim McEvoy couldn't be my lawyer, he checked in with me about my mental health and to make sure I was getting sound legal advice. Tim McEvoy is a good man.

The proceedings began with an assistant commonwealth's attorney calling cases involving high crimes and misdemeanors. Some of the defendants didn't show up. Some attorneys had been assigned cases at the last minute and weren't prepared. I'd seen this all before when I covered the court as a young reporter.

The grand jury cases went second, and Theo Stamos and her assistant, Carlton Davis, stepped to the prosecution table. Owing to my polyneuropathy, my legs had become extremely tense and unresponsive during the long sit before I was called. I willed myself to get up and walk with confident strides to the defense side of the podium; I didn't want to look unsteady or like my knees were buckling from fear.

I greeted the judge with a "Good afternoon, your honor," and the charge was read. I did not have to enter a plea. My next hearing would be at 9:00 a.m. on January 5. I seemed to recall Theo Stamos saying that my trial was expected to last two days. What in the hell had I done that would require a two-day trial? I walked to a seat on the left side of the courtroom and numbly filled out some paperwork. I asked the bailiff to fill out a card with the date for the next hearing, and he graciously did so. I have a compulsion about not relying on my memory. The compartment in my car console was filled with old business and appointment cards.

Scott Ziegler's hearing came right after mine. They talked about setting his trial in July. I doubted my money could comfortably last that long.

Leaving the courtroom to go to booking downstairs, I was accosted by Evan Goodenow of the *Loudoun Times-Mirror* who asked me if I was being "railroaded." I told Evan that I'd have something to say to everyone later.

A sympathetic bailiff got me on the elevator that goes to the booking area on the first floor. There, Deputy Elliott sat me down and began the paper-work, asking me a series of questions and recording the answers on a form:

Address. Not a tough one; I had been living in the same place for the past thirty-three years.

Height: I was 6'2" at my peak, but I have shrunk to 6'1". (I think Deputy Elliott put 6 feet.)

Weight: 264 as of that morning (I'm working on it).

Hair color: Deputy Elliott took a look at my bald head and charitably wrote "Gray."

Prior arrests and convictions: None.

Religion: Presbyterian by birth, though I hadn't attended church in a long time. There was no designation on the form for Presbyterian. Deputy Elliott decided on Protestant. Close enough.

Tattoos: No. Having green ink under my skin has never appealed to me, and I've never seen a good one.

As I answered these questions, I looked at the desk in front of me. There were photos and reports concerning the people who had sat in this chair before me. Most were wearing orange. Most were accused of serious crimes.

How in the hell had I ended up here?

Fingerprinting was done digitally by placing my hand on a glass plate. Deputy Elliott told me to relax as he took my hand and ran my palms and fingers over the glass. A couple of times the computer noted that the images were not acceptable, so we did it again.

There's a reason mug shots look so bad. In my case, the mug shots were taken with two "dummy" cameras affixed to the wall. I was asked to face forward, then turn left and right. The cameras were affixed to the wall at a height that made me stretch and strain in unnatural ways so that the cameras could maintain their focus. I looked at my images on the digital screen after the photos were taken. I hoped these never saw the light of day, a television screen, or the front page of a newspaper.

Scott Ziegler entered the room after me. He spent ten years as a police chaplain in Virginia Beach. We agreed that there probably hadn't been a more unlikely pair being booked in this room at the same time. As Scott shook my hand, he confided that his wife was not doing well with this whole affair. He would be leaving via a rear entrance to avoid the media. I understood. I would go out the front door and face the media. As a public information officer, I had done this for superintendents in the past. I was proud—I can't say happy—to do this for Scott.

As I exited the courthouse, the media pack had grown, making a line the width of the courthouse lawn. There was a microphone stand set up a short distance from the door. As I looked at their eager faces, I realized how the turkey must feel at Thanksgiving. Viewing the uneven ground in front of the microphones, I worried about keeping my legs steady. I didn't want to appear drunk.

As forcefully as I could, I said that I would make a statement, but take no questions.

I said that Loudoun County Public Schools; the interim superintendent, Dr. Daniel Smith; and the Human Resources Department had treated me fairly and professionally.

I stated that, contrary to earlier reports, I was on leave *without* pay.

I stated that I planned to plead not guilty.

As I walked away after making this statement, Nick Minock ran up behind me and offered me his private phone number should I wish to call and confide in him. Given our past history, I gave Nick a hard "No."

I'd rather piss on a spark plug than trust a piece of filth like Nick Minock.

One cameraman used his phone to get a walking shot of me as I headed for the street. I reminded my legs, again, to stay steady. The cameraman then began filming the Christmas tree in front of the courthouse.

I guess this was to provide a juxtaposition between the happiness of the holiday and the shitty time Scott and I had just endured.

Pre-Planned Holiday Fun

We had already scheduled a trip to the Gaylord National Resort hotel in Washington's National Harbor to take in the annual Christmas events. My wife, myself, our oldest daughter, her husband, and our four-year-old grandson all took part in this small bit of normalcy.

The centerpiece of this extravaganza was an area full of ice sculptures depicting scenes from the movie *A Christmas Story.* You had to don special parkas to go into the viewing area because it was kept at eight degrees to preserve the ice. All the scenes from Cleveland Street in the movie were rendered from huge chunks of ice. There was the "electric sex" leg lamp in the window, Ralphie's infamous battle with Scott Farkas, and Ralphie with soap in his mouth.

My daughter bought an "all-you-can-ride" ticket for the indoor sledding hill. After one trip on a rubber tube down this slick incline, my aging body decided once was all I could ride. The muscles in my midsection were screaming, and my feet banging off the side barriers left me happy that I hadn't broken something when I reached the bottom. Watching my grandson go down the tubing hill—fear at the top, jumping up and down in elation at the bottom—gave me a feeling of Christmas cheer that had obviously eluded me this holiday season.

Another thing that gave me hope was when an LCPS principal, Andrew Stevens, spotted me and offered some words of encouragement. He was the first LCPS employee I had seen since my suspension, and I greatly appreciated his sentiments.

The next morning brought a minor tragedy.

Like Ralphie, my grandson whiffed on his visit with Santa. Once we were past the photo area, he wanted desperately to go back to make a better impression. Sensing an imminent meltdown, Pappy took him for rides up and down the escalators. On the ride home, it was clear that the escalators were the thing my grandson found the most entertaining part of the hotel. When we were alone, my wife said "we" paid $800 for this trip. (When it comes to "us" spending on family things such as weddings and vacations, I usually discover the amount spent long after the fact.) Basically, I had paid $800 to watch a four-year-old enjoy riding up and down the escalator.

It was worth every penny.

Place of Meditation

Old Stone Church is about a mile from my house. Built in 1820 and rebuilt in 1838 after a fire, it is the prototypical idyllic country church. Surrounded by lush farmland and mature trees, it boasts an ancient cemetery. It can be reached only by a half-mile country lane off the main road. My neighbors, Bill and Martha, graciously allowed anyone who wanted to see the church to cut through their property using this road, which doubles as their driveway.

This sanctuary was abandoned for many years when Cora Bell Crim formed the Old Stone Church Memorial Association in 1927 to preserve it. The limestone church is immaculately maintained, the cemetery regularly mowed and weeded. A short distance from the church, a large pavilion was erected to host the Memorial Association's annual August picnic.

One of the many oddities in the cemetery is a small obelisk made of small stones and seashells. Originally erected in 1923, it was constructed to represent countries from around the world. Vandalized through the years, replacement shells were painstakingly put in place from 1980 to 2001.

It is the kind of lovingly created monument that I treasure.

Though isolated, the Old Stone Church provided me with personal encounters that sharpened my perspective on my situation. On December 18, a particularly cold day, I spotted a man kneeling over a fresh grave in the new section of the cemetery. The profound look of sadness on his face and the amount of time he lingered told me that he was enduring something much worse than I was.

On the same day, I encountered a man in a car packed with Christmas wreaths. His family originally owned the 180 acres surrounding the church. He comes, every year, to decorate the graves of his ancestors for the holidays. This was a living embodiment of the permanence and emotional sustenance such places provide. We all need to acknowledge the past and those who made our world, even with all of its flaws, possible.

Something from my past always enters my thoughts when I walk to the Old Stone Church.

In the early 1980s, the Cracker Jack Old Timers game was held at Washington's RFK Stadium. Liberally abusing my status as the sports editor of *The Winchester Star*, I made sure that I got a press pass to this event. It was literally as if the entire roster of the Baseball Hall of Fame (Hank Aaron, Stan Musial, Warren Spahn, Bob Feller, Brooks Robinson, Early Wynn, Billy Williams, Al Kaline, Jim "My real name is not 'Catfish'" Hunter, Lou Brock, Ralph Kiner) was walking around the field.

One Classic featured Bobby Thomson, who hit the "Shot Heard 'Round the World" to win the 1951 National League pennant for the Giants, and former Dodger Ralph Branca, who threw the pitch Thomson hit. More than thirty years later, they were still reliving that one moment—Thomson with relish, Branca with weariness—for what must be the ten thousandth time. Branca said he once asked a priest why he was chosen to throw the infamous pitch. The priest replied, "God gives us no more than we can bear." I thought of Ralph Branca a lot as I stood before a small, wooden cross on the hillside near the church. I told God, he must have chosen me for this particular assignment for a reason, and that I was up to it.

I would also occasionally see a large blue heron, who would take flight whenever I walked within a hundred feet and soar majestically to a new place of solitude. A Google search showed that spotting a blue heron "traditionally symbolizes luck, prosperity and determination."

For once, I took Google's word for it.

First Meeting with Jennifer Leffler

December 21: the shortest day of the calendar year, one of the longest of my life. Clichéd, yes, but in this case more than fitting.

I asked several lawyers who they would recommend as my defense attorney. They all give me a list of three or four names.

The only name on every list was Jennifer Leffler.

Central casting did me a big favor in finding a lawyer to handle my case. Our initial meeting showed that Jennifer was smart and compassionate. She thoroughly understood how to (justly) manipulate the system to her clients' advantage. Jennifer is a petite, slender, attractive young woman. Her father is a prominent retired attorney, Rod Leffler. Tackling the law is in her blood.

Jennifer was also a former Fairfax County assistant commonwealth's attorney. She was named a Top Lawyer, through a vote by fellow attorneys, by the *Washingtonian* magazine each year between 2017 and 2022 and was named a Rising Star by Super Lawyers. Jennifer allowed that defending a client who is not guilty is much harder than defending one who is.

I liked her immediately.

Another thing I liked was that she didn't sugarcoat the potential pitfalls in my case: The legal proceedings could last nine months. Her fee could be up to $30,000. (It ended up being $35,000 and worth it.) I told Jennifer that, under no circumstances would I enter into a plea agreement or waive my right to a speedy trial. She accepted this but told me that I would have to keep an open mind regarding what the prosecution might offer.

Jennifer said that she would call Theo Stamos that afternoon and let me know how it went at the end of the day. For the first of many times, Jennifer Leffler was good to her word.

After talking to Jennifer for an hour, I walked around downtown Fairfax for another hour. Halfway through my walk, I remembered a question I had meant to ask Jennifer and headed back to her office where my car was still parked. Mary Herbert, Jennifer's assistant, brought an excited Jennifer out to see me. Jennifer said it was a good thing that I had come back because she had talked to Theo Stamos and thought that she had discovered what led to my indictment.

Theo was obsessed by the fact that LCPS did not say the incident at Stone Bridge was an "assault" in the original communication Tim Flynn sent out on May 28, 2021. On the stand, Theo had hammered me about when I had become aware that this incident was indeed an assault. I had answered, honestly, the following October. My focus on May 28 had been on the sheriff's cruisers with blue lights in front of a high school with a parent running amok in the office. Stick with me for the next part, it's convoluted.

Theo had an email from Chief Operations Officer Kevin Lewis to the superintendent's cabinet that included my boss, Joan Sahlgren. This email had been written sometime during Memorial Day weekend 2021. In this email, the word "assault" was mentioned. I had not been copied on this email and had no knowledge of it. Theo surmised that Joan had told me about this email, that I had knowledge of the assault, and therefore that I had lied on the stand when I had said I had no knowledge of the assault from the beginning.

I sat stunned on Jennifer's couch. I had already surmised what Jennifer assured me of; there was no way this was going to hold up in court. Julia Judkins had been right. They were going to offer me a deal to turn on my colleagues—in this case, Joan and Kevin—and hope that the dominoes would begin falling so more indictments could be issued. This was why my life had been turned inside out. I was stunned, relieved, angry, and puzzled all at once.

Jennifer later summed up her conversation with Theo Stamos in an email. "Theo told me that she did not feel good about the prosecution, but she thought it was a righteous prosecution. She also told me that she told her boss that she could not guarantee conviction, but that she was to go forward with the case anyways."

Fuck you and the horse you rode in on, Theo Stamos. Sorry you were conflicted.

The "righteous" comment fit in with something Scott Ziegler told me. He had heard Theo say she was doing "God's work" in this matter outside the courtroom during one of his proceedings. When a prosecutor feels conflicted about pursuing a case she doesn't think she can win, but does so anyway at the behest of the Almighty (and the attorney general of the Commonwealth of Virginia), you've got a real problem. When a judge wasn't in the room to stop this prosecutor from bullying and berating witnesses and trying to concoct thin conspiracies for a grand jury, you've got a critical problem. This shouldn't happen in a democracy.

Driving around metropolitan Washington can be incredibly frustrating; only LA's traffic is worse. It took me three hours to drive from Fairfax to my home in Winchester after leaving Jennifer's office. I was sitting bumper-to-bumper on Interstate 66 when Brenda called in tears. She had had a total emotional breakdown during physical therapy for her knee and felt like a fool. She said that she was awake the night before worrying that I would be sent to jail, leaving her alone. Listening to Brenda sob on the phone, my heart broke, and my anger rose. A reluctant prosecutor was doing concrete emotional damage, not only to me but to everyone in my family. I was not comforted by the fact that Jason Miyares thought fucking up my life was worth taking a political risk.

Glenn Youngkin Tooting His Own Horn

An op-ed written by Jim Geraghty, a senior political correspondent at the *National Review*, appeared in *The Washington Post*. It detailed a conversation with Glenn Youngkin about 2023, which Geraghty dubbed a make-or-break year for the governor.

Near the end of the piece, Youngkin talked about LCPS and the special grand jury. "The governor said he finds opposition coming out of Loudoun 'ironic:' 'We've got indictments coming down from the grand jury. They turned a blind eye to clear violations, to literally sexual assault, going on in the school district, and they hid it.'"

We've got indictments coming down.

Fuck you, Glenn.

You won't get any further indictments out of me.

The Death of My Mom

On December 29, 2022, my brother called to say that my mother had died the previous night. She died alone in her sleep with no obvious signs of pain or struggle when staff found her. Probably the easiest death any of us could ask for.

Her dementia had advanced rapidly, and she had refused meals for several days. Death hadn't appeared imminent because she had exhibited such behavior before and rebounded. My brother, oldest nephew, and niece spent a considerable amount of time with her the night before and had observed no overt signs of distress. Her hospice attendants said that she could die at any time or linger for several months. There was no real way of knowing. Based on this assessment, my brother drove my nephew to his home in Las Vegas. My brother didn't find out about mom's death until the next morning.

My brother and I talked about whether I should fly to California. He would front me the price of an airline ticket. (The thought of taking charity from my little brother wounded me.) That was not the real problem, however. Due to Southwest Airlines' recent scheduling debacle, and with the air-traffic grid hopelessly tangled, there was no guarantee I could get a flight back before an upcoming court hearing. We agreed that the attorney general's office would love to charge me with jumping bail if I gave them any reason to.

I could be dramatic and say my lack of money and court proceedings denied me the opportunity to comfort my mom in her final hours. That would be a lie. Nobody could have predicted that she'd die that night. And I really don't know if it would have meant anything to her if I had been there. I was alone with my dad when he died in 2016. I can't say it was a transformative experience or that anything profound happened. He simply inhaled and didn't exhale again. Still, I took comfort in the fact that dad hadn't been alone at the end and that I had fulfilled my duty as his eldest child.

Mom was a contradiction, as most people are. Harboring deep anxieties, she lashed out in anger when threatened. She could be judgmental of neighbors and others in her social orbit. I think she did this out of fear. Mom was always very insecure about her status in life and tried to carve out a place where she was detached and above it all. I recognize some of her worst traits in me and, as I get older, try to—if not eliminate—at least mitigate them.

Mom was also a fierce defender of those she loved. When dad had been forced to go into what was euphemistically described as "memory care," mom had gone with him, even though we knew it was a terrible decision. She essentially lived as the only normal person in what can only be described as a lunatic asylum. She tried to "normalize" dad's behavior and dress him in business casual—a routine that was almost impossible—as his mind deteriorated rapidly. At times, mom had uncontrollable fits of rage, punctuated by uncharacteristic streams of profanity. She could process what was happening to her husband of nearly sixty years on an intellectual level but could never get there emotionally.

Mom gave birth to me when she was twenty-three, eleven months after being married. We had essentially grown up together. My regret about her death was that I didn't have a chance to say a final goodbye before she was cremated. There was no closure concerning her death during the months to come.

After mom's death, I found myself mentally going through some of the life anecdotes my parents told me. Mom and dad related two versions of how I received my unique first name. At the time my mom was pregnant, dad was stationed at Fort Lee, Virginia, as a second lieutenant. Walking around a nearby battlefield, they came across a monument to Confederate General Wade Hampton III, "the richest man in the Confederacy." Being young and clever, they decided to add a "y" to Hampton's first name so there were five letters and a descender in both my first and last names.

The alternate explanation (and the one I prefer) was that I was named after Wayde Preston, a popular TV cowboy of the late 1950s. Preston was a Tom Selleck type, sporting the same kind of mustache that has adorned my face since 1976. I'd rather be named after an obscure celebrity than a traitor and enslaver.

I loved my parents.

As the years go by, I try to judge them less and love them more.

They made mistakes.

I've made many of my own.

They did the best they could with what they had.

That's all you can do.

A New Year, the Start of My Hearings

January 2023 was a month of legal maneuvering. Jennifer Leffler came up with several promising legal strategies, none of which reached their promise. My spirits would rise every time she found a gaping hole in the prosecution's case. The legal establishment's job, however, was to spackle over these holes, no matter how gaping and obvious they were.

The Bill of Particulars

Jennifer and I had a quick conversation about what to expect during my first hearing on Thursday, January 5, 2023. Jennifer said she would file a demand for a bill of particulars to finally find out what *exactly* I had been accused of doing. She would also ask for a change of venue, most likely to Fairfax County. Theo had stated that the "taxpayers of Loudoun County" were the victims of my crime (whatever that crime might have been). Jennifer asserted that these "victims" could not produce a fair jury pool. Fairfax also had a quicker docket and a more-diverse jury pool less acquainted with the furor in Loudoun.

Theo would ask for a May-June trial date; Jennifer for March-April.

Jennifer speculated that it was an inconsistency between my testimony and Joan's that led to the perjury charge. I hoped this was not the case. Joan was a great boss and a good friend. I knew she would have felt incredibly guilty if something she said had put me in this position.

Jennifer and I decided it would be best if she spoke to the media after the hearing.

My Initial Hearing

As was my custom, I parked at North Street and changed from my green mountain shoes into shiny black footwear. I always wear lightweight, rubber-soled shoes when I drive. I've seen professional drivers do this at racing events, and it seemed like a good idea. My neuropathy also makes my feet numb, and I feel more connected with the brake and gas pedals when I have rubber soles on.

It was an unseasonably warm day on January 5, 2023, (fifty-nine degrees as I left the car at 8:30 a.m.). It was like a day in early April—bright sunshine, no breeze—as I walked the couple of blocks to the courthouse, dreading the media scrum that I knew was waiting at the entrance. I stopped for a second to exchange pleasantries with the worker taking down the artificial Christmas tree in front of the old courthouse, delaying the inevitable. Rounding the corner, I saw two tripods with TV cameras mounted on them, but only one reporter.

Once inside, I connected with Jennifer, and we headed for Courtroom 2A, where the preliminary hearing would be held. While waiting for the courtroom to open, Jennifer approached Theo Stamos for some preliminary bargaining. As Jennifer later related to me, Theo told Jennifer that she might still bring up the conflict-of-interest issue concerning Jennifer representing me. Jennifer had represented an LCPS cabinet member, Kevin Lewis, before the special grand jury. Technically, she could have been disqualified from representing me. Carlton Davis's incompetency had opened the door to her becoming my attorney. (During a December phone conference he said—without Theo's knowledge—that he saw no problem with Jennifer representing me.) Jennifer let Theo know that ship had long-since sailed, and Theo backed down. Jennifer said she would file a motion to move the trial to Fairfax. Theo stated that she would oppose it. The bill of particulars didn't seem like it would be a problem.

As Jennifer spoke with Theo, I found myself at an oak table sitting across from a genial man whose case was also set to be heard that morning. In the course of conversation, the man said he had been driving down Route 7 at sixty-five miles per hour—a moderate rate where this thoroughfare was concerned—when the man in front of him deliberately slowed down to twenty, repeatedly. The man to whom I was speaking thought maybe this motorist was trying to cause an accident so he could file a lawsuit, something that was not uncommon. In what my fellow defendant admitted was a lapse in judgment, he followed the slow driver and berated him publicly. Now he was pleading guilty to a misdemeanor for disturbing the peace with the provision that his record would eventually be wiped clean. The man said that defending himself was growing too costly and that the court hearings, which seemed to go on forever, were affecting his work.

"That," I thought to myself, "is exactly how plea deals work."

Inside the courtroom, I was the first case up. Theo told the judge, Douglas Fleming Jr., whom I had not seen before, that the earliest she could go to trial was June, after Scott Ziegler's trial. Checking with the court docket, it was determined that the earliest my two-day trial could be held was June 20. Jennifer argued that this would put me under financial duress because I was currently on suspension *without* pay. The judge allowed that, while the scheduling was important to me, the trials already on the docket were just as important to the parties involved.

Fair point.

It just stiffened my resolve to have the trial held in Fairfax.

When asked if this would be a jury trial, Jennifer replied, "Yes." While expected, this utterance made me nervous. I'd seen enough jury trials to know such things can go horribly wrong.

Still, I trusted Jennifer's judgment. She distrusted Loudoun's judges, and I couldn't argue with her on that point. Loudoun's judiciary had made some rulings regarding LCPS that defied logic. The stink of partisan politics hung over the Loudoun County court complex.

While Jennifer and Theo were holding a conversation after the hearing, a man wearing a mask approached me. He quickly identified himself as

Jim Barnes, the former public information officer for the Loudoun County government. Jim told me that I'd stood by him years before when he went through a tough time and now he wanted to be here for me. I was genuinely touched by this. I knew I was grasping at rays of hope, but they kept coming.

I found comfort in that.

While this was happening, Scott Smith arrived and began a long and amiable conversation with Theo.

The appearance completed, Jennifer did some informal briefing with the gathered press on the lawn outside the court complex. She faced an expanded media scrum that now included all four Washington network affiliates and assorted members of the local media. She was totally on point and got our main talking points across quickly in a confident, telegenic manner:

- I was under financial duress.
- I still didn't know what I was charged with.
- We would seek a venue change to Fairfax.
- I would plead "not guilty."

The media didn't pick up on the talking points as I'd hoped. There had been a gruesome shooting involving a three-year-old that yanked most of the reporters at the courthouse in another direction. Tape of Jennifer's interview was edited by staff back at the station, who had no idea how to put it into context. *The Washington Post* ran a disappointing article that was convoluted and haphazard.

Jennifer also related to me that Carlton Davis was leaving the prosecution team to take a position with a law firm in Washington, DC. I hoped this was a case of a rat abandoning a sinking ship.

Walking with Jennifer back to her car, we had a moment of collective paranoia. A jacked-up Ford F250 with smoked-glass windows stopped beside us for what seemed like far too long of a time. As it moved down the street, I saw that it had orange and blue "Don't Tread on Me" plates. After going a short way down the street, the truck turned around and headed back toward us. When the smoked glass on the driver's side was rolled down, it was just a very nice African-American man wondering if he could have the parking space Jennifer was about to vacate.

My paranoia was increasing.

Walking back to North Street, I decided to make a pit stop even though I didn't really need it. North Street was once Leesburg High School. It was a ramshackle affair during the time LCPS administrative headquarters was there, including the first five years of my tenure. My office was in a corner of what was once the gym. I could see the old windows and high ceilings through the holes in the drop ceiling over my makeshift office. The basement was referred to as "the garden level" and regularly flooded as rainwater would cascade down flights of outside stairs. The superintendent's office was in the former cafeteria's kitchen and featured a barely concealed grease trap under the chief executive's desk. Once school administration departed, a large amount of money was spent to turn North Street into a luxury senior center.

Walking through the center, my ears caught the sound of poker chips hitting a table. This was a sound I recognized from the Saturday-night games my maternal grandfather had held for years in his basement. For a moment, I wondered if they would deal me in. Over the urinal, there was a flyer stating that there would be a birthday party for Elvis the following day from noon to 2:00 p.m. I don't have a thing for the King, but a party right then couldn't hurt.

Leaving the building, I realized what I'd been trying to do: avoiding calling Brenda.

Sitting in the front seat of the car, I called home and told Brenda that the trial could be June 20—our worst-case scenario. She said she was fine with that, but I could clearly sense that she was not.

Avoidance continued on the way home as I took the scenic route and stopped to buy a Mega Millions ticket at the Berryville 7-Eleven. I played my happy song, the Beatles' "Ob-La-Di, Ob-La-Da."

Once in the door, Brenda told me, near tears, that she was not OK. She had applied for a part-time job at Winchester Medical Center.

I do not deserve Brenda Kay Fertig Byard.

Brenda called my attention to that day's horoscope in *The Winchester Star*. "Today is like a reality game show, all hype and edgy music. You've a talent for keeping your cool. Be methodical, stay in communication with your team and respect the clock. You're favored for the win!"

The horoscope was compiled by someone named Holiday. I decided that Holiday was right.

I took encouragement from wherever it came.

A Motion to Dismiss?

Jennifer had a long conference with Scott Ziegler's attorney, Erin Harrigan, who Jennifer said was very bright and capable. Erin was filing a motion to dismiss on January 26. If this motion was accepted, my case would also go away.

Jennifer disagreed with Erin about a motion to recuse all of Loudoun's judges from hearing Scott's case. It was Jennifer's feeling that this could fail, with the end result being several very angry judges. She wanted to keep emotions out of my legal proceedings and stick to the facts.

I couldn't have agreed more.

My change of venue would be argued on January 24 or 25. The earliest trial date in Fairfax was February 14 to 15. Overlooking the romantic implications, trying my case on these two days would have greatly relieved our financial situation.

Jennifer wanted to win on the trial level and not have to strategize about an appeal. I wholeheartedly agreed.

The Right Lawyer

Jennifer left a message late Tuesday afternoon saying that she'd had an "epiphany" that might lead to the early dismissal of my case.

Since the special grand jury heard testimony in secret, the transcripts of testimony before it were secret. Only the "attorney for the commonwealth" or the defendant could request the transcript. If Theo and Carlton Davis had listed themselves as "special counsel for the grand jury" and not "attorney for the commonwealth," they were not entitled to the transcript. Without the transcript, they would have no proof that what I said had been a lie.

The case would have been dismissed.

I was absolutely stunned.

Could Theo have made a mistake this stupid? It was the legal equivalent of going to work and forgetting to put on your pants.

Jennifer and I talked at noon on Wednesday. Jennifer said that she had talked to the ever-helpful Carlton Davis who, as usual, had been more helpful (to us) than he should have been. Davis told Jennifer that he was trying to "make it easier for you" by having Jennifer request access to the transcript and then agreeing to share it with the prosecution.

To quote Theo Stamos, "Yeah, sure."

"Here's a loaded gun, shoot my client."

Jennifer said under no circumstances would she be requesting the transcript.

I agreed.

Jennifer said Theo and Davis could have presented their evidence to a regular grand jury and removed this obstacle but didn't. She was sure they would still try to get the transcript.

Jennifer said that there were some conflicting statutes regarding such testimony, and she was still trying to work things out.

A ray of hope is a ray of hope.

Life Outside of the Hearings

After years of rejecting the idea, I finally submitted to therapy. My paranoia and anxiety had reached an alarming level. Life, and death, had given me some lessons in perspective about where my current troubles fit into the grand scheme of things.

The Need for Therapy

While LCPS wouldn't pay me, I was still eligible for the Employee Assistance Program (EAP). Lisa Boland sent me the contact information, and I called the 1-800 number. I couldn't register online because my LCPS email had been decommissioned. After answering the usual biographical questions, the courteous operator asked me what kind of services I required.

"Psychological counseling."

I was connected with a counselor who identified herself as La Tanya, and she actively listened as I unloaded what was on my mind. After some time, she went where most people wouldn't. She asked me if I was a man of faith. I didn't go to church, but I prayed religiously every day. When the garage door came down signaling the beginning of my morning commute, I asked for God's protection for the people and animals—living and dead—who are, and have been, important in my life. There was a list of about eighty people and creatures that I would work through in relative order of importance. (The animals outranked many of the people. I truly love animals.) I always finished with the words "God give me the strength to get through this day. Amen."

I told La Tanya that I needed all the strength I could get.

We talked for more than an hour and, my permission given, explored some pretty philosophical territory. La Tanya also confirmed something I had already known without me mentioning it.

I was holding in a huge amount of anger.

The previous Saturday, my wife, oldest daughter, and I had gone to lunch at our favorite restaurant. I could feel growing apprehension as we got further into the short drive. In my mind, I vowed that if anyone at the restaurant said something insulting about my present situation, I would beat the unholy shit out of them. (I'm not a fighter or big-time tough guy, so this was an odd thought for me.)

At the restaurant, something truly wonderful happened.

Mark Merrill, the former CEO of Valley Health and a fellow Our Health board member, stopped by the table to offer Brenda and me a message of support. At first glance, I'd always thought Mark Merrill a cold, officious person. I guess you have to project that image when you run a major hospital system. He is, in fact, a very warm, caring man.

I was proud to have a friend like Mark Merrill.

I was ashamed of my anger.

Adrenaline spikes were something else I had been experiencing. I started lifting weights in 1973 to support my laughable football career and have stayed with it, religiously, ever since. The Sunday after my suspension found me in the gym lifting far too fast and furiously. During a bench press, something in my left shoulder popped so loudly that other people jerked their heads around reflexively to see what had happened. I was so adrenalized that I ignored whatever had just happened and did ten more reps with a few extra just to show I was OK.

I was not OK.

Paranoia was working its way into my thoughts. Late at night, a mouse in the attic would make its presence known. The ice machine in the refrigerator would drop a load loudly into its storage receptacle. The house creaked and groaned, as houses will. I started listening for the next sound, the one that would signal that someone had broken into the house. (I have a robust alarm system, so this really wasn't plausible.)

I briefly considered buying a gun.

I discarded this idea quickly. Experience as a crime reporter had taught me that guns were usually used on someone you know in a fit of rage or on yourself in a moment of depression. I had never considered suicide. I was filled with rage. I didn't want to combine that with a firearm. The only potential there was to make a bad situation tragically worse.

My decision not to buy a gun was validated on the Thursday night after my indictment. A car was lingering way too long on the other side of the rural road in front of my house. The driver, a man, was outside of the car. I opened the door and yelled at him, asking what he was doing there. What followed were scampering feet, a slammed door, and a car tearing off into the darkness. My grandson was standing behind me and had taken in the entire incident. He looked up at me and said, "That's inappropriate behavior Pap."

When he FaceTimed with my son-in-law later that night, the first thing my grandson said was, "Pappy got real mad and yelled at some guy." A four-year-old had been startled by my behavior.

The next morning, I went across the road to see if there was any evidence of the driver from the night before. All I found was a couple of dead bushes where the back of the car had been. Had a gun been present, I could have shot a guy for doing something weird with dead bushes.

Sleep was a problem.

Sleep had always been a problem.

A woman I was once involved with told me I couldn't get a good night's sleep because I was a control freak, and I couldn't control what happened in my dreams.

She was right.

When I sleep deeply, which isn't often, my dreams dredge up my deepest anxieties. I'm back at the newspaper, on deadline, using a technology I can't understand while my coworkers mock me. It can be very real and vivid.

I would wake up sitting bolt upright and sweating.

Having constant anxiety about my uncertain legal future had increased the realness of these dreams. I found my mind racing to the point that it was impossible to sleep when my head hit the pillow. When I would get out of bed the following morning, I couldn't really tell if I'd slept or not. (Brenda would complain about my loud snoring, so I suppose, on some level, I'd at least been unconscious for some amount of time.)

In the too much information (TMI) department, I had explosive bowel movements. Nothing painful or distressing; just all of a sudden, Ka-pow! My body was judo-slamming me and saying, "Dumbass! You are going through a life-altering, stressful situation!"

La Tanya said that she would schedule six free sessions with a local therapist.

I realized that I should have done this years ago.

La Tanya also suggested that I get a weighted blanket, also known as an "anxiety blanket" to help me sleep. I went to a local department store where I'd seen these blankets displayed. The sale price of $90 was beyond my current restricted budget. One day I was surprised to see the UPS guy at my front door carrying a compact—and apparently heavy—box. My youngest daughter had sent me a weighted blanket. After a brief try, Brenda said there was no way we were going to sleep under this every night.

I ended up using the blanket when I watched TV. It really did help.

First Therapy Session

Numbness is the highest form of stress.

That was the biggest takeaway from my first session with Keri, my therapist, on January 20, 2023.

We met in her plain office in a dilapidated house on the edge of Purcellville. Keri's job was listening, which she did quite well, and offering the occasional insight. I went through the chronology of events that had led me to her office. Like most people, she couldn't believe what had happened to me.

I expressed that I hadn't experienced any real emotional outbursts, such as crying or a display of temper (with the exception of the dead bush guy). Keri said that the trauma was still very recent, and it would take time to process.

We agreed to meet again in a week.

Later that night, I watched the season premiere of *Real Time with Bill Maher*. One of the guests was South Carolina Congresswoman Nancy Mace, who seemed, on the whole, like a reasonable sort. Reasonable until she talked about the school system in Virginia that hid a rape and arrested the father of the victim for trying to talk about it. This was now the catechism of the Right derived from hundreds of mentions on Fox News.

I pulled the weighted blanket up around my chin and felt numb.

Back to Work for Brenda

Brenda and I drove to Fairfax. She had an interview with the Claude Moore Charitable Foundation, Virginia's leading educational charity, for some part-time work. When she came out of the meeting ninety minutes later, Brenda had a commitment from Claude Moore and a statement of interest from George Mason University.

I don't deserve Brenda Kay Fertig Byard.

I spent the time that Brenda was in her meeting wandering through a nearby shopping district. I come from a long line of community wanderers. I had an unfortunate great uncle, Roy, who had been struck by a Stanley Steamer as a child during the early twentieth century. His injuries had led to him undergoing brain surgery, which was not the highly refined art it is today. The result was diminished mental capacity, a pop eye, and a verbal handicap that led to him drawing out his words when he spoke. Uncle Roy would wander around town with a shopping cart all day, collecting various "treasures." He lived in a room at the back of my grandmother's house where these objects were displayed. I remembered cleaning out this area after his death as one of the great traumas of my young adulthood.

As Brenda and I drove back to Winchester, I realized I was a shopping cart short of being Uncle Roy.

Funeral for a Friend

Life didn't stop even though my professional life was on hold because of the hearings, something underlined by the funeral held at the end of January for a dear friend.

As I entered the church, a local grand dame of Republican politics said she "has to give me a hug" and added, "I don't know what this is all about." I replied, "It's about Glenn Youngkin wanting to be president." She feigned ignorance of the governor's motives.

I let it slide.

During the service, the priest said we shouldn't ask why my friend, Adrian, had suffered so greatly. But I was certainly asking. I've always wondered why the pious seemed to suffer while rank bastards and downright evil people ran around free, inflicting themselves on others.

This was one of many questions I intended to ask God, assuming there is a heaven and assuming I ever get there.

Given recent events, I tried not to assume too much.

The day before the funeral, I had visited Adrian's wake and was stunned by the amount of work that had been done on his body. No amount of mortician's magic could mask the amount of suffering he had endured. The Knights of Columbus, of which Adrian had been a devoted member, had an honor guard at the funeral home that staged an elaborate changing-of-the-guard ritual while I was there.

I tried to comfort Adrian's widow, Toni, but she seemed more intent on comforting me. She had wanted to get in touch with me before Adrian died, but he didn't have names associated with the numbers on his phone. She had really wanted me to see him. I told her it was OK, that Adrian and I had texted and that we had always been in a good place. Toni said that Adrian had purchased a present for me and that it was somewhere in their house. If she ran across it, she would send it to me. I felt it was just as well that the present was in an undisclosed location. Receiving it at that time could only have triggered more raw emotions on top of the many raw emotions I was already experiencing.

It was better left for another day.

After the funeral service, another woman, who had been on a state oversight board, approached me. We'd known each other for years. The woman said that she resigned from the oversight board because, since Youngkin's election, everything had become political.

I believed it.

Going down to the social hall, I ran into my longtime friend and colleague Scott Mason. Mason, who had worked four decades as a photographer at *The Star*, caught me up on what had been happening with former staffers.

The news wasn't good.

One woman, an extremely talented graphic artist, had died at sixty-nine after suffering for seven years from Stage 4 breast cancer. Brave to the end, she had become a life coach for those suffering from the disease.

Another former reporter, younger than both of us, was suffering from Stage 4 cancer. A few months later, he died at fifty-two.

A former photographer had Parkinson's disease.

Mason and I talked about some of the wrecks, fires, plane crashes, and tragic situations involving disabilities and disease we had seen through our years at the newspaper. We concluded that being alive and healthy made us among life's fortunate.

I later went through the inventory of some of the horrible things I had witnessed. I thought particularly about a tragedy I covered in the spring of 2000 involving an elderly gentleman who had lived right down the road from my house.

The man's wife, suffering from dementia, was being housed in an assisted-living facility. Every so often, he would go there, "kidnap" her, and bring her home. The spring of 2000 had been particularly rainy. When he got her home after one of the kidnappings, her wheelchair had become stuck in the mud. Unable to move his wife, the elderly man shot her in the back of the head using a rifle he kept in the house. He then covered her with a tarp to keep the body dry. Inside, he carefully set up food and water for the couple's dogs and secured them in an area so that they could not get at his wife's body. He then went to the backyard, set up a lawn chair away from the house and an outbuilding, and blew his brains out with the rifle.

Before this last act, he had set out tools from the outbuilding for those who would have to clean up the gruesome scene he would leave in his wake. He also wrote a detailed note explaining what he had done and why. What drove this story home more than other such tragedies was that the elderly man, like me, was a graduate of the University of Missouri School of Journalism. He had left journalism for a career in public relations, which I was about to do at the time.

This episode put my life into perspective. My future couldn't possibly be that bleak.

Could it?

PART V

Pretrial

Pinning Down the Arguments Against Me and Fighting for a Venue Change

With the opening hearings out of the way, it remained for us to find out, finally, exactly what the prosecution was charging me with and to fight to get a fairer venue.

Second Court Hearing/Dodging the Media

On the day of my next court appearance, I semi-purposefully gave myself an adrenaline rush. More than a week before, Jennifer's secretary, Mary, had emailed a letter to me stating that Jennifer wanted me to be in court for my next hearing, January 26, 2023. I took note of the time, 1:00 p.m., and committed it to memory. A little after nine in the morning, I searched the email account and found the letter.

What if the hearing had been at nine? I'd already be late. A truly horrible error.

I opened the letter, and my eyes immediately fell on 9:00 a.m. This was, however, the time of my June 20 trial. The letter confirmed that I was due in court at one o'clock that afternoon. Still, the very temporary shock of the 9:00 a.m. had given me a profound chemical reaction that shot through my body. It felt like all my muscles were on edge, and my heart raced.

For the first time in weeks, I didn't feel numb.

Checking the mailbox, I noticed two vultures circling lazily overhead. That couldn't be good.

Under the guise of justifying my procrastination, I took the scenic route to court, following a maze of country back roads, rather than jumping right on to Route 7. Knowing that I was headed toward a media scrum and arguing lawyers, I felt that my procrastination was more than justified. One of the houses I passed on this journey was a small, white structure no more than ten feet from the railroad tracks. It was inhabited by an old man who adorned it with a flag depicting Donald Trump holding an AK-47 and riding a tank into political battle.

A short distance away was a farm that once had a hand-painted "Trump Country" sign affixed to its fence. This house belonged to someone who had taken part in the January 6 insurrection.

I couldn't believe I had been indicted before Donald Trump.

I used my turn signal on rural roads, even when there was no one behind me. I stayed well within the speed limit, which was fairly rare for me. I didn't need any more entanglements where the law was concerned. I felt my paranoia was justified when I spotted two Loudoun County Sheriff's Office deputies conducting a speed check at the bottom of the mountain leading into the county. Even though I was going slower than sixty, I checked the rearview mirror for blue lights for several miles after passing them.

I parked at North Street and began my familiar walk to the courthouse, wondering how many of my media friends would be there.

I saw Scott Ziegler walking toward the courthouse entrance, which was guarded by several members of the media, cameras ready. I sped up, hoping that Scott would act as a blocker, and I could slip in quickly behind him.

This strategy was only partially successful.

WJLA-TV reporter Scott Taylor stuck a microphone in my face just before I pulled the door back. Taylor asked me if I regretted not answering the probing questions he'd put to me months before concerning the Stone Bridge incident. I said nothing. In my mind I was thinking, "Oh yes, Scott, not answering your questions was one of the greatest regrets of my life! If only I'd answered. You—as the Washington area's greatest arbiter of truth— would have prevented me from falling into the terrible circumstances I find myself in today."

Nobody ever confused Scott Taylor for a great journalist.

Jennifer argued our bill of particulars to find out what I was accused of lying about. Before the hearing, Theo Stamos told Jennifer that she was going to enter numerous statements that I had allegedly lied about. (Apparently, I was George Santos now.) Jennifer argued that Theo should state, exactly, what the special grand jury had indicted me for. What was that statement?

Jennifer wanted a specific statement attached to the indictment.

Jennifer argued that, if Theo tried to enter multiple statements and one of the statements was not found to be perjury, didn't that mean the whole case would go away?

Theo's new second chair, Brandon Wrobleski, argued the motions for the commonwealth. He stated that the prosecution had "no intention to hide the ball."

OK then, what was I being charged with?

Wrobleski said the prosecution couldn't provide specifics because it would "divulge its theory of the case."

Which was?

Judge James E. Fisher rejected Jennifer's motions, but allowed that she could refile the part about the statements if Theo's reply to the bill of particulars was deemed insufficient.

Filing for a Change of Venue

In February, Jennifer Leffler filed a change-of-venue motion in Loudoun County Circuit Court asking for the trial to be switched to Fairfax County. The logic she set forth was well-reasoned.

"According to EO4, as well as numerous statements issued by both the Governor and the Attorney General, citizens of Loudoun County were deceived by the administrators of the Loudoun County school system. This alleged deception is at the root of the Defendant's indictment for perjury. Thus, citizens of Loudoun County cannot 'stand indifferent' to this case, as required by law, because they are alleged victims in this action.

". . . In characterizing the citizens of Loudoun County as victims of the alleged cover-up by LCPS officials, and by indicting the Defendant for allegedly furthering that cover-up by LCPS officials, through his testimony before the special grand jury, the Governor and Attorney General have adopted and systematically publicly disseminated the theory that Loudoun County residents, as stakeholders, are interested parties in this case. Both the Governor and Attorney General have routinely referred to the entire jury pool in Loudoun County as victims of the alleged cover-up by LCPS and the Defendant, as the spokesperson for the county. As such, Loudoun County residents are per se disqualified from serving as jurors in this unique case.

". . . The government had an opportunity to control the narrative and not influence emotions of Loudoun County residents by designating them as victims in this matter. However, at every opportunity, the Governor and the Attorney General have promised the citizens of Loudoun County that they will get justice for the wrongs that Loudoun County families have suffered as the result of the alleged cover-up by LCPS. By seeking justice for Loudoun County residents, the government is implying that those residents have been injured, and thus 'disqualified from jury service because prejudice is inherent.'"

Seemed like perfect logic to me. Unfortunately, logic had regularly been defied in this case.

In a text message, Jennifer told me a large box of documents had been turned over as part of discovery. She asked me if I would like to make an appointment to go through them at her Fairfax office.

I made an appointment for ten the following Tuesday morning.

A Romantic Gesture

On the day before Valentine's Day, I threw financial caution to the wind, took the rolled-up quarters from the blue vase in the guest bedroom, and cashed them in at the bank. I went to Costco and bought two dozen roses for my wife.

Brenda's eyes welled up when I gave them to her.

I am sorry to the core of my soul for all I've put this woman through over the course of four decades.

Of Madness and Strategy

From February to April, I went through the mountains of special grand jury testimony at the law offices of LefflerPhillips in Fairfax. I did not go through this material in any kind of chronological order. I just picked up a thick stack of papers and started reading. There were more than a dozen formidable piles of information laid out across a conference table. Sometimes, I would pick up a large stack at the beginning of the day and opt for a smaller stack at the end because I thought I could finish reading it before the office closed.

Anyway, that was the extent of my research "method."

A Journey of Discovery

I was happy I splurged on those roses for Brenda, because I ended up spending Valentine's Day in the conference room of Jennifer's law office in Fairfax, going through special grand jury transcripts. The ever-helpful and polite Mary Herbert gave me red sticky tabs so that I could flag documents I thought Jennifer might find useful. For the next five and half hours, I skimmed through hundreds of pages of special grand jury transcripts and legal documents. This was not quite the daunting task it may have seemed at first. Much of what had been turned over was "filler" that had nothing to do with my case or was just tangential (read bullshit) to my situation.

I noted that on the special grand jury witness list, I was witness number twenty-four of forty-six, hardly a position that would have suggested any importance.

After completing my work with the transcripts, Jennifer and I had a frank talk about what was before me. After reading my testimony on August 2, 2022, she thought that I had said nothing incriminating and that Theo Stamos's questioning had been over the top. She contemplated setting a meeting with Theo to point out how absurd Theo's conduct had been and to ask if Theo wanted to risk the embarrassment of a jury trial. Under normal circumstances, Jennifer said she would take this trial to a jury with confidence that she'd get a not guilty verdict. Given the politically charged nature of Loudoun County, however, she didn't know if such a verdict was a certainty.

Jennifer didn't think the motion to change venues would succeed given the lack of success with previous defense motions associated with the special grand jury. There was a chance that it would be impossible to seat an impartial jury in Loudoun, at which point the venue would have to be switched. Despite my raised hopes from earlier, in a similar vein, she didn't think a judge would grant a pretrial motion to dismiss the case. The fact that the special grand jury had issued the indictment meant it pretty much had to go to trial.

There was a chance that a judge could order a "motion to strike" before the trial went to the jury. This would mean that, in the judge's opinion, the prosecution had clearly not made its case.

Jennifer got out the statute concerning perjury and said that this was a charge that was very hard to prove. The fact that I uttered a falsehood would have to be attested to by two or more people. Someone would have to attest that I stated that I was going to lie to the special grand jury. I knew there was zero chance of either of these things happening.

Taking a Strategic Loss

Jennifer had already told me that we would lose our motion to change venues to Fairfax before I arrived for the hearing on this matter. I was OK with that. This was all part of the process. Though I was worried about having to wade through a media scrum, I was relieved that there was no media in sight when I arrived at the courthouse.

Going through security, Deputy Fanelli, who oversaw security, greeted me by name. When the courthouse security detail can greet you by name, and you're not a lawyer, that's a sure sign that you're spending too much time at the courthouse. I checked the board and saw that we were in Courtroom 2A. When the bailiff opened the courtroom, I asked him who the presiding judge was. Plowman. I knew right then that our motion was going nowhere.

When our turn came, Jennifer argued that casting Loudoun's population as victims of the school division by Youngkin and Miyares made the county's potential jury pool appear to be tainted. Why not move the trial to Fairfax, where Jennifer and Theo both have offices, to remove any appearance of bias? I could tell from Plowman's comments and questions that Jennifer was getting nowhere.

Arguing for the attorney general's office was a new face, Jason Faw. He pissed me off by saying my crime should be tried in the building where it occurred. Faw made it sound like I had shot somebody in the courtroom's corridors. (Never mind the fact that he failed to mention the word "alleged.") Faw was also Plowman's former assistant commonwealth's attorney; two on one. While I was steaming on the inside, I did my best to maintain a placid exterior.

As expected, Plowman denied the motion to change venues.

In the lobby outside the courtroom, I was approached by an attorney who had represented one of the school board members before the special grand jury. He told me the charge against me—although I still didn't know exactly what it was I was charged with—was bullshit. He also served up a bit of information on the departed Carlton Davis. Davis had never appeared in a courtroom until he had been appointed to the prosecution team for the special grand jury.

As we reached Jennifer's parking space, she said that she didn't want me to be disappointed. She told me that we would lose this motion because that was what she believed, and she didn't want me to have false expectations. Jennifer added that she believed we would ultimately win at trial. I had never doubted Jennifer's legal instincts and didn't doubt them as we parted.

Walking back to North Street, I experienced one of those moments of coincidence that gave me strength during this time and the feeling that somehow life was looking out for me.

I bumped, almost literally, into Jo Ann Pearson, a retired teacher from Broad Run High School. Jo Ann told me that my case had been a major topic of discussion at the Loudoun Retired Teachers Association luncheons and that this group was 100 percent behind me. If the retired teachers were on your side, who could be against you?

A lot of good people believed in me. That had to count for something.

Plowman Paranoia

I had severe reservations about Judge Jim Plowman having anything to do with my case based on his record as Loudoun County commonwealth's attorney—specifically a case involving Freedom High School Assistant Principal Ting-Yi Oei.

In August 2008, Oei became aware of students sending around a semi-naked photo of a young woman on their phones. The photo showed the torso of the young woman with her hands folded across her naked breasts. You have to remember that these were the days when cell phone technology was new, especially to a middle-aged man like Oei. Naively, Oei asked a student to send the photo to his cell phone so that it could be downloaded to a computer as part of a record of the incident. Oei testified that it was the first time anyone had sent a photo to his phone, and he was very unfamiliar with the technology involved. Oei said that the transfer was not done secretly and other school officials were there as the photo was sent to his phone.

The student who provided Oei with the photo was later suspended for pulling down another student's pants. As is usually the case, something unrelated to the initial incident put Oei in the crosshairs. The suspended student's mother went to the sheriff's office with details of the photo incident, and Oei was charged with failure to report suspected child abuse. When that charge didn't stick—Oei had reported the photo to his principal—he was charged by Plowman's office with possession of child pornography. The case was dismissed in April 2009, and the charges expunged in May 2011. The school board paid Oei's legal fees and assigned him to administrative duties that would allow him to finish his career.

In an NPR interview after his ordeal, Oei speculated on why he was charged. "I think there may have been issues of conflict between the Commonwealth's Attorney's Office and the school system about what they think the Commonwealth's Attorney's Office should know about what goes on in the schools."

For his part, Plowman never apologized or backed down from the reasons these dubious charges had been filed.

And that was why I was paranoid about Jim Plowman.

Death, Million-Dollar Bathrooms,
and Pole Dances

Matters as serious as death—it gets no more serious than that—and as mundane as the configuration of bathrooms assaulted my imagination. When we face something as serious as death, I don't know why we waste so much time on where people pee. I couldn't help but feel that we would all look back *at the end of our lives and wonder how we could have been so petty and stupid.*

Dealing with Death

During the morning of March 9, 2023, I put a down payment on the marker for my parents' graves at the family plot in New York. In keeping with their frugal ways and disdain for all things extravagant and flashy, I went with simple gray granite for the lowest price of $4,670. You can buy more expensive stones that are "guaranteed," but how much can granite really age? I was also reckoning that the last time I, or any member of my family, would see this marker was at the burial. The last time I had visited this site had been three decades ago for the burial of my grandmother's ashes.

Besides, whatever the marker, it had to be more dignified than the closet in my guest bedroom and my brother's garage where the cremains of my father and mother, respectively, had been residing.

In the afternoon, I made the trek to Berryville for the visitation of the wife of a friend, Mike Sipe. I had known Mike since he was fifteen, when he was the star athlete at Clarke County High School and I was sports editor of *The Winchester Star*. His wife, Stacy, had died after an eight-month battle with cancer.

I met Mike in the funeral home's reception room. He said that that morning his mom had pulled out the family Bible. Inside was an article I'd written about Mike while he had played football at Shepherd College. I told Mike that I had never considered my writing holy scripture.

I was reminded that my work—however routine it may have appeared to me at the time—had value and meaning.

It was good to be reminded of that in times like these.

Glenn Youngkin on CNN

Glenn Youngkin was the guest on a CNN town hall on March 9, 2023, "The War Over Education." Jake Tapper moderated. "Typical" Virginia parents, students, and teachers were in the audience to ask Youngkin questions. As the cameras panned around the room, I noticed that LCPS Interim Superintendent Dr. Daniel Smith was in the room.

The Youngkin that appeared on this telecast was different from the rabid version that had appeared before the Administration Building during election season. He had his moderate, family-friendly persona on; his voice was higher and more aw-shucks than when he was in campaign mode. The red vest was nowhere in sight. He used the hour-long program to repeat his standard talking points no matter the question. Tapper asked follow-ups to the questions that were hardly hard-hitting. Mostly, he grunted what seemed like assent as Youngkin disgorged his talking points.

I wanted to reach into the screen and slap Jake Tapper.

Youngkin started off by saying that Virginia was the recognized national leader in education before becoming the epicenter of controversy. "The big question we ask is, 'How did we get here?'"

Well, Glenn, I have some thoughts . . .

The governor said previous "progressive" administrations lowered expectations and pitted child against child based on race, myths, or religion using materials not consistent with their values. The pandemic exposed the abuses heaped on students as parents saw what their children were being taught, according to the governor. He then repeated the mantra that got him his narrow gubernatorial victory: "Parents deserve—not only to be at the table—but they deserve to have the head seat at the table." Later Youngkin added, "When parents are engaged with their children, they can make good decisions together." Maybe in your sitcom fairy land Glenn, but it's a different story in the real world.

Another take on Youngkin's philosophy on parenting: "There's a basic rule here, which is that children belong to parents, not the state, not the schools, not to the bureaucrats, but to parents." Children as property. Spoken like a true CEO.

Loudoun County didn't come up directly until a question from James Miller, of Ashburn, who asked about sending his children to schools that were safe. Youngkin's answer: "What we've seen in Loudoun County is really representative of all of the issues that we've been talking about tonight. And that is a school district that embraced equity, embraced divisive concepts in teaching and parents saw it and stood up and said 'Wait a minute, time out.'"

Then Youngkin blathered a word salad that spoke directly to my situation.

"And then it was coupled with the fact that there was a young woman who was sexually assaulted in a school and the superintendent moved that child—without telling the families—to another school and another young woman was sexually assaulted. It took a new governor, an executive order, an attorney general in Jason Miyares—investigation for nine months—in order to get an indictment of what was a cover-up.

"See there's a basic truth that I believe, that school boards, that superintendents and administrators need to be held to: one, is that parents matter, transparency is critical and they do have a responsibility to tell parents and to tell the police when there has been a crime, violent crime. This issue is at the heart of why we, as administration, worked so hard to pass bills to make it mandatory that, in fact, that the violent crime is reported to police and can't be covered up again, just like it was."

Let me dissect and clarify Glenn's talking points here:

- The victim wasn't transferred here, her assailant was. And, under state and federal law, you can't tell third parties when a student is involuntarily transferred for whatever reason, whether they are victim or perpetrator.
- There was no "cover-up." LCPS reported what it could, when it could.
- The singular use of the word "indictment" showed me just

how much importance higher-ups placed on the indictment of yours truly.

- LCPS told the "police," or in this case the sheriff's office, about the incident in Stone Bridge's bathroom minutes after it happened. No legislative action was necessary.

Youngkin's performance on CNN drew tepid reactions from other media. At best, it was labeled ineffective.

$11 Million Bathrooms

There's a scene in Mel Brooks's *Silent Movie* set in the men's washroom of the evil conglomerate Engulf and Devour. Engraved over the sink are the words "Our Toilets Are Nicer Than Most People's Homes."

I thought of this scene after the LCPS Department of Support Services gave a presentation titled "Safety and Privacy in School Restrooms." The gist of this initiative was that LCPS would spend $5.3 million in fiscal year 2023 and $5.6 million in fiscal year 2024 to create all-gender bathrooms at all levels of schools.

This effort leaned heavily on Policy 8040, Section C, which stated that LCPS shall "modernize school restrooms and locker rooms to improve student privacy and to promote the creation of single-user restrooms that are available to all students in a ratio appropriate for the enrollment and size of the school." The presentation stated that the planned restroom conversions were being done with "on-going feedback on operational and facility aspects" from a principals' advisory group. I'll bet the principals had some feedback. The redesigned bathrooms would feature floor-to-ceiling stalls. I could only imagine the horrors that might go on in there. The presentation noted "Student Behavior," "Supervision—During Class and at Class Changes," and "Teachers' Hesitance to Intervene" were among the "challenges" the new bathrooms would present. To help with these challenges, the refurbished bathrooms would include vaping and air-quality monitoring and occupancy sensors. No cameras.

Toilet attendants might have been a much more cost-effective way to go.

Fox News picked up the story of the $11 million—$10.9 million, actually, but what's another $100,000—bathrooms, and the outrage machine kicked into gear.

Joint Therapy Session

Brenda had not been able to escape the claws of stress that my case brought. She joined me in therapy and, as we attended our second joint therapy session, I cajoled Brenda into expressing some of her anger. She told Keri that she just wanted this to be over so we could move on, the verdict didn't matter. I offered that, in the unlikely event we lost at trial in June, I would appeal the decision. Brenda wasn't on board with this. I told her and Keri that I would fight to protect my name and reputation. Brenda replied that the people who knew me wouldn't be moved by the verdict one way or the other and that the whole matter would soon fade from the public's consciousness.

While I conceded these points, I wouldn't concede on the appeal. As I would tell Brenda later, I had taken all the shit I was going to take in this life, and I wouldn't take that.

After the session, we went to an upscale country store for which Kyle had gotten us a gift card. I bought six $8.95 chocolate bars to place in the family Easter baskets.

Why not?

Brenda and I then went to a screening of *The Lost King*, a tale of a woman obsessively searching for the burial site of England's King Richard III. She defied the experts by locating Richard and then was screwed out of the credit by pompous academics. Still, she found personal fulfillment and a sense of worth from her lonely quest.

This story resonated deeply with me as I was in a master class for lonely quests.

I would definitely be appealing should it come to that, and I would get Brenda on board somehow.

A Startling Reference

On March 27, 2023, *The Washington Post* published an article on the rising number of Freedom of Information Act requests in the metro DC area. LCPS's count had gone from thirty-one in 2019 to 224 in 2020 to 554 in 2021 and 403 in 2022; statistics that, with the exception of 2022, I compiled.

The article noted that five LCPS lawyers and communications staff had recently undergone online training to handle these requests.

I used to do these by myself.

I wondered if I was missed.

The article quoted "spokesman Dan Adams." Dan is a very good man, but it was jarring to see someone else offering comment for LCPS.

A Terrible Phone Conference

While I was reading through the court documents during a March 28 visit to LefflerPhillips, Jennifer Leffler stopped by the conference room to say she was going to have a phone conference with Theo Stamos about my case. By the sound of Jennifer's raised voice coming through the closed door, I knew things weren't going well. Theo still refused to say exactly what I was charged with. Jennifer said she would now have to file a bill of particulars, and we might not know until thirty days before the June 20 trial what I was accused of.

Jennifer offered that she might have made a mistake by mentioning the words "prosecutorial misconduct" to Theo. That set the prosecutor off.

Jennifer said I would still be found innocent if we got a fair jury. "If everybody follows the law, there's no way you're convicted of this."

Her voice was not quite as confident as I would have liked it to be.

Drag Queens and Pole Dances

Virginia Lieutenant Governor Winsome Sears was a guest panelist on the March 31, 2023, edition of *Real Time with Bill Maher*.

As I watched one of my favorite programs, I braced for a mention of LCPS or my situation.

Much to my relief, it didn't happen.

Sears did hit on a controversy supposedly plaguing America's schools. "If I don't want my child given lap dances at school by a drag queen, I don't want it done. That is happening."

Maher reacted incredulously. He said he was aware of drag queens reading to students but wasn't sure about the "lap dance" part.

"There are drag queens doing pole dances," Sears doubled down.

"In school?" asked Maher.

"Bill, you gotta read more," replied Sears.

Specifically, you have to "read" Fox News.

As is typical with Fox, there was a shred of truth in this story that had been extrapolated to its illogical extreme.

On March 22, 2023, the Pride Club at Forsyth Technical Community College in Winston-Salem, North Carolina, held a pride festival at a restaurant on campus. Attendance was not mandatory. It was not done in a public elementary school.

Here's where things got complicated.

Forsyth Technical serves students as young as fourteen. This event was advertised with free pizza, but didn't mention drag performances. As the college later noted, "parents of children under 18 were not notified of this in advance."

As should have been expected, right-wing activists attended this event and videoed it. A drag queen was depicted apparently giving a lap dance to a young girl. The video showed up on Libs of TikTok, a far-right, anti-LGBTQ account.

After investigating this incident, I had some questions from the perspective of a school public relations professional.

Who was the genius who approved this event with no parental warnings or restrictions? This had potential media disaster written all over it.

What was the drag queen thinking when they gave a lap dance to a kid? There are always, always cell phones present. You are providing a viral moment the Right will use to denigrate and destroy you. You are living down to their worst expectations.

For all the disparagement of the right-wing media echo chamber, the far Left continually gives them more ammunition than they can use. The college and the drag queens had no one but themselves to blame for this fiasco. This was the type of incident that only throws fuel on the culture war fire that engulfs ordinary people's lives like mine.

Sears used this incident to segue into the standard talking points about education she and Youngkin use. "I'm a parent. I'm a parent all day. I get to decide what happens in my child's life. Not you. Not you. Not the government. Not anybody. I don't co-parent. I had this child. Anything happens to Little Johnny, you're calling me, as you should."

With April Showers Came Witnesses and, Finally, the Reason for My Indictment

Preparing for the trial that perpetually seemed on the far horizon consumed a great deal of my time. As the trial grew closer, some of the players in Loudoun's ongoing media circus began to resurface.

Witness List

The first thing I saw when I entered my makeshift office at LefflerPhillips was the witness list for the trial from Theo Stamos. Some of the names from LCPS were expected: Stone Bridge Principal Tim Flynn, Director of High School Education Nereida Gonzalez-Sales, Director of School Administration Doug Fulton, Chief Operations Officer Kevin Lewis, and Director of Communications and Community Engagement Joan Sahlgren. The witness list said that these witnesses could be found at 21000 Education _Drive_, Ashburn. It's Education _Court_. A small point, but it showed the prosecution's eye for detail or lack thereof.

One name was conspicuously missing, Scott Ziegler.

State Police Special Agents Eric Deel and Wanda Beard were listed. I had never met them, but they may have been present for special grand jury testimony.

Scott Smith was on the list. Knowing his propensity for violence and flying off the handle, having him on the stand could actually work to our advantage.

Stone Bridge SRO Tavis Henry and Sheriff's Office Detective Corrine Czekaj also could offer testimony about the chaotic nature of Stone Bridge on May 28, 2021. That could help me.

Former LCPS Division Counsel Stephen "Steve" DeVita rounded out the dozen witnesses. The prosecution said his whereabouts were unknown. Steve and I had remained friends and communicated on Facebook. I knew where he was.

I didn't think I would volunteer that information.

Finally!

On Good Friday, more than six months after I had been secretly indicted, the Virginia Attorney General's Office finally revealed what I was indicted for in an email to Jennifer.

"On August 2, 2022, the defendant testified before the Special Grand Jury impaneled to investigate allegations of sexual assaults in the Loudoun County Public Schools, to include the Stone Bridge High School and Broad Run High School. When questioned, Defendant repeatedly testified under oath that he was unaware of an alleged sexual assault that occurred at Stone Bridge High School on May 28, 2021, until after the sexual assault at Broad Run High School occurred on October 6, 2021."

This was true.

I did not know that anyone had been charged with a criminal offense in connection with the Stone Bridge incident until after the October 6, 2021, incident at Broad Run. There were some cherry-picked snippets of testimony that followed this statement that really proved nothing. What I told the special grand jury, repeatedly, was that I didn't know if the Stone Bridge encounter had been classified as an assault or consensual sex until after the October 7, 2021, sheriff's office media release.

I noticed the email to Jennifer was signed by Assistant Attorney General Jason A. Faw with Theo Stamos copied. I wondered what that was about. Had Theo been replaced as the lead prosecutor?

My brother and I talked about the prosecution's assertions the next day.

He likened it to someone who continued to raise the pot in a poker game, even though they had a weak hand, hoping that their opponent would refuse to call the bluff and fold or make a strategic mistake.

I vowed to do neither.

Ian Prior Resurfaces

Going through the news on Tuesday, April 11, I found an article stating that the US Department of Education (DOE) Office for Civil Rights (OCR) was opening an investigation into the 2021 LCPS sexual assaults at the behest of—wait for it—Ian Prior. Prior filed a complaint in January through his role as senior advisor with the America First Legal Foundation, citing LCPS's alleged failure to respond to the sexual assaults as required by Title IX. "This is about protecting students from sexual assault and sexual harassment," Prior told the local Fox affiliate. "And it's important the politics are taken out of this, and they do a thorough investigation to make sure the problems are remedied."

If there was one thing I knew, Ian Prior was all about taking the politics out of things.

What I found especially interesting was that Scott Smith apparently wasn't on board with this investigation. Smith gave his own statement to Fox 5: "The U.S. Department of Education now declaring that it will investigate LCPS for potential Title IX violations is meaningless. It's like the National School Board, who branded me a domestic terrorist, saying that they are going now to investigate the harm put upon my family—it's biased, and the only result that the USDOE will come to is that Loudoun did everything right, in order to protect it from truth and reason. You have to question why now, over a year later, that suddenly the federal government is interested in this problem. Is it to root [out] wrongdoing or is it actually to make an effort to protect the wrongdoer, the Loudoun County School Board, that adopted the harmful left-leaning policies that the federal government actively agrees with regarding the education of our children? Any investigation by the federal department of education is an absolute farce, and any conclusions it may come to [are] completely untrustworthy."

The reason the DOE was taking up this matter was a request from Ian Prior. If Scott Smith had a beef with anyone—and Lord knows he had many—it should have been with Ian Prior.

LCPS's statement on the DOE's investigation followed the standard statements it had been making all along. "Loudoun County Public Schools has received a Notification of Complaint from the United States Department of Education Office for Civil Rights, and will duly assist OCR in this process."

The Virginia Attorney General's Office stated that it wouldn't comment on pending litigation. I have to wonder what they were thinking in Richmond about an investigation that could blow up the special grand jury's findings.

A Good Day

You should learn something new every day.

On this sunny spring day in April, I learned that groundhogs could climb trees. I was out on my walk when I startled a groundhog, who quickly shimmied up a tree until we were looking at each other eye-to-eye.

Later in the day, I dropped by an antique shop in Stephens City. The proprietor had set aside some specialty baseball cards that he sold to me at a reduced price.

In the evening, Brenda and I went to a trendy restaurant for which my brother purchased a gift card. Nothing on the menu looked intelligible. A helpful waitress told us one of the items was steak.

As it turned out, a very good steak.

These were the small things that made up a "good" day for me in my purgatory.

Oh yes, Glenn Youngkin "suspended"—read abandoned—his 2024 presidential campaign. Unable to crack 1 percent in the polls, and with his top political consultants bailing, Youngkin bowed to reality, saying he would shift his focus to the 2023 General Assembly elections.

"Listen, I didn't write a book, and I'm not in Iowa or New Hampshire or South Carolina," Youngkin told *The New York Times*.

Yeah, Glenn, but you're still up my ass.

In the coming weeks, Youngkin adopted the attitude of a reluctant prom date in the back seat as he discussed his presidential aspirations. "Maybe I will, maybe I won't. Maybe I will if I'm asked nicely [or begged a whole lot]. I'm flattered and honored just to be asked."

Juli Briskman Gets It

At the April meeting of the joint school board-board of supervisors committee, Algonkian District Supervisor Juli Briskman offered the kind of common-sense wisdom that Loudoun's leaders had rarely voiced during the past two years. "I don't believe that we have a systematic issue in our schools with sexual assault. Charges and arrests came very late in my opinion and communication failed."

Exactly.

I'd known Juli for years, since she had been a young reporter at *The Winchester Star*. She was obnoxious then but, full disclosure, so was I. In the decades since leaving *The Star*, she'd grown into a compassionate, able public leader.

Although her obnoxious side would occasionally resurface, which was what vaulted her into politics.

On October 28, 2017, Juli was riding her bicycle near the entrance to the Trump National Golf Club in Loudoun when President Trump's motorcade rode by her. Juli gave Trump the finger as his limousine passed. The image was photographed and went national. She lost her job as a marketing analyst for Akima, a government contractor, but gained a fan base.

I vowed to contact Juli Briskman when this was all over.

Maybe she could help me give Glenn Youngkin the finger.

Learning Likability

Jennifer Leffler invited Brenda and me to a meeting at her office.

The first thing Jennifer said was that she had consulted a neuropsychologist and that she didn't think portraying me as someone with a bad memory or cognitive disability would be a viable strategy.

That was a relief. The inevitable reports of my lack of mental acuity would have haunted me the rest of my life.

Jennifer then started questioning Brenda about her observations on my mental state in May 2021 and before my special grand jury appearance in August 2022. Brenda related that I was stressed by my workload and noted the number of calls we had received on our home phone line from principals seeking help when they couldn't find another administrator. She noted the school board meetings that would get me home at one in the morning and the constant Teams meetings at night and on the weekends when emergencies arose. She told Jennifer that she didn't remember me ever discussing the sexual assault at Stone Bridge High School. Brenda added that I was not stressed the morning of August 2, 2022, before my special grand jury testimony, and she said that I stated it would probably be the kind of routine testimony I had given before.

After speaking with Brenda for a time, Jennifer said my wife would make a strong, sympathetic witness and that she would like to put her on the list of potential witnesses. I felt more than a little bit of alarm. Brenda had suffered more than enough from this affair despite having no role in it. In another example of the strong woman she is, Brenda said she was ready to testify.

I trusted my wife's intuition.

I trusted Jennifer's professional judgment.

Case closed.

Speaking of closing the case, Jennifer said that it was her hope that neither Brenda nor I would have to testify. She thought the prosecution's case was so weak that the judge could accept a motion to strike—ending the case in our favor—before the defense presented its case.

Next, Jennifer told me that I had to express uncertainty on the witness stand. The special grand jury did not like the fact that I had given my version of events and stuck to it with an authoritative tone. Jennifer said I had to win the jury's sympathy without lying.

What she suggested was that, if the prosecution asked if anyone mentioned that the Stone Bridge incident on May 28, 2021, was a sexual assault, I would say, while I didn't remember anything specifically, that was a possibility.

My defense would rest on the following facts, which were all true:

- My training had always taught me that a crime is not alleged until a charge is filed. Until a charge is filed, any talk about assaults would be only rumor and hearsay.
- I had no idea a charge had been filed in the Stone Bridge case until October 7, 2021, when the sheriff's office sent out a media release about the incident at Broad Run.
- It was my thought—and it was—that dubbing the Stone Bridge incident an "assault" before the sheriff's office's determination would be prejudicial, which would affect possible school board discipline and future prosecution.
- In reviewing my May 28, 2021, emails in preparation for my August 2, 2021, testimony, I saw no mention of the words "sexual assault," which was absolutely true.

Jennifer said that I shouldn't mention that my feelings on whether the Stone Bridge incident was a sexual assault were "immaterial." What I thought didn't matter because—no matter what I thought—I was not authorized to include the words "assault" or "sexual assault" in messages to the public. She said others would testify to that point.

Jennifer said I would have to soften my demeanor so that I didn't appear to be confrontational or overly authoritative. Brenda chimed in to say that this had always been a problem for me, even with family matters. The two women then tag teamed me about needing to not appear so cocksure and to allow some vulnerability and doubt to seep into my potential testimony.

Jennifer said she would coach me, at length, to project these qualities before the trial. The idea was to present truthful, believable testimony without looking rehearsed.

Jennifer offered a ray of hope about a pretrial motion she was filing that could kneecap the prosecution's strategy before the trial began. Regarding the special grand jury testimony, Judge Plowman had ordered that transcripts not be disseminated without a written order from him. The prosecution had given Tim Flynn and Joan Sahlgren copies of their testimony without such an order. Jennifer would file a motion saying Flynn and Joan should be excluded as witnesses as a result of this transgression.

Without Joan Sahlgren and Tim Flynn, their star witnesses, the prosecution would have to abandon the case. Jennifer said that this motion was usually a slam dunk since this was a clear violation of a judge's order. However, given her experience with Loudoun's judiciary, she wasn't 100 percent confident. Jennifer added that having Judge Plowman decide on this motion could actually be to our advantage since it was his order that was violated. At any rate, such a motion could help us get an adverse verdict dismissed on appeal because of a prosecutorial or judicial error.

Brenda stiffened visibly at the mention of the word "appeal." Jennifer assured her that she believed I would be found not guilty.

Brenda and I drove away from Fairfax both comforted and anxious, the perpetually paradoxical state we now inhabited.

A Month of Lunacy, Surprises, and a Betrayal

It was not enough that I was going through rigorous preparations for my upcoming trial. I discovered the prosecution might try to revive a long-ago accusation of perjury against me made by a local lunatic. The local lunatic, whom I choose not to identify, had posted incendiary remarks about LCPS by the thousands on a multitude of unrelated websites and comment sections. After starting his public rants against LCPS in 2014, he branched out until his list of enemies included a state legislator from a faraway district, an NPR host, and newspaper editors throughout the mid-Atlantic.

His primary target, however, was LCPS. Over the years, he had filed 124 FOIA requests and sued the school division multiple times.

The local lunatic's "perjury" charge against me resulted from a FOIA request. He had asked me for information and copied nineteen people to make sure his request was noticed. I gathered the information, which had no real relevance, hit reply all and sent it to everyone.

Well, almost everyone.

In hitting "reply all," which is my least-favorite technological function, I had neglected to check if the local lunatic was copied.

He was not.

Attorney Julia Judkins and I discovered my mistake when preparing for a court hearing. The local lunatic was sent the information he requested along with an apology for my error. During the hearing, Loudoun County Circuit Court Judge Jeanette Irby ruled that my error was just that, an honest clerical error and not perjury. This didn't stop the local lunatic from calling me a "perjurer" online for years. I consulted a respected attorney to see if I could sue the local lunatic for libel. The respected attorney told me that even if I won such a case, I would get nothing but legal bills for it. The local lunatic was broke. This was not worth my while. I respected the respected attorney's opinion and let the matter drop.

The local lunatic couldn't let it go.

He called the Virginia State Police demanding an investigation. Thus it was that, in 2015, I gave an interview to a State Police investigator who, after the interview, declined to file charges. I considered the matter done.

Done until a cold, gray spring day in 2023.

Jennifer Leffler emailed me to state that the prosecution might seek to enter the 2015 State Police report into evidence as proof of my history of lying. She said that this was nonsense and that it wouldn't be entered unless I made the mistake of mentioning it in court.

I vowed not to do this.

I hate "reply all."

This report was the reason why former LCPS Division Counsel Steve DeVita was on the list of potential witnesses. Steve is a great guy whom I wouldn't mind seeing. But not under these circumstances.

Julia Judkins wrote a memo memorializing the reasons I *didn't* commit perjury. Although it would cause Jennifer consternation, I almost would have liked to see Julia get on the stand to defend me. She's a fierce advocate who drives the local lunatic—I would say "insane," but he's already there.

I made contact with Julia on Facebook, and she said that she had contacted Jennifer to let her know that the "perjury" evidence was inadmissible.

Julia Judkins is a true friend.

The Reappearance of Mike Chapman

Politicians are the epitome of cooperation during an election year. Loudoun County Sheriff Mike Chapman was no exception.

During a quarterly update on crime to the Loudoun County Board of Supervisors, Chapman trumpeted the fact that the sheriff's office and LCPS were experiencing better communications.

"I am pleased to say that the Loudoun County Sheriff's Office senior-level collaboration with Loudoun County Public Schools has been much better since the appointment of Dr. Smith as the interim superintendent. It has been refreshing and completely different from the previous administration. This is evidence that effective communication is possible at our most senior levels, and the way things should always work."

Chapman's rhetoric was particularly galling to me since it had been his partisan arrogance that caused the communications breakdown in the first place. According to Mike Chapman, things couldn't be better where work with the school division was concerned. "This collaboration has become even better since the appointment of Dr. Smith. He and I have met personally to discuss the [Memorandum of Understanding] and are in direct contact on safety issues related to Loudoun County students and the schools."

The supervisors took Chapman to task for the manner in which he used Alert Loudoun, a county-funded system to share emergency information. The sheriff's office had used Alert Loudoun to disseminate a 1,600-word essay on a study that did not favor the conversion of the sheriff's office to a professional police department. Chapman had also used Alert Loudoun to criticize Democratic Commonwealth's Attorney Buta Biberaj. The system was not used, however, when Dulles Town Center, Loudoun's major shopping mall, was closed by a shooting on April 2, 2023. Chapman's rationale was that the shooter had been arrested and that there had been "no risk" to the general public because law-enforcement personnel had surrounded the building.

I can attest through painful personal experience that Mike Chapman was very selective about what his office communicated to the public.

A Random Act of Perspective

You never know when random acts of perspective will pop up to alter your view of the world.

Brenda and I were going to spend the next couple of nights at my youngest daughter's house while her husband was at a conference. I went to the gym for an early morning workout, something I almost never do.

A man came up and addressed me warmly in a halting voice while I was at the gym. I didn't recognize him until he introduced himself, Todd Hill.

Todd coached Winchester's Handley High School to a state runner-up finish in football in 1999. He moved to Loudoun County High School in 2007 and coached the Raiders to a 51-39 record and five playoff appearances before he had to give up coaching in 2015 after undergoing a spinal operation. Despite his health issues, I've always known Todd as a boisterous, upbeat man who had a warm welcome for me whenever I visited County.

The man standing before me on this sunny Sunday morning was greatly diminished.

Todd told me that more than a year before, he had been in a gym class when a student kicked a volleyball that struck him in the temple. The result was a traumatic brain injury (TBI) that forced him to retire after a year of attempting to regain his health. Todd said that he'd made 140 trips to a specialist in Richmond for rehab. There was a chance that a blood vessel at the back of his head had constricted, and surgery might be necessary. Todd could no longer drive and relied on his wife to get him around.

Todd embraced me warmly and told me that I was a good man and that my troubles would pass. I was overwhelmed.

Watching out of the corner of my eye, I saw a once-robust man struggle to bench press a small amount of weight. His wife then told him it was time to go and tenderly led him away.

My troubles were nothing compared to Todd Hill's.

At the end of the day, I reflected on how terrible things happen to good people, how wonderful things happen to bad people, and how weird things happen to people like me.

Considering what happened to Todd Hill, I was fortunate to only be dealing with weird.

A Missed Slam Dunk

I was greeted by the ever-friendly Deputy Fanelli as I entered the courthouse for a hearing on our motion to exclude testimony. I asked him where he was from. Fanelli said that his family was from Southern Italy originally and that he grew up in Utica, New York. I mentally filed these facts away for our future interactions.

Jennifer Leffler was confident as we met outside the courtroom to discuss the motion to exclude the testimony of Joan Sahlgren and Tim Flynn. A well-placed Loudoun attorney assured her that Judge James Fisher would see things our way.

He didn't.

Not that Jennifer didn't give a good argument. She even weaved in a sports reference, which I always appreciated. "Mr. Byard has a right to have this court call balls and strikes." Jennifer admitted that Virginia case law was thin on the matters she was arguing before the court, but that several federal cases were clear about the inappropriateness of prosecutors disseminating grand jury testimony without judicial approval and to influence witness testimony.

As soon as Fisher began speaking, it was obvious he wouldn't be ruling in our favor. He didn't want to take part in developing a statute Virginia didn't have. "The Virginia experience is quite different," said Fisher.

No shit, your honor.

While things didn't go our way, Jennifer and I both noticed that Theo Stamos looked nervous and anxious. Jason Faw sat next to her at the prosecution table and was obviously doing some emotional hand-holding.

Theo argued that the prosecution providing testimony was standard operating procedure and that the only requirement they had placed on the witnesses was "to tell the truth."

After the proceeding began, Scott and Jessica Smith entered the courtroom and sat in the front row. I noticed that she was wearing several layers of what appeared to be workout clothes. After the hearing, Theo talked to Scott and Jessica. As they made their way down the two flights of stairs to the main lobby, I watched them from the courtroom lobby. Scott Smith turned his head back a couple of times to fix a malicious stare at me.

"I am not the source of your dysfunctional life," I thought as he stared.

I hadn't done anything to provoke this volatile piece of work and simply watched the couple leave.

I then took a seat at the head of the stairway as Jennifer, Theo, and Faw sat around a table at the other side of the lobby to talk about upcoming motions and the trial. I sat, eyes closed, and tried to pick up on any stray bits of conversation I could.

Going over the jury instructions, they talked about whether I should be referred to by my full name or simply as "the defendant."

Whatever.

Faw gave me a bit of encouragement when I heard him say, "There's no smoking gun in this case."

The name Kevin Lewis came up a few times.

The lawyers' conference took far longer than the preceding hearing. When it was over, Jennifer and I departed through the lawyers' entrance to avoid any media that might be lurking outside.

A Tale of Two Witnesses

Jennifer and I spoke in the parking lot after the adverse ruling.

She said that the prosecution would seek to declare Joan Sahlgren an "adverse" witness. In a motion filed on May 11, prosecutors said giving Joan this label would allow them to ask her "leading or challenging questions" during the trial.

The motion, which would be heard on June 8, resulted from Joan refusing to meet with prosecutors and conveying to them that she thought the special grand jury process was "one-sided" and "unfair."

A report on the motion in *Loudoun Now* offered another reason for the motion's filing. "Prosecutors said in the motion that because Byard is on unpaid leave with no resignation to date, it is assumed he will return to his position if he is acquitted of the perjury charges." The document also noted that Joan and I had had a close working relationship and that she relied on me for information regarding school communication. "It is the specific nature of the close working relationship that the two individuals had, and that Mr. Byard would be returning to if acquitted, that makes Mrs. Sahlgren unique."

It was flattering to think that the attorney general of Virginia was speculating about my future employment. I had contacted nobody at LCPS about what I intended to do when the trial was over. I made sure to make a note to tell Jennifer about that.

I felt truly sorry for Joan. I know she has a good heart and a hard time testifying in court. The trial wouldn't be easy for her.

Tim Flynn was another matter.

Flynn's lawyer wouldn't allow him to talk with Jennifer. Beyond that, the lawyer told Jennifer, "He wants to see Wayde convicted."

People had warned me for years about Flynn, how he was an egotistical ass serving only his best interests. I had always given him the benefit of the doubt. That benefit ended in a Leesburg parking lot.

Jennifer said that Flynn's attorney quickly tried to recant the "hoping I'm convicted" remark. Too late. The damage was done. Jennifer said she would use the statement to cast doubt on Flynn's testimony.

Good.

Jennifer said she was getting angry.

Even better.

What made Flynn's betrayal particularly galling was that he was one of the first to reach out expressing support for me, leaving a phone message on the day of my indictment. We subsequently communicated on Facebook. The following are messages Flynn sent:

December 12, 2022, 6:22 p.m., "Thinking of you. If you need anything give me a call."

December 28, 2022, 4:32 p.m., "Merry Christmas. Santa not good to redsox."

January 31, 2023, 7:10 p.m., "You doing ok?"

February 1, 2023, 12:37 p.m., "Very sorry for all of this. It will all work out positively! Call if I can help in any way."

A Few Motions Forward, a Few Steps Back, and a Ghostly Encounter

A trial is certainly never a straightforward affair. During the month of June, my legal team and I encountered steps forward and just as many steps back.

Upcoming Motions

As she headed for court, Jennifer caught me on my cell phone as I walked toward the Old Stone Church. She told me that since I hadn't talked to Blankingship & Keith for the infamous report, I shouldn't fear its contents. There were no statements from me in the report that could contradict what I had said before the special grand jury.

We would be in court on June 8 for a hearing on Joan being declared an adverse witness and motions Jennifer would be making. One motion would ask that my case be dismissed because of seven instances during which Carlton Davis gave inappropriate testimony to the special grand jury. Davis showed his inexperience in court by admitting he knew that he was doing something wrong before the special grand jury, as previously noted. It was Jennifer's hope, and mine, that his self-incrimination would bring everything to a screeching, if unsatisfying, halt. At this point, I wanted to be found "not guilty" by a jury. I didn't want to win on a technicality due to a prosecutor's self-admitted stupidity. As with previous motions, this relied heavily on case law not related to Virginia. It would probably be rejected, but we had to go through the motions (pun intended).

The other motion regarded my bill of particulars. We would try to clarify again what, exactly, I was being charged with. Jennifer said that her dealings with the prosecution were becoming more contentious. They were hinting that they were going to accuse her of some sort of professional misconduct. We agreed that the prosecutors were becoming more desperate.

The Appealing Disposition of Scott Smith

Scott Smith filed an appeal to his August 2021 conviction for disorderly conduct in Loudoun County General District Court. I couldn't imagine—other than publicity—why he would be doing this. The terms of that conviction were a ten-day jail sentence to be suspended contingent on a year of good behavior. The year had already passed; let it go. A charge of resisting arrest against Smith in relation to the June 22, 2021, school board meeting was dismissed because of a paperwork error.

The disorderly conduct charge stemmed from Smith's confrontation with a woman in the school board meeting room as the June 22 meeting had disintegrated into chaos. "I think he's lucky he didn't get slapped, never mind arrested," said Judge James Howe Brown in setting Smith's appeal trial for September 25. This observation did not go over well with Scott Smith.

"How the fuck does a judge say I deserve to be slapped," Smith told the media after the hearing, a quote only one outlet was bold enough to record.

Smith also offered comments more suitable for a family newspaper. "The problem with our justice system across our land is it's no longer fair. It's not fair. I'll keep fighting this and I will win. But in the meantime, it's just more pain on me and my family. It just holds back our healing. It's ridiculous. Our governor needs to step up and do something."

According to a quote from the ever-helpful WJLA-TV, Smith was disappointed with Glenn Youngkin, as well as the legal system. "My feeling is we had another leftist judge in here. That's worse than what I did. Cussing? He cursed. I am tired of Loudoun County judges. I am tired of the law system here. I am absolutely tired of it and it's finally time after two years—I have yet to hear from our governor, Glenn Youngkin, about any of these matters."

Well, Scott, I wouldn't be sitting by the phone waiting for that call.

In July 2023, Scott Smith summed up his feelings toward Youngkin for *The New York Times*. "I've turned on Glenn Youngkin . . . People say 'The right used you.' I look at it more like a drunk one-night stand: I got what I wanted; they got what they wanted. Youngkin got elected. I got a special grand jury."

Jessica Smith shared her victimhood status with the media. "Enough is enough. They need to stop attacking us. We did nothing wrong. All we did was speak out because our daughter was raped at school and nobody did anything."

This statement led to several observations on my part. Who was attacking Scott and Jessica Smith? At the time of the June 22, 2021, school board meeting, their daughter's case was still under investigation. They didn't speak out. Nobody was arrested for anything that was said that evening.

Loudoun's New Superintendent

On June 2, Dr. Aaron Spence, Virginia Beach's superintendent since 2014, was named LCPS's new leader during a special school board meeting. The vote was 6-2-1, with Tiffany Polifko and John Beatty opposed and Denise Corbo absent. Corbo tried to enter the meeting remotely, but her motion to do so died for the lack of a second. Her fellow school board members appeared to have finally gotten wise to her flimsy excuses for participating remotely.

In addition to his experience in Virginia Beach, Spence had been a superintendent in North Carolina, had held administrative posts with Houston Independent School District and Virginia's Chesterfield County, and had been a high school principal in Virginia's Henrico County.

He also apparently had some balls. In 2019, he filed a complaint against two of his school board members for creating a hostile work environment.

Spence's wife, Krista Kuehne Spence, appeared to be well-matched with her spouse. She generated controversy for this January 1, 2020, Facebook post: "Happy New Year to all I hope this year is a wonderful one filled with love and happiness for everyone . . . except for Trump. he can go F**k himself."

The date for Spence taking over in Loudoun hadn't been set, so he could wrap up business in Virginia Beach. That meant my fate with LCPS might be determined by Daniel Smith. Either way, I told Brenda that there was a strong possibility I'd work for neither.

Preparing for Motions Day

I used June 4, an overcast Sunday, to review the motions for Thursday's hearings.

Jennifer Leffler would again ask the court to make the prosecution say exactly what I said that had led to the perjury charge and what relevance my statement had legally. "The defendant previously filed a motion for a bill of particulars which was denied by this court. At the time of the filing, the defendant had not requested nor received discovery from the commonwealth. That is no longer the case. The original motion asked for the commonwealth to be ordered to identify both the false statement and how the statement was material to the hearing. The current motion only identifies the statements."

Good points.

Jason Faw, on behalf of the commonwealth, kept dancing in his reply. "The commonwealth has never maintained that the defendant made a singular false statement to the special grand jury. The defendant testified he was unaware of an allegation of a sexual assault occurring at Stone Bridge High School on May 28, 2021, until months later when a second sexual assault occurred at Broad Run High School on October 6, 2021. The defendant established this through a number of direct statements and adoptions by agreement." I had no idea what "adoptions by agreement" meant.

As far as Joan Sahlgren being declared an "adverse" witness, Jennifer wrote: "The commonwealth has failed to show how Ms. Sahlgren has a personal interest in the outcome of this case. She has maintained her employment with LCPS throughout this ordeal. There is no evidence her employment will be affected by the outcome of this trial. The Defendant has never been Ms. Sahlgren's superior, nor would he be if he returned to his employment with LCPS."

Jennifer filed a dismissal motion based on statements Carlton Davis made to the special grand jury. On June 14, 2022, Davis said the following during the "questioning" of Scott Smith: "I'll just tell you: From my perspective—I wasn't involved with anything going on here. I live in Arlington. I have two kids, and I had one kid in public school in Arlington at the time—I saw you on TV, and I thought, 'Oh, look at that angry parent, and at the school board about Critical Race Theory and gender issues. That's what I thought, because that's what the narrative was out there . . . But at least the narrative I had of just of a parent of a seven-year-old in public schools is you had the media, the sheriff's office, the school system, all of these people were treating you like you were the problem. Now, that's the narrative I had just observing this on TV."

If you're having trouble following that word salad, refer back to Davis's history of competence.

On September 22, 2022, Davis offered the following statement to a school board member: "I think you were left out, is my personal opinion . . . And I think there's a problem down at 21000 Education Court, and the problem does not necessarily rest with the Board despite what a lot of, you know, outside observers think, and I know holy hell was rained down on you guys at these board meeting(s), I've watched some of them."

On October 6, 2022, Davis said this to Atoosa Reaser: "I'm not sitting here, thinking that Atoosa Reaser should have done anything differently. I'll just be clear. I told the grand jury the same thing. I don't think you guys knew anything. Okay? That's pretty clear to me. Information was kept from you. Information was concealed from you . . . But you weren't told. You weren't told. That's the bottom line."

Other statements are cited but, as was often the case with Carlton Davis, they included philosophical meanderings. I will stipulate, however, that they didn't reflect well on the prosecution.

In response to this motion, Theo Stamos wrote: "The Motion to Dismiss deliberately misrepresents these exchanges as direct communications with members of the SGJ [special grand jury]. On the contrary, each is an instance of a series of questions and answers directed to a witness before the SGJ."

I have to think Theo Stamos was cursing Carlton Davis as she wrote this.

A Day of Half Victories

I donned my new Shaquille O'Neal shirt and departed for court. I discovered that the shirt looked white inside and blue in sunlight.

Magical.

I'd take all the magic I could get.

The sky was murky as a result of smoke drifting south from the Canadian wildfires. This seemed fitting as I was in a murky mood; unable to resume my life until after the trial.

As I rounded the corner of the old courthouse, I spotted a TV remote van and braced for the reporter associated with it. To my great relief, there were no reporters present in the customary media area. Looking around more closely, I saw a female camera person shooting me from behind a fence at the corner of the courthouse property, trying to look as inconspicuous as possible as one can with a large TV camera in front of them.

I have my paparazzo. They must have a very sad existence to be assigned to stalk me.

The first person to catch my eye as I ascended to courtroom 2B was Theo Stamos. She was talking to a group in a girlish voice not at all reminiscent of the sour, aggressive tone she had used on me during my grand jury testimony. She sported a black pantsuit that, unlike my shirt, could not change colors, accented by leopard shoes and two strings of pearls.

The next person I spied was Joan Sahlgren, who looked haggard and somewhat unkempt. We nodded noiselessly to one another. Joan and her lawyer, Kelly King, were present to testify about the prosecution motion to have her declared an adverse witness.

Scott Smith showed up in an outfit that was the opposite of Theo's stylishness: camouflage shorts with a tan T-shirt and baseball cap.

The first motion to be heard was that concerning my motion to dismiss based on Carlton Davis's inappropriate comments. Judge Fisher, who was again on the bench, seemed engaged as Jennifer Leffler made her arguments on my behalf. Fisher rested his chin in his hand, raised his glasses to his forehead, and seemed very attentive. Fisher said, while he found Jennifer's argument "interesting," he was having trouble finding a "nexus" between

Davis's words and my testimony.

Theo began her rebuttal with the poetry of Carl Sandburg, whom she noted that, like herself, was a native of Chicago:

"If the facts are against you, argue the law.

"If the law is against you, argue the facts.

"If the law and the facts are against you, pound the table and yell like hell."

At the end of the arguments, Fisher ruled against us but wryly noted that no one had pounded the table.

Next up was the motion to declare Joan adverse.

Jason Faw questioned Joan and tried to state that I was in a mentorship role to Joan. Joan quickly shot that notion down, saying that I provided only "helpful information" to her. She added a bit of befuddlement to her testimony when she couldn't recall when I was placed on suspension. Joan's guesses on this dramatic date were sometime in September, October, or November. (Actual date: December 12; I certainly hadn't forgotten.) Joan said I was her second in command and would run the office in her absence but answered "I don't know," when asked if she knew if I would return to work if I was acquitted. Honestly, I didn't know the answer to that question either.

Joan said she hadn't characterized the special grand jury as one-sided, as the prosecution stated. "I wouldn't characterize it as one-sided or unfair." Joan did state she had been surprised a judge hadn't been in the room when she had testified.

Jennifer noted there was no nexus between Joan's opinions and my employment. I liked how she worked in the word "nexus" given its earlier use by Judge Fisher. Jennifer said that Joan and I only worked together for a year-and-a-half and hadn't worked together in six months, adding that Joan would make a good witness for the commonwealth.

Faw rebutted by stating that his questioning of Joan involved leading questions, such as those asked of an adverse witness and that this made his point that she should be declared adverse.

Fisher said he would not rule on this issue but would defer this decision to the trial judge, adding he didn't know who this would be.

Not a win, not a loss. I'd take it.

Jennifer next took up our renewed motion for a bill of particulars stating exactly what I said that was perjurious. She said the prosecution's memorandum of record left open the possibility that the jury could consider a statement other than "I did not know of the alleged assault until October" when it made its deliberations.

In Faw's rebuttal, he called the memorandum of record the bill of particulars, a slip I found somewhat revealing. He promised that the commonwealth wouldn't stray from the charges it had made in the memorandum of record in prosecuting me and could be called short during trial if it attempted this. "Yeah, sure," in Theo Stamos's words.

"It seems to me that the commonwealth has shown the cards," Fisher said, before proposing a compromise. Fisher could issue a pretrial order limiting the commonwealth to charges it had stated in documents already filed. These documents didn't have the specificity we wanted, but they at least narrowed what the prosecution could bring before a jury. He could issue a pretrial order binding the commonwealth to the charge outlined in the memorandum of record. While not as limiting as a bill of particulars, it would basically give us what we wanted. I realize I'm using somewhat-confusing legal terminology here, but somewhat-confusing legal terminology is what lawyers use to screw people.

During the following conversation, Faw said some interesting things:

"I've already written my closing argument." Wow, really? So much for tailoring what you say to the evidence presented. He also stated that perjury could be proven through the testimony of two witnesses or the testimony of one witness and "corroborating evidence." At this point it was becoming obvious Joan wasn't going to help their case much. The prosecution was relying on Tim Flynn and corroborating evidence.

Jennifer agreed to Fisher's compromise while reserving the right to object to wording proposed by the prosecution. She submitted proposed language for the pretrial order to Faw before we left the courthouse, but he rejected one word, wanting something mushier. They both talked to the clerk and asked her to get the precise language that Fisher suggested.

Faw also made this observation: "Joan Sahlgren was a punt."

In the parking lot, Jennifer said today felt like a win. She remained convinced we would win at trial, and I was due a karmic payback for all that I had been through.

Jennifer added that having Faw as the lead prosecutor would work to our advantage. He was wooden and not nearly as polished as Theo.

Jennifer said we might get some real help from Director of School Administration Doug Fulton. After the sheriff's office press release of October 2021, I had called Doug, who was on vacation in Finland, to ask what the hell was going on. In an interview with the prosecution, Doug had said that I had no knowledge of the boy's arrest or his transfer or the details of the case.

The prosecution dropped Doug from its witness list.

We wouldn't.

Continuing Irony

Donald Trump was indicted on June 9, 2023, for the mishandling of classified documents.

Glenn Youngkin issued a tweet demonstrating his willingness to kiss MAGA ass and his total lack of a moral backbone: "These charges are unprecedented and it's a sad day for our country, especially in light of what clearly appears to be a two-tiered justice system where some are selectively prosecuted, and others are not."

A justice system where some are selectively prosecuted? I have some thoughts on that subject Glenn.

Youngkin then returned to his primary theme of "parental rights." I'll give him this, he knew how to stay on message. "Parents in Virginia know firsthand what it's like to be targeted by politically motivated actions." Uh, Glenn, Scott Smith was still waiting for your call. Just because you wouldn't have anything to do with someone on a personal level didn't mean you couldn't use them as a political prop.

Having waved the bloody flag of parental rights, Youngkin returned to the plight of poor, persecuted Donald Trump. "Regardless of your party, this undermines faith in our judicial system at exactly the time when we should be working to restore that trust."

Like the way you were restoring trust in education, Glenn?

By the way, you've put a pretty significant dent in my own faith in the judicial system.

Predictably, Youngkin's assertion that a rich, privileged White man, who had long avoided the consequences associated with his reprehensible and illegal behavior, was being persecuted drew predictable reactions.

"It's interesting, as a Black American, to witness this sudden Republican interest in unequal systems of justice," tweeted University of Maryland Assistant Professor Christoph Mergerson. "Palpably bad faith. Extra points for the critical race theory dog whistle. Glenn Youngkin knows his audience."

Well said, Christoph.

I just hoped that none of Youngkin's "audience" ended up on my jury.

Back to Training Camp

Brenda was falling into depression.

"This has to be over," was her constant mantra.

She said that what we were going through was worse than death; I assured my wife it was not. Brenda was convinced that the prosecution had a bombshell surprise they would drop on me during trial. The rules of discovery argued against this, but I had to acknowledge that this case continually defied the rules.

Ten days before the trial, I told her we'd take a Saturday road trip to an undesignated location just to get out of the house.

Shortly before noon, I steered onto Interstate 81 for the location I'd chosen, Carlisle, Pennsylvania. Brenda didn't know where we were going and didn't seem to care. She dozed off for the most part as we headed north.

I had gotten to know Carlisle during my days at *The Winchester Star*. Dickinson College, which boasts one of the most beautiful campuses you'll ever see, had hosted the Washington Redskins training camp for thirty-four years.

Carlisle is a quaint town that's seen a lot of history, having played host to George Washington, Benjamin Franklin, and Molly Pitcher, among many Revolutionary luminaries. On the day we visited, there was a group of reenactors around the courthouse restaging the 1863 Battle of Carlisle, part of the Gettysburg campaign.

We stopped by Bedford Street Antiques, where I bought a 1959 Clem Labine baseball card for 20 percent off. Any time you can get one of the "Boys of Summer" for 20 percent off, you seize the opportunity. The man running the baseball card booth had a collection of several hundred thousand baseball cards that filled several closets and his basement.

It was always nice to talk to a fellow obsessive.

I selected the lunch spot, the Gingerbread Man, a local landmark located in a large alley next to the courthouse. This was the place where sportswriters and Redskins used to hang out back in the day, when members of the media and professional athletes still intermingled socially in such spots. The Gingerbread Man is a faux nineteenth-century establishment featuring dark wood, stained glass, and unnecessary Victorian sculptures. The fare was pub food with burgers as a staple, and music from a jukebox that only played oldies.

I loved it. Brenda tolerated it.

On the way home, we stopped at a mall in Hagerstown, Maryland, where

Brenda bought a new bedspread set and clothes for our grandson.

I didn't ask if we could afford it. Anything to make Brenda happy, no matter the cost.

My wife was becoming melancholy, bordering on depressed.

I would do anything to restore her happiness.

Still Among the Living

There's a wooded access road between the Old Stone Church property and Misty Meadow Lane, which I added to my daily walk to lengthen it. I was on this isolated thoroughfare when I heard a loud gunshot nearby. Some of my rural, hillbilly-survivalist-MAGA neighbors are fond of AR15s. They are in the shoot-first, ask-later camp when it comes to firearms.

Looking down at my bright, white T-shirt, I saw only some minor spaghetti stains from the previous night's dinner. No growing blood stains like you see in the movies. I decided that Misty Meadow Lane would get along just fine without me and turned around.

I was entertaining the thought that I was a ghost until I unlocked and locked the gate on the road leading to the church.

Ghosts couldn't do that.

I looked to the side to see if I still had a shadow. (A key indicator of being a ghost that I remembered from *The Sixth Sense*.)

I had a shadow.

As was my practice, I waved to all the drivers who sped by me on the main road. They waved back. Case closed on the whole ghost thing.

As I began the final week before the trial, I had to admit that I was not in good shape mentally or physically. I was physically exhausted by midafternoon. When I would fall into a deep sleep, I would have bizarre, hallucinatory dreams that would wake me up in a sweat. Brenda had taken to leaving for the guest bedroom in the middle of the night as I snored, grunted, and moved about.

I could see the finish line. I just had to give it one last push.

It was going to take everything I had to get there.

A Predictable, Non-Offer Offer

On June 15, Jennifer Leffler emailed me the following communication from Assistant Attorney General Jason A. Faw:

"Jen,

Theo and I have spoken and believe there is value in meeting one last time in an effort to try to resolve this matter prior to trial. That does not include dropping the charge. However, we'd like to discuss it in person. Are you available at either 3pm today or 10am tomorrow morning? If you are willing to come to our office, we have space, if not, we can walk over to you.

Please let me know."

Jennifer attached the following note with this offer:

"Do you want me to meet with them? I don't see the harm in it, other than wasting my time. We don't have to agree to anything."

I replied:

"I see no harm in meeting, though I agree that it is probably a waste of time.

"I am not going to plead guilty to anything.

"It can't hurt to say we listened to their offer and exhausted all options.

"Please let me know what they say."

They were panicked. That was my interpretation, anyway.

Theo and Faw walked over to Jennifer's office for a three o'clock meeting. It's always a sign of weakness to journey to the other party's home court.

I called Jennifer after the meeting to find out what had been offered.

"Nothing good," was the reply.

Theo and Faw had offered for me to plead guilty to perjury with the proceedings continued for two years. At the end of the two years, the charge would be reduced to obstruction of justice, and I'd be fined $100. Basically, they would get the conviction they wanted, then, after everybody had forgotten about it, it would quietly go away.

Oh, and I'd get fired and lose more than $100,000 in back pay and legal fees.

Jennifer's advice? Reject the deal.

I took my attorney's advice.

Trial Beginnings

After months of anticipating the trial, there was a rush of activity in the days just prior. I was coached on being an effective witness. As I got a window into the people who could sit in judgment of me, a dramatic video came to light. Hurry up and wait had been replaced by a flurry of hurry.

Victim, Not Hero

Brenda and I traveled to Jennifer's Fairfax office for a three-hour trial preparation session.

Jennifer critiqued my responses during prep with the common observation being that they needed to be shorter.

Jennifer said that she had been through hundreds of my emails between May 28, 2021, and mid-October of that year, which had been turned over by the prosecution as part of discovery. There had been no mention of the May 28 "assault."

That would certainly help my case.

We went over Jessica Smith's July 7, 2021, visit to the LCPS Administration

Building. This was what Jennifer was most worried about at the moment. Ultimately, Jennifer came to the conclusion that Jessica Smith's testimony could be classified as "hearsay." I had no direct knowledge of what happened at Stone Bridge High School on May 28, 2021. At the end of the day, it didn't matter what people told me.

Jennifer went over what would happen if Brenda testified.

Brenda said that she was afraid she might cry on the stand.

A display of genuine emotion would work in our favor, according to Jennifer. While she never recommends that clients cry on the stand, if it happened naturally, fine.

While the judge for my trial was supposed to be a mystery, Jennifer thought she knew who it would be. During the previous day's plea-bargain conference, Jason Faw had let slip that it would be Judge Fisher.

I asked Jennifer what her advice would be about continuing my career— albeit briefly—with LCPS. "I wouldn't go back there if I were you. No job is worth this." She also didn't think the school division would pay me the $35,000 in legal fees I'd already paid her.

The Washington Post contacted Jennifer about a plea deal being imminent. I wondered where they got that idea. As Brenda and I were having dinner at a nearby Cheesecake Factory, Jennifer texted that *The Post* wanted a quote from us for a trial preview story on Tuesday. Could I suggest something? Over appetizers, I texted back: "After more than six months of waiting, we look forward to arguing this case in court. We feel confident the facts, when put in context, will exonerate Mr. Byard."

"I like it," Jennifer texted back.

My brilliant attorney's approval meant everything to me.

As we left her office Friday, Jennifer gave me a two-page guide on how a model witness should act on the stand. The bullet points:

- Be truthful;
- Be precise;

- Listen more than you talk;
- Make clear what you don't know;
- Be polite;
- Avoid absolutes;
- Resist attempts to summarize;
- Be careful of repeated questions;
- Pay attention to documents;
- Listen to the question asked;
- Think about how to answer the question asked;
- Answer only the question asked;
- Stop and wait for the next question.

Diving into the Jury Pool

At the end of the trial-preparation session, Jennifer gave me five sheets of paper listing the eighty-two potential jurors for my trial. The people listed on this document reflected Loudoun's population as well as the chasm between the county's economic classes. Software engineers were the most-represented job description. Next, were government contractors, followed by government employees: people employed by the State Department, Parent Office, and local government. There were a few teachers—LCPS and private school— and a smattering of what I called "Average Joes and Janes."

Jennifer asked me to research these people online and give her my opinion of them. Her sixteen-year-old son, Brooks, an aspiring lawyer, was also scouring the Web. I separated the potential jurors into three categories: "Yes," "No," and "Maybe." The "Yeses" and "Maybes" had thirty-two and thirty-nine entries, respectively. I assigned the "Nos" only to people who had an obvious red flag.

The Dunkin' Donuts cashier, bartender, secretary, delivery truck driver, and produce sorter all got a quick yes. I trusted the wisdom of average people. They tended not to overthink. They were wary of the government, especially when they trained the big guns on an average citizen for an incomprehensible offense.

I placed college professors and researchers in the Yes category. An analytical mind would see that the prosecution's case simply didn't make sense. I wanted to have a college student on the jury because there was a chance that they were a former LCPS student and part of my cult of personality. An LCPS teacher could be an effective juror because they could recognize a lot of the administrative bungling around me, and they wouldn't like Tim Flynn when Jennifer got done with him. I also gave a thumbs up to retired women. They could empathize with Brenda if she was put on the stand.

Software engineers, government workers, and contractors went into the Maybe pile. These folks had the biggest online presence, with virtually all of them having a LinkedIn account or biography on a company website. My feeling was that a tech type's logic would see through the flimsy nature of the prosecution's case; it simply was not logical. On the other hand, tech types could be socially maladroit and unresponsive to emotional arguments. They might not respond to my "victimhood." Government workers could fall into two camps: those "gung ho" types who believed in the infallibility of their mission, and the disgruntled who were sick of bureaucratic bullshit. The disgruntled might be skeptical of anything a government representative, such as a prosecutor, told them.

Retired men got a hard "No." They were among LCPS's most vocal critics. Retired military men who were also retired in general, got a double "No." I carefully looked at addresses. I was leery of people who lived in Western Loudoun. This area voted Republican, and there were large homeschool and Mormon communities there. While I don't want it to sound like I was profiling and stereotyping, I was profiling and stereotyping. Political correctness be damned with my ass on the line.

Another definite "No" involved two teachers from private, religious schools. One wrote on her biographical page about how the Lord guided her teaching.

The Almighty had nothing to do with creating the ungodly mess at Stone Bridge.

A Feeling of High Confidence

Jennifer and I had two phone conversations on Saturday, June 17.

The first concerned the local Fox affiliate video of Scott Smith's arrest on June 22, 2021. During the melee, during which Scott Smith was thrown to the floor by deputies, Jessica Smith screamed about her daughter being raped. During my special grand jury testimony, I said that I witnessed Scott Smith's arrest. The prosecution would say that Jessica Smith's screaming was evidence that I knew an "assault" had occurred. Jennifer Leffler said, if asked, I would answer that Smith's screaming didn't register with me because of the chaotic nature of that evening.

And that was the truth.

Jennifer's second call came after I had traveled to my oldest daughter's home in West Virginia. Analyzing the "perjurious" statements I had made, she thought she could get them all dismissed on a motion to strike. The trial could be over before our defense even began. I had the phone on speaker. Brenda was heartened by what she heard.

Jennifer said the only wild card in her optimistic assessment was Judge Fisher.

Eve of the Trial

Jennifer and I spoke at ten in the morning on June 19, after she texted me before seven to set up a time. She had to call me back after the appointed hour because her phone was ringing under a pile of papers when I called at the appointed hour. It was a good sign, I suppose, when your attorney was buried under a pile of paperwork on the eve of the trial.

Apparently, Jason Faw was full of shit; Fisher wouldn't be our judge. Jennifer had done a little networking with her legal colleagues, and it appeared that Douglas Fleming Jr. would be presiding. Jennifer considered this good news since Fleming was considered the most defense-friendly judge on Loudoun's bench.

Theo objected to the possibility of Brenda testifying. In an email, Theo stated, "Your description of what Ms. Byard is intending to testify to strikes me as irrelevant and inadmissible testimony. If you would like to proffer her testimony to the court before the trial gets underway, and the court rules in our favor, then of course she would be free to remain in the courtroom. Otherwise, the rule on witnesses will apply." Brenda, who was in West Virginia babysitting our grandson, was confused when she read this email. Jennifer said we'd get word to Brenda on whether she could be in the courtroom during my trial after tomorrow's ruling. Jennifer added that juries tended to try to connect who in the gallery was connected to the people involved in the trial. Having them connect Brenda with me would be a plus.

I couldn't argue that point.

Jennifer reminded me to say I "heard" something, not that I became "aware" of it if I testified. Something along the lines of "I can't sit here under oath and swear that I hadn't heard that, but I don't remember."

Jennifer went over various testimony scenarios until it felt like my head would explode.

Tuesday, June 20, 2023: First Day of the Trial

On the way into the courthouse, I received good wishes from Bob Barnard of WTTG-TV and Neal Augenstein of WTOP Radio. Deputy Fanelli, the pride of Utica, New York, was, as always, amenable as I went through security.

At the top of the stairs outside the courtroom was half of LCPS's senior administration. I felt embarrassed to have had to duck into the bathroom before reaching the upper level.

Young Brooks had done his homework, combining my fifteen pages of jury notes with his research. We had a thorough analysis of potential jurors. Given the short time frame, our "analysis" relied heavily on first impressions and stereotypes.

Entering the courtroom, Jennifer was greeted enthusiastically by the chief bailiff, Deputy Shakib. He had worked with Jennifer's father in Fairfax. Jennifer and I agreed that his presence boded well for us.

Judge Fleming took the bench after Deputy Shakib gave the customary "All rise . . ." Fleming, an older man (a phrase that also describes me), was stooped and had a gray beard and salt-and-pepper hair. He possessed a deep voice, and his overall demeanor was one of a friendly grandfather.

The first order of business was to take up the bill of particulars/memorandum of understanding controversy. This was to have been worked out by Judge Fisher, but the clerk who was handling the paperwork was on vacation. Fleming had no paperwork to work from.

Your justice system at work, a competent, well-oiled machine.

Fleming was unmoved by the prosecution's effort to have Joan Sahlgren declared an adverse witness. "I'm unconvinced being someone's supervisor makes someone adverse." Fleming also offered some bits of wisdom that made me feel he'd be a fair, impartial jurist. He said he wanted to walk off the bench at the end of the day smarter than when he came on, and he wanted to respect citizens' time when it came to serving on a jury. When an attorney had an objection, Fleming wanted them to stand and say two words citing the legal foundation for the objection. He didn't want attorneys doing long-form orations in front of the jury.

The attorneys argued over whether Brenda, as a potential witness, could be in the courtroom for the entire proceeding. Siding with Theo, Fleming ruled that she would have to wait outside like any other witness. Theo argued that Brenda's testimony might be an attempt to set up a diminished capacity defense.

The judge stepped off the bench to successfully track down Judge Fisher's written orders. The prosecution would be limited to the statements listed in the memorandum of understanding. At 9:53 a.m., I was formally arraigned. In the firmest voice I could muster, I pleaded not guilty. Before I was allowed to make this plea, Fleming asked if I understood the charges against me, was I using drugs or alcohol, was I satisfied with my counsel, and did I want a jury trial.

- Sane? Check.
- Drunk? No.
- On drugs? No.
- Liked my lawyer? Definite yes.
- Was I willing to place my fate into the hands of my fellow citizens? We'd wait and see on that one.

At 10:07 a.m., thirty-four potential jurors entered the courtroom. Following Jennifer's lead, I stood as they came in. There were so many that they overflowed the jury box and spilled into the spectator area at the rear of the courtroom.

"Diverse" was the word that popped into my mind as I gave them the once over. They wore shorts, T-shirts, a hijab, and business casual. One man sported a ponytail, and there were the unruly hair and beards common among tech types. I recognized some of them from their LinkedIn photos.

I felt detached as the proceedings went on, almost like a spectator at a play. Was this normal? I'd been in courtrooms many times before and tried to maintain an air of objectivity as a member of the press. I couldn't be objective now. This was my life on the line. Despite all the games going on in my head, I attempted to project an image of calm.

Jury Selection or, As It Is Formally Known, *Voir Dire*
Like almost every term involved with legal proceedings, there's some Latin

involved. The term involved in jury selection is *voir dire*, "to speak the truth." The process of picking the jurors began with the candidates speaking the truth about what conflicts they might have about sitting impartially on my jury.

One juror said that they knew Kraig Troxell, one of my potential witnesses.

Two said they knew Doug Fulton, another of my witnesses. Another knew LCPS Deputy Superintendent Ashley Ellis, who would testify for the prosecution. To make sure the potential jurors knew who the witnesses were, Fleming had each of them stand in the gallery. When Jessica Smith's turn came, she strode out like a model walking the catwalk.

Fleming said that the scheduled two-day trial might bleed over into a third. Did this present a problem for anyone? Six hands went up. The judge asked the potential jurors if they had formed an opinion of this case "beyond a reasonable doubt." Fleming said that he understood if a juror had some opinion about this case because of the publicity it had received. "If you have a sanitized mind, I'm going to have the clerk . . . take your pulse." I liked this folksy observation. He added that "suspicion or probability of guilt" was not a reason for conviction.

At 10:35 a.m., Jennifer, Theo, Jason Faw, Judge Fleming, the court reporter, and I went to an area beside the bench that was only partially visible to the potential jurors. Those who had stated conflicts came up one by one to be questioned and to determine if they could serve as an effective juror. Here's what this small parade of humanity produced:

- One gentleman had several family members who had flown in from India and become seriously ill. Excused.
- Two women had undergone serious dental surgery and would miss long-scheduled follow-ups if they served on the jury. Excused.
- A young woman said she had to fly to a conference in New York on Thursday; a conference for which she was one of the prime organizers. She was afraid it would affect her

performance review if she was late for the conference. Excused.

- Another woman was in charge of a beach weekend at her in-laws' house where she would be the hostess. She was leaving early Thursday morning. If the trial ran long, she said she would become very, very stressed. Her father-in-law was a former school security officer at an LCPS high school whom I knew well. She was excused, but I wished she hadn't been.

- A young man wearing an orange T-shirt with the word "Golf" on it said he'd seen a good deal about the case in the media and may have formed an opinion. Fleming offered this bit of wisdom, "We're not required to show that Wayde Byard is a bad person." That said, I didn't want this guy. At least he wore his good T-shirt. Excused.

- A University of Virginia student wearing a hoodie and shorts said he might not be able to serve because his residency was really in Charlottesville, which was not part of Loudoun County. Later, he came back to ask about an obscure point of law regarding juries that a classmate had told him about (the gist of this legal nugget being that he shouldn't serve on a jury). Both sides agreed he should be dismissed.

- One juror was related by marriage to school board member Denise Corbo. Hard No.

- A juror that I really wanted was a special education professor from George Mason University. He had knowledge of school law, had worked with LCPS on special-education cases, and had a grasp on how complex it was to work with secondary students. The prosecution had him excluded.

- One man's wife worked at Freedom High School when potential witness Doug Fulton was principal there. He had bumped into Doug on a staff work day when Doug distributed food as a symbol of his appreciation. He ended up on the jury.

- Another man was a former Stone Bridge parent who had a long conversation with Tim Flynn at a "Battle of the Bands" competition. He was not on the final jury.

After this long sidebar, the clerk put all the jurors' names into a plastic box and Fleming randomly selected two. These jurors would automatically be excused by "lottery." The defense and prosecution each got to exclude five jurors, no questions asked. The lottery was to protect the names of those who had been struck by counsel. It was kind of like when they give one guy in the firing squad a blank cartridge without telling him it's a blank. You can walk away from the experience untainted.

At the end of this process, Fleming announced we had our jury of thirteen, including an alternate.

Based on the research Brooks and I had done, I felt we had gotten our "No. 1 draft pick" seated on the jury. She was a medical student, a member of an ethnic minority, likely non-Christian, and LCPS-affiliated (she was a graduate of a Loudoun high school, and her mother taught at another LCPS high school). Neatly dressed in a black suit, she had a pleasant face accented by glasses. This young woman would serve as my bellwether throughout the trial. If I saw her nodding in agreement with a prosecution statement or taking copious notes when a prosecutor was talking, I'd know I was in trouble.

One juror who made me nervous was a "Karen" type: She sported an "I want to see the manager haircut," suburban mom casual clothing that did not come at a casual price, and an attitude that could kill at fifty paces.

It was amazing how judgmental I could be based on superficial impressions.

Before breaking for lunch, Fleming told the jurors they couldn't ask one another "What do you think so far?" They could take notes on testimony, but these notes would be collected and destroyed at trial's end.

PART VI

The Trial

The Trial Proper

The preliminary work done, the trial proper began. Up next? Testimony, side-bars, hearings without the jury present, and a lot of things you can't fit into an hour of Law & Order. *There was no high drama, but some low comedy managed to find its way into the courtroom. If my future hadn't been hanging in the balance, I don't know if I would have watched this.*

The Fight Over Joan's Adversity

Before opening arguments, the court decided whether Joan Sahlgren was an adverse witness.

Joan was more composed than during her June 8 hearing. She testified that she had my work number on her cell phone and that I hadn't been fired. Joan also testified that our media consultant, Dr. Lori Muehler, hadn't advised her to push back against Glenn Youngkin's Executive Order 4.

Jason Faw admitted that Joan was not hostile. She said my return to work was a possibility. "Nobody in this trial or planet is in the position Ms. Sahlgren is in," offered Faw. Fleming said this relationship alone would not create an adverse interest. "One wonders if this makes any difference at all. That being said . . ."

Fleming declared Joan an "adverse" rather than a "hostile" witness. The prosecution could ask her leading questions, but not display overt hostility —a death by a thousand cuts as opposed to having your throat slit.

Opening Arguments

It was decided that the day's proceedings wouldn't go past five so that jurors could vote in the primary elections, even though virtually nobody voted in Virginia's primaries.

Theo Stamos began her opening argument at 2:44 p.m. She used a large TV screen and featured a PowerPoint presentation. The opening title, in a sickly yellow color, struck me in its starkness: COMMONWEALTH VS. WAYDE BYARD.

Theo used a phrase she would use several times, "this very courthouse," in explaining the scene of my "crime." She moved through a timeline of all the events that led to my supposed cover-up of a rape:

- In the spring of 2021, LCPS (actually the school board) sought to implement Policy 8040, defining the rights of transgender students.
- Between August and October 2021, a student involved in an alleged sexual assault was moved from Stone Bridge High School to Broad Run High School.
- In January 2022, Governor Youngkin signed Executive Order 4.
- In March 2022, the special grand jury was impaneled.
- On August 2, 2022, I testified before the special grand jury.

Theo then stated that on May 28, 2021, Stone Bridge's principal "Dr. Flynn" had a problem on his hands and did "something he has done many times before" (called me). She said Flynn told me about a "sexual assault" and that this information should have been included in the initial message to the community. Theo noted that Superintendent Scott Ziegler, Deputy Superintendent Ashley Ellis, and Joan all had a part in conceiving the original message and that the only reason they were involved was because the incident involved a sexual assault. Despite this, Theo noted that the original message focused on a disruptive parent. "Nothing to see here, move along."

Theo then moved on to a videoconference meeting, on the Teams platform—that I hadn't been a part of. She noted that Flynn used the phrases "anal penetration" and "rape" during this meeting. Theo went on to say that the boy involved in the Stone Bridge incident had been quietly transferred to Broad Run and that this quiet was shattered on October 6 when LCPS became "the epicenter of quite a big news story."

Theo then asked several questions:

"Was there a cover-up?"

"Was there a lack of transparency?"

"Were people withholding information?"

Theo concluded that the evidence would show that LCPS administrators "resolved to lie" and that lies were material to the special grand jury being convened and its work that followed.

In her opening arguments, Jennifer said our defense would be based on common sense and that I was "the fall guy," a term I absolutely detested. In my view, a "fall guy" was a hapless stooge, served up because he was too stupid to offer a credible defense. I had never wanted to be publicly labeled "hapless" or a "stooge." Who would?

Jennifer was barely into her opening argument when Theo objected to questions Jennifer would ask the jury to consider. Fleming called a sidebar, and the clerk switched on the noise-canceling machine, which sounded like the static that came out of televisions in bygone times after the broadcast day ended. Theo was animated in the pantomime that I observed from my seat, which had a much better view than the jury.

When Jennifer resumed her opening, she hit on the materiality of the charges against me. What, if anything, could I have done differently on May 28, 2021, if I'd known about a sexual assault? Afterward, Jennifer and I agreed that Theo was trying to throw my attorney off her game through the opening-statement objection.

The Prosecution's Star Witness

Tim Flynn was the first person Theo Stamos called to the stand. In short order, her questions established that:

- Flynn was a six-year veteran of the US Army Reserve.
- He had been employed by LCPS for sixteen years and was in his fifth year at Stone Bridge.
- He and I had a cordial relationship, "We've been work friends, friends on Facebook." We also bantered a lot about sports.
- Flynn stated that I'd called Bingo over the public address system as a surprise for students and that I'd allowed a teacher to use my image on a T-shirt as a fundraiser.

Theo then focused on May 28, 2021. Flynn said two assistant principals told him about a sexual assault in a bathroom. He testified he'd seen "nothing like this. This is unique." Flynn recounted Scott Smith's demeanor when he arrived at the school. He said that Smith was enraged and wanted the boy who did this. Messages were coming from the nearby library about students and staff being alarmed by the intensity of the confrontation in the office and the strong language being used. Flynn said that Smith asked "Who the fuck are you?" when they first met in the office and that SRO Tavis Henry had to intervene to end this interaction. Eventually, Smith was removed from the building. Flynn characterized this as a "huge disruption to school." Later in his testimony, he said that Smith had indicated that he wanted to "go after the boy who did this." Flynn added that students and staff were so upset, the school's United Mental Health Team had been called in.

Between 2:30 p.m. and 3:00 p.m., Flynn said he contacted me as he had many times before. The gist of Flynn's testimony was that he had a "crystal-clear memory" and that he had told me everything about the May 28 incident, including the fact that it was a sexual assault. However, some things leaked into his testimony that showed his memory hadn't been all that clear. Flynn was asked if I was on the Teams videoconference during which the alleged concept of sexual assault was discussed. "I don't recall" was the response. (I wasn't.) He said there were two Teams calls—at 3:30 p.m. and

7:30 p.m. that day to discuss the assault. Flynn said that the second Teams call occurred when he was at home; he remembered having to quiet his dog and children so that he could participate.

The alleged second call would become a huge deal in my defense.

Flynn also confirmed that he uttered the words "it went sideways" to me, which were the words that stuck in my mind.

When Jennifer Leffler cross-examined Flynn, she attacked his "crystal-clear memory" and tried to prove that he was covering his ass. Jennifer asked why he had met with prosecutors twice and refused to meet with her. Flynn said he did so on the advice of his lawyer.

Jennifer asked him if he was positive about the second Teams call. Flynn replied in the affirmative. Jennifer asked Flynn if he was familiar with the concept of UTC code. He was not.

This would become a key part of Jennifer's closing argument.

Jennifer asked Flynn if he had shared teaching assistant Elaine Rosales's email with his superiors during the Teams call. This was the email in which Rosales expressed concerns that the boy would do something everyone would regret. Flynn answered that he didn't share the email. Jennifer asked why. Flynn answered he thought this was a case where a teacher's assistant was having a classroom management issue.

Jennifer asked Flynn why he mentioned a previous incident at Tuscarora High School involving the female victim of the May 28 incident. Flynn answered that the Tuscarora incident involved something that happened in a Leesburg park. He added that he didn't have all the details on that situation. "There were a lot of questions to be answered."

Flynn then answered some questions that helped my defense.

Flynn stated that he would not have asked me to mention the sexual assault in his initial message to the Stone Bridge community. That could have compromised an ongoing investigation by law enforcement.

Flynn said the primary topic of our conversation on May 28 had been Scott Smith's behavior. He later said that principals have the right to alter the verbiage of draft messages I send them. Flynn encapsulated my motivation behind the draft communication, "[I] need to set him up for success."

Flynn agreed that he had mentioned that this was a boyfriend-girlfriend situation gone wrong to me on May 28.

During his testimony, Flynn turned a deepening shade of red. He fidgeted and took several swigs from a bottle of water. These were the kinds of mannerisms I hoped the jury noticed.

Leaving the courtroom, everyone who saw him told me he appeared shaken.

If this was the prosecution's "star" witness, the prosecution was in trouble.

Tavis Henry's Testimony

The former Stone Bridge SRO is an imposing African-American man. He's the kind of solid, middle-linebacker type who conveys instant authority. He was wearing a sharp, earth-toned suit as he took the witness stand.

Prosecutor Jason Faw questioned Henry. Faw laid out the alleged reason that I hadn't mentioned the words "sexual assault" in my draft message: "He does not want his name attached to that."

Henry said that in the initial interview of the female victim in the assistant principal's office, the victim's friend had done most of the talking. He added that the female victim and the boy in this incident appeared to know one another. "These people were seen together." In fact, Henry had seen them together on a regular basis and added that they were with each other all the time.

Asked what the boy was wearing at the time of the May 28 incident, Henry described it as a "kilt." Henry later testified that video footage showed the boy and girl entering and leaving the downstairs bathroom where the alleged assault took place, together.

Henry said that Scott Smith showed up thirty minutes after the alleged victim came to the office and "changed the dynamic of the investigation." Smith refused to show ID at the main entrance and was extremely angry. Henry said he used his de-escalation training to calm Smith down before allowing him into the school. Once inside, Henry said that Smith confronted everyone in the office and that Henry was "100 percent" focused on Smith.

Henry testified that Flynn was "riled up" after a confrontation with Smith and wanted to know when the Smith family had left the Stone Bridge campus as he considered a no-trespass order.

Henry testified that the school administration did not know where the boy was while all this was transpiring. The administration undertook a search of classrooms where the boy had been and searched video cameras in an effort to determine his whereabouts. He was finally located in the bus loop as he attempted to board a bus to go home.

The prosecution's examination of Henry ended at 4:48 p.m., and with that ended the first day of the trial.

Jennifer began cross-examination of Henry the following morning. As the day began, I noticed Theo Stamos looked haggard. She'd ditched the two strands of pearls she wore the previous day; nothing to clutch. Was the pressure of the trial getting to her? Did Theo feel she was losing? Was this just wishful thinking on my part?

Jennifer established that I was not at Stone Bridge on May 28 or the days that followed.

Henry confirmed a conversation that he had with Flynn on May 28. "When I talked with Dr. Flynn, I said the girl said she was raped." How was this helping, Jennifer? My attorney was testing my faith in her. Jennifer recovered by getting Henry to testify that the boy and girl were "within each other's space" when he previously observed them. As I sat at the defense table, my feeling was that the "consensual sex" line of questioning was bombing.

Jennifer delved into the specifics of the Tuscarora incident with Henry. Faw objected. Fleming asked Jennifer, "Do you wish to lay a foundation?"

Jennifer did. Fleming allowed Henry to testify about what he had told Flynn about another alleged assault. As a result of this conversation, Jennifer asked, did Flynn or Henry comment on the alleged victim's credibility?

Theo objected and everyone involved went to the left side of the bench for a sidebar. Sidebars were becoming the majority of my trial. When the transcript was converted to print form, I wondered how the court reporter would describe the long intervals when the hissing of the noise-canceling machine filled the courtroom. During this sidebar, it appeared that Fleming was lecturing Jennifer in fatherly tones. Jennifer later confirmed this and said she found this condescending. Theo nodded in agreement as Fleming talked. Faw stood separate from Theo at the edge of the group and looked resigned. It appeared he had clearly been assigned the role of second-stringer.

The objection was sustained. After fiddling with her pen, Jennifer asked Henry a few more questions. She asked which was worse on May 28, the parent behavior or the alleged assault. The prosecution objected, and the objection was quickly sustained.

Henry's testimony ended on a bad note for us.

Still, I didn't think the prosecution had landed any devastating blows.

Corrine Czekaj

Loudoun County Sheriff's Office Detective Corrine Czekaj was the prosecution's next witness. She looked smart and professional as she took the stand, wearing pants and a long-sleeved, white sheriff's office shirt, her handcuffs and sidearm clearly visible. She accented this ensemble with serious black work shoes and a shoulder bag of the type detectives use to carry their laptop and official investigative notes.

This woman was all business.

Her testimony was also all business—a just-the-facts recitation of the timeline concerning when the female victim was treated and the boy arrested.

Jennifer asked the detective if she had ever emailed me. Detective Cze-kaj's succinct answer: "No."

Kevin Lewis

Next up on the prosecution's witness list was LCPS Chief Operating Officer Kevin Lewis.

Theo Stamos examined Kevin, who appeared as relaxed as his business-casual attire. Theo started by asking Kevin about the now-infamous Teams video meeting on May 28. Theo asked Kevin about the boy wearing girls' clothing that day. "I don't recall" was Kevin's answer. Why had he mentioned Policy 8040 in his email? Kevin replied because it was under review by the school board.

Kevin soon made a statement to Theo that I had made during special grand jury testimony: "I'm not sure what you are asking me." Theo was speaking more quickly and in a louder tone. As was her habit, her questions were soliloquies that left it up to the witness to determine what she was asking. Kevin's speech was slow and measured, which made Theo appear somewhat hysterical by comparison. Theo was also wandering away from the podium, creating problems when it came to her being heard clearly. Fleming admonished her to return to the podium.

There was the inevitable sidebar to argue about what Kevin could testify about. He sat and smiled as the legal parties decamped to the side of the bench and the noise machine turned on. Jen lost her objection, and Theo started hammering on Policy 8040 again. "I don't mean to be obtuse about this . . ." (Actually, she did).

Theo talked about May 28 and the incident in the bathroom. "We didn't know about the incident," said Kevin. He was summoned to the school because of the unruly parent. Theo asked Kevin about UTC. He replied, "something about the time."

Jennifer objected to Theo leading the witness and, for once, the objection was sustained. Two other objections followed and were also sustained. Maybe Jennifer was making some inroads with Fleming.

Theo shifted her attention to a rally outside the Administration Building on August 10, 2021. Kevin said he couldn't recall a specific rally on that date. There had been numerous rallies and counter-protests outside the Administration Building that summer. Theo asked if Kevin was concerned about a possible thunderstorm that day.

Another sidebar was called, after which it was announced that the prosecution would have no more questions.

Jennifer's cross-examination was brief.

Had Kevin communicated with me? No.

Had there been a Teams meeting at 7:30 p.m. on May 28, 2021? No.

Was I on the Teams meeting that did occur concerning the May 28, 2021, incident at Stone Bridge High School? No.

No further questions.

As Kevin left the stand, I had to wonder why he had been called at all.

The "Adverse" Joan Sahlgren

Next up for the prosecution was my boss, Joan Sahlgren.

Jason Faw started the questioning and offered Joan, who was suffering from allergies, some water. She refused. He asked Joan about her prior employment. She said she formerly worked for a trade association representing the paper industry. Faw said he wouldn't make any Dunder Mifflin jokes. The attempt at humor predictably fell flat.

Joan went through the exercise of identifying my position on the LCPS org chart. She stated that I was in charge of the office when she was out. Joan stated that I was the FOIA officer. Faw asked if my job entailed "Being aware of what was going on." Joan replied: "I think that would be a bit broad."

Faw began zeroing in on May 28. Joan began coughing—and apologizing for doing so—before Jennifer got the bailiff to hand her the extra water bottle in her purse. (It's amazing what Jennifer had in her purse. More on that later.)

Joan corrected Faw when he referred to the mass email communications system as Connect Ed. That term had gone out about a decade ago, the correct terminology was Blackboard Mass Notification. This was a small point, I know, but I had to wonder if all the small mistakes the prosecution was making were having an effect on the jury's confidence in their case.

Joan said she wouldn't have put a rape allegation in the May 28 message.

Faw began hitting Joan with her special grand jury testimony. He said that I was the one who was filling her in on what was happening at Stone Bridge. Joan replied that others were giving her information. "I also said it could have come from other people."

"Can you give me some context?" said Faw as he began shuffling through papers on the prosecutor's table. I wondered if the jury was observing the confusion at the prosecutor's table. Small things . . .

Faw reviewed a paper copy of Joan's special grand jury testimony and stated that she knew about the sexual assault, "Facts that would pertain to a public message." "I don't think I would agree with that," was Joan's reply, adding that the main problem on May 28 was the disruptive parent.

Faw handed Joan emails that had passed between us on May 28. In one of the emails, she complimented me on my work. I already knew there was no "smoking gun" here and had to question the relevancy of Faw's actions.

Faw handed Joan my email from October 8, 2021, where I alerted senior administration about questions from Luke Rosiak of the *Daily Wire*: "All, I believe this should receive immediate attention." Joan replied, "I don't know. I don't remember. I would have to reread the article. I don't know," when asked about her reaction to this message.

Joan was asked to recall the summer of 2021 and if she initially linked the October 6 arrest at Broad Run with the May 28 incident at Stone Bridge. Joan said that she didn't make this linkage.

There ensued a lot of stage whispering and paper shuffling going on at the prosecutor's table. Jennifer leaned over and whispered, "They're mad."

Faw attempted a more direct tactic with Joan. "Do you remember saying under oath . . ."

Jennifer objected and Fleming sustained, admonishing Faw like a naughty child. Theo asked for the judge's indulgence while she and Faw conferred. They decided they would ask more general questions about "Mr. Byard." Joan gave a general vote of confidence to my abilities. Jennifer objected at this point (but not about my general abilities). "I think this line of questioning has been asked and answered." She was overruled, but the whispering among the prosecution continued before its questioning quickly ended, and the jurors were granted their eleven o'clock break.

When they came back, Jennifer cross-examined Joan. She quickly established several facts:

- Did Joan know if I was the one who told her about the sexual assault? "I do not."
- Joan didn't know if she was on the Teams meeting and didn't know if I was on it.
- I would not have been allowed to send out a message about a sexual assault while an investigation was still in progress.
- The most common questions from the media during the summer of 2021 concerned the suspension of Tanner Cross, Policy 8040, and CRT.
- Prior to October 6, there were no media inquiries about the assault at Stone Bridge.
- Did I have any authority regarding student discipline? Placement? Criminal investigations? Joan answered, no, no, and no.
- Joan said she heard Scott Ziegler's statement on no sexual assaults happening in LCPS bathrooms during the June 22, 2021, school board meeting, but didn't know if I had heard it.

The prosecution asked Fleming for some time before it began its redirect questioning. "Just briefly, your honor," said Faw. There was obvious confusion among our opponents. After "briefly," Faw began hammering a familiar line of questioning. Did Joan, and more specifically I, have any interest in why the parent at Stone Bridge was so irate? "We're very concerned with student privacy," was Joan's answer.

Things went on in this vein for a bit longer before Joan was dismissed from the witness stand. She may have hurt my defense a little, but certainly not much. She had not provided the prosecution with the "smoking gun" that they so desperately needed.

A Prosecution Witness Who Earned My Sympathy

The prosecution stated it would have "documentary evidence" from its next witness.

This evidence was offered by Josh Hetzler, an attorney for the Founding Freedoms Law Center in Richmond. Founding Freedoms, the legal arm of the Family Foundation, was launched on July 1, 2020. Its mission is "to engage in the legal arena to preserve and promote the fundamental principles of life and liberty in the Commonwealth of Virginia."

Hetzler was a handsome young man in a nice suit who appeared a bit sullen and shaken on the stand (I would later learn why). He was there to introduce a video clip of the August 10, 2021, rally outside the Administration Building. The video depicted noted firebrand, and former state senator, Richard "Dick" Black, under a large, temporary shelter of the type that springs up on the sidelines of youth sports events. Black was using a portable sound system to berate LCPS's administration about its treatment of "a father who was getting up to speak after me (at the June 22, 2021, school board meeting)." Black said—actually shouted—that this father was going to talk about his daughter being sodomized by a boy wearing a dress.

Before showing the clip, Faw fussed over the various technical options through which it could be shown. Amateur hour.

Under prosecution questioning, Hetzler said he didn't film the video clip, which had been posted to YouTube on August 19, 2021. "It's not my video clip. I didn't take the video." Hetzler said that he hadn't heard Black make these allegations before August 10 and allowed that he had heard Black speak several times, maybe ten, but couldn't name exact dates. Hetzler said that he was at the June 22, 2021, Loudoun County School Board meeting.

Under cross-examination, Jennifer asked Hetzler if he had seen me at the August 10 rally. "I don't remember seeing him."

Later, Brenda told me that she had spoken to Josh Hetzler before his testimony. He, his wife, and fourteen-month-old son stayed with friends in Loudoun the night before his testimony. Josh fell down the stairs of his friend's house while carrying the baby. He and his wife spent the night before his testimony in the hospital while his son was tested for a concussion. Fortunately, the baby was fine.

Josh told Brenda he didn't know why he was there.

I didn't either.

I was sorry he had to endure every parent's worst nightmare to provide meaningless testimony.

A Not-So-Special Special Agent

I'll state up front that my impression of Special Agent Eric Deel of the Virginia State Police is that he's a nice guy. That's saying something when someone testifies against you. He's about my age and drew a duty—serving a special grand jury—that you get at the end of your career. This was not a task for an up-and-comer.

Deel took the stand wearing a bright red shirt, which didn't fit the typical style of law enforcement. His unconventional style was reflected in the manner he answered questions—vaguely—not in the crisp, clipped diction I'd seen law-enforcement types use on the stand in the past. Deel said he couldn't remember how long he had served the special grand jury. He affirmed that I was sworn in to testify under oath and verified a copy of my testimony transcript, which was later given to the jury. When asked how many witnesses appeared before the special grand jury, Deel estimated fifty.

It was decided that Deel would need to testify later in the trial and that he should remain in the courthouse. He came back to the stand twice.

The line of questioning for his second appearance was a newspaper article from *Loudoun Now* published on August 17, 2021. The article detailed Scott Smith being found guilty of disorderly conduct and resisting arrest for his scuffle during the June 22 school board meeting.

Part of my everyday duties had been to compile a twice-daily media report for senior administration. I did this using Meltwater, a digital clipping service. On a busy day, I'd forward twenty to thirty stories, scanning the headlines to see what could be of interest to senior administration and doing very little in-depth reading. Near the end of the brief story in question, it mentioned Smith's "anger about an alleged assault of an immediate family member inside a bathroom by a person identifying as gender fluid." Nowhere did it say "sexual assault," which was a point Jennifer would reinforce when Jason Faw incorrectly said the words "sexual assault" in relation to this article during his closing arguments.

Deel said he clicked on the link in the email on June 8, 2023, after being provided the link by the prosecution. He testified that it was the only email he had read in conjunction with my case. Deel said he didn't know if I had read the article.

Another Hail Mary from the prosecution.

Deel's third appearance came as a witness for the defense. Only the noise-canceling machine had been a greater presence at my trial.

Deel looked shaky as Jennifer cross-examined him. Deel said he served subpoenas for LCPS emails, but that he only reviewed one: the email containing the *Loudoun Now* article supplied by the prosecution.

Had he seen any document connecting me and the words "sexual assault"? No.

Deel was present when Theo Stamos questioned Tim Flynn about the 7:30 p.m. May 28, 2021, Teams call, but he didn't ask Flynn about this matter himself. Deel said he didn't know what UTC meant.

Did he inquire about why Flynn mentioned an incident involving Tuscarora High School and the girl involved in the Stone Bridge incident? "I asked him no questions."

Theo Stamos then cross-examined Deel. She established that he'd been a member of the Virginia State Police for thirty-four-plus years. This was the second time he'd served as an investigator for a special grand jury, although he'd presented evidence to a regular grand jury on many occasions. Theo stated that the special grand jurors were the primary investigators of evidence in this case, not Deel. "You weren't investigating if this perjury occurred?" Theo asked. "Yes ma'am," was the reply.

Jennifer looked a little concerned as Deel left the stand, but I didn't think any damage had been done to our case.

Jessica Smith

At 12:25 p.m. on the first day of my trial, the jury decided it would hear one more witness before going to lunch: Jessica Smith, mother of the victim at Stone Bridge.

Fashion tip: Don't wear Crocs to court. The first thing the jury heard from Jessica Smith was the sound of her footwear moving toward the witness stand after she was sworn in. Squish. Squish. Squish. Squish. Squish. Squish.

Jessica's black Crocs matched her all-black ensemble: black blouse, black pants accented by a serious bun. She spoke in a loud, aggressive manner.

Jessica said that she owned a plumbing business with her husband. Her husband, Scott Smith, was a constant presence in the courtroom, as was his handler, Ian Prior. Scott Smith wore a short-sleeved shirt, neat tan pants, and an ever-present baseball cap. Prior modeled suburban dad chic: high-end jeans, button-down shirt, and sports coat. I noticed his Don Jr. beard and perfectly coiffed, camera-ready hair were growing increasingly gray. As I viewed this political odd couple, I couldn't help but come to the conclusion that Ian Prior was a world-class hypocrite. He wouldn't take the time to spit on someone like Scott Smith under ordinary circumstances. Scott Smith was only a prop to him; something to help grab airtime with Laura Ingraham and Tucker Carlson.

Theo Stamos's first question resulted in an ever-increasing number of sidebars. "Are you testifying with the support of your daughter?" During the following conference next to the bench, Theo looked nervous and broken as Judge Fleming spoke to her. Jason Faw also looked nervous. I watched Jessica Smith on the stand, her eyes were blank. Her demeanor reminded me of a shark's: lifeless, but ready to strike.

I hoped she was not about to take a chunk out of me.

Theo asked Jessica if she "had occasion" to go to Stone Bridge High School on May 28, 2021. Affirmative.

Did she attend the June 22, 2021, meeting of the Loudoun County School Board? Yes, it was the first time she had attended a school board meeting in person. Jessica added that her daughter had led the Pledge of Allegiance at a January school board meeting.

Jessica said that Scott Smith arrived first at the June 22 meeting and that she witnessed the altercation that led to his arrest.

After some technical wrangling, on par for the prosecution, the video of Jessica Smith screaming at the June 22, 2021, school board meeting was shown. Jessica Smith verified its veracity and looked smug as she spoke. The video shown in court was not, however, the one I saw on my phone the previous Saturday. It was a generic video of the incident stripped of the identifying Fox News graphics. The sound was indistinct. During my special grand jury testimony, I said that I was "a few feet" (meaning thirty or forty feet) from Scott Smith as he was arrested. The video panned around the area of Scott Smith's arrest, but I was nowhere in the frame. Jessica Smith saying the word "rape" was clearly audible, but the sound was nowhere as crisp as it had been on the Fox video. My brother and I talked about this later. He speculated that Fox had pulled up a specific soundtrack (they had a sound-board at the meeting) and had enhanced it for broadcast.

The murky sound was not helped by feeding the audio through a projector. The resulting muddy audio conveyed a true sense of the chaos of June 22. There were the sounds of people trying to hold public comment using a portable public address system. The final shot was of Doug Fulton having a verbal confrontation with the ever-present local lunatic.

Later in her testimony, Jessica was asked how many people were in the school board meeting room when the video was shot. "A lot, 300 people maybe." She added that the atmosphere in the room was chaotic.

Jennifer said that she was not going to question Jessica Smith about the video.

I concurred. Let it speak, or not, for itself.

Theo turned to Jessica Smith's visit to the Administration Building in July 2021.

I remembered this brief meeting well. I was called from my office, which was then adjacent to the building's lobby to talk to someone seeking information. Jessica Smith, a receptionist, and I were the only people in the lobby, which I remembered being somewhat dark and cool.

Jessica Smith testified that she had asked me for an "incident report." She said, correctly, that I had told her incident reports were kept by the sheriff's office, and she would need to seek the report from law enforcement. Jessica Smith described my attitude toward her as "dismissive."

She didn't utter the words "sexual assault."

Jessica Smith testified that she didn't speak to me or Tim Flynn on May 28.

After her testimony concluded, my assessment was that Jessica Smith had done no major damage.

The worst the jury could conclude from her testimony was that I was "dismissive."

Keeping Me from Being
My Own Worst Enemy

During the following lunch break, Jennifer Leffler produced the peanut butter and jelly sandwiches and apple slices that she kept in her purse. You could tell she coached youth sports.

After they completed lunch, the jury was instructed to read my special grand jury testimony. I reread it. Doing so convinced me that I should accept a piece of important legal advice that I was hearing around the lunch table: I shouldn't testify on my own behalf.

Taken by itself, my special grand jury testimony wasn't damaging. It showed, however, that I was combative and could be goaded into saying much more than I should. Jennifer, Mary Herbert, Jonathan Phillips (Jennifer's law partner), and legal savant Brooks Graham (Jennifer's son) were unanimous in their verdict that I shouldn't take the stand.

At 2:35 p.m., the bailiff confirmed the jury had read my special grand jury testimony, and at 2:40 the trial resumed.

Ashley Ellis's Notes
Deputy Superintendent Dr. Ashley Ellis was the only person who took notes during the infamous May 28 Teams meeting.

Accurate notes.

This would become very important to my defense.

Theo Stamos asked Ashley to read her notes, which she had recorded in a steady, clear hand. There were three major phrases noted:

- "Anal penetration."
- "Oral sex."
- "Police handling."

Ashley did not write down the words "sexual assault."

"When was the last time you heard about anal penetration at one of your schools?" Theo asked.

Ashley was asked about an email involving the composition of the May 28 Blackboard Connect message to the Stone Bridge community. "Can we say, confined to the main office, not sure that is true," she had written. Ashley testified that she didn't recall why she wrote this. "I'm guessing. I don't have context."

She added that the disruption in Stone Bridge's main office was the main focus on May 28.

Theo asked Ashley if, as the number two administrator in the school division, she was routinely involved in the crafting of school messages. "I'm rarely involved in drafting a message about a disruptive parent."

Theo switched the focus of her questioning to October 2021. She began asking the compound, word-salad questions that got witnesses tangled up during the special grand jury. Jennifer successfully objected to the overly complex form of these queries.

Had Ashley read negative articles about LCPS? "They were very unpleasant. It was a horrible situation."

There were questions about the Blankingship & Keith report and the Title IX investigation or lack thereof.

Had Ashley had conversations about her job security? No.

Jennifer Leffler then cross-examined Ashley Ellis. The facts she elicited were short and to the point:

- There was no 7:30 p.m. Teams meeting on May 28, 2021. "I do not recall this at all."
- She and I had no direct or indirect conversations about the May 28 incident.
- I was not on the Teams meeting.
- The superintendent's cabinet was privy to information that other employees (read me) were not privy to.
- Ashley wrote down the most important words from the May 28 Teams call, including "alleged inappropriate act" and "no trespass." She did not record the words "rape" or "alleged sexual assault."
- Ashley did remember Tim Flynn telling her, "The girl arranged to have sex in the bathroom."

Ashley said that she had no inquiries about the arrest of the male Stone Bridge student until October.

When Theo asked Ashley further questions during redirect, Ashley said "[I] don't have a clear time line in my head" about the incidents related to the events of May 28, 2021, at Stone Bridge High School. Theo's other questions had nothing to do with me.

I thought to myself that I might be the only defendant who was basically a spectator at my own trial. What seemed like hours went by without my name being mentioned.

Ashley is a tall woman in her forties with a girlish smile, sensible bob haircut, and friendly manner. You can definitely picture her as the popular English teacher she once was. Ashley looked emotionally pained and stricken as she left the courtroom after her testimony.

The opposition spontaneously confirmed how devastating Ashley's testimony was to the prosecution's case. Shortly after she left the stand, Brenda saw Ian Prior hustle Scott Smith into a small conference room at the entrance to the courtroom. The sound of Smith shouting "Liar! Liar! Liar!" could be heard through the closed door.

The Resting of the Prosecution

After Corrine Czekaj returned briefly to the witness stand to detail the charges filed against the boy involved in the Stone Bridge and Broad Run incidents, the prosecution rested. I really hadn't seen any major damage that their witnesses had done. Tim Flynn certainly hadn't helped. They had provided no documents to prove I knew about a sexual assault before October 7, 2021.

With the jury out of the courtroom, Jennifer Leffler began arguing her motion to strike: stating the reasons why the commonwealth had failed to prove its case and why the trial should end in my favor.

A Jarring Reality Check

At the end of the trial's second day, Judge Fleming conducted a hearing that destroyed any sense of overconfidence the defense may have been feeling. We rebounded with some brief, but strong witnesses and a reference to an obscure time measurement that looked like it could undermine the testimony of the prosecution's star witness.

A Judicial Knockout

In the weeks leading up to the trial, Jennifer thought she had a good chance of having the trial end on the motion to strike, which was heard with the jury out of the courtroom. That hope evaporated during the first two days of the trial as Judge Fleming's statements made it clear that he wanted this case decided by a jury.

Jennifer's points in her argument to strike seemed valid:

- The prosecution needed two witnesses, or one witness with corroborating evidence, to "turn the scale" against me. She said that Flynn was the only witness and that no corroboration had been presented. No one, other than Flynn, could say what we had talked about on May 28, 2021.
- Jennifer noted that I couldn't be placed at the rally where Dick Black made his speech.
- Jessica Smith couldn't place me close to her at the June 22 school board meeting.
- There were no emails showing that I knew about a sexual assault before October 7.
- There was no evidence that Flynn told me who Scott Smith was. Zero.

Judge Fleming smiled and nodded as Jennifer made her argument. "Maybe," I thought, "the motion to strike had a chance." Glancing at the prosecution table buoyed this hope. With no pearls to clutch, Theo was wringing her hands.

Fleming called the jury back into the courtroom to ask if they wished to go on with testimony into the night. He wanted to know their tolerance for extending the day. "If I'm causing someone to miss a twenty-fifth anniversary dinner, I want to know."

Jennifer told the court she would call three or four witnesses for the defense. An initial poll of the jury showed one juror wanting to push through, with the rest falling into the "indifferent" category. If the jury stayed, Fleming said pizza could be provided. "I can't promise a Michelin meal."

Theo Stamos piped up at this juncture, noting she was the "senior person" in the courtroom. She estimated the trial would go on to 9:00 p.m.

or 10:00 p.m. "I don't disagree," said Fleming. The jurors quickly decided that they had had enough and were dismissed until nine in the morning on Thursday.

With the jury out of the courtroom, Jason Faw rebutted Jennifer's motion to strike. He stated my quotes cited as perjury constituted corroboration. Faw said that I "can't hide behind the splitting hairs that his attorney is hiding behind." Faw noted that the judge had to view the motion to strike in a light most favorable to the commonwealth. He added that I was indicted for one count of perjury because the commonwealth couldn't indict me eight times.

Faw said my guilt or innocence was a matter for a jury, not a judge. Fleming looked stern as the prosecutor said this. Faw quickly recovered and said the verdict was "a jury question, your honor."

Faw presented much of what he would say in his closing argument using PowerPoint to make his points. He cited the *Loudoun Now* article: "That would cause any reasonable person to ask questions." Faw noted that I was the "one person paid by taxpayers to know what's happening."

Jennifer had the final word. She said the commonwealth was bound by their witnesses. They didn't have two or more witnesses or one witness and corroborating evidence to show I had committed perjury. There was the matter of Ashley's notes, which didn't mention "sexual assault." There were no media inquiries regarding sexual assault before October 2021. Most of the prosecution witnesses said they had no interaction with me.

Jennifer's argument ended, and Fleming took a moment to consider the motion to strike. The attorneys shuffled papers. Faw began packing up for the day. (Or was he packing it in on the trial, knowing the motion would be granted?) Outside the courtroom, I heard people talking loudly and laughing.

What happened next was not a laughing matter.

Judge Fleming gave the prosecution a road map to my conviction, going through my nine statements and witness testimony to show how I could be convicted of perjury. "We're here because it's very material," Fleming said of the evidence. Jennifer got up to object to the depth in which Fleming was discussing the case, but Fleming waved her off.

"The jury will decide," was Fleming's ultimate ruling. The motion to strike was denied at 6:04 p.m.

I was relieved that I had taken Jennifer's advice to seek a jury trial rather than a verdict from the bench.

At the back of the courtroom, Scott Smith seemed happy as Ian Prior led him away.

I was weak at the knees as I obeyed the bailiff's command "All rise" as Fleming left the courtroom. Jennifer said she hoped karma was at work and that tomorrow would be much better.

The walk back to Jennifer's parking place was glum. My attorney said she was reconsidering having me testify. Neither Brenda, who saw how devastated the defense team was as it left the courtroom, nor I got any sleep on Wednesday night. I got up at 1:30 a.m. to write a page-and-a-half of talking points about whether I should, or should not, testify.

The Final Day of the Trial

I'm a creature of habit and a seeker of omens.

On the final day of the trial, June 22, I dressed in the only suit I owned, a brownish-gray, two-piece model with vague pinstripes. I accessorized this with a tan shirt and a brown-and-tan patterned tie. I wanted to convey calm and neutrality through earth tones. I hoped the jury saw nothing but calm in my demeanor.

As I arrived at North Street early on a drizzly morning, I was mildly upset to find I had forgotten my small bottle of Gatorade Zero. I am superstitious and want to have the same things with me every day when facing a major crisis. As a compensating factor, I found a clean, open porta-potty at St. James's Episcopal Church. I didn't know if my bladder was going to hold out for the two blocks to the courthouse, and the relief this way station provided was palpable.

Outside the courtroom, Jennifer and I reaffirmed our original assessment on me testifying. I wouldn't take the stand.

At 9:10 a.m., the defense started calling witnesses.

Aaron Smith and the Importance of UTC

LCPS Chief Technology Officer Aaron Smith spent the first two days of the trial reading a novel while seated on a hard oak chair outside the courtroom. Each time I walked by Aaron, I noted that he'd made significant progress in his reading. He told me it would have taken a year to get through this book, given his casual reading habits.

Aaron's first bit of business on the stand was to define Coordinated Universal Time or Universal Time Coordinated (UTC). In the old days, this was referred to as Greenwich Mean Time. Basically, it's the measure by which the world regulates clocks and time.

Computer servers, such as the one used for Teams videoconferences, are set to UTC. Aaron explained that the 7:30 p.m. time code on the Teams call was the UTC time and that the actual meeting was held at 3:30 p.m. on May 28, 2021. There had been no second Teams meeting involving LCPS's senior administration and Tim Flynn that day. During his testimony, Flynn had been adamant about the second meeting, just as he had been adamant about the things he had allegedly told me. How could a juror be sure of what Flynn said he told me, when his memory of the second Teams meeting was so obviously wrong? Flynn didn't strengthen his credibility by remembering quieting his dog and ushering his young children out of the room during the second, imaginary, meeting.

Jennifer asked Aaron if I could have destroyed any of my emails. While staff can delete emails to clear their individual accounts, something I regularly did, LCPS's Department of Digital Innovation holds all emails for years so that they are available for possible litigation. Aaron said that he had turned over every single email the commonwealth asked for.

The prosecution had no questions for Aaron Smith.

Michele Bowman and a Devastating Blow for the Prosecution

Michele Bowman, the media relations and communications manager for the Loudoun County Sheriff's Office, and I are long-standing colleagues. As she took the stand, I noted that her demeanor was haggard and tentative. Michele was a trusted, reliable colleague. She and her former boss, Kraig Troxell, had always shared bad news about LCPS in advance so that my office could prepare communications for the affected school community.

Under Jennifer's questioning, Michele said she had searched the Alert Loudoun system, which the sheriff's office used to communicate news to the public, for any release on the May 28, 2021, incident at Stone Bridge. There was no such release. Michele added that such releases were kept in an electronic file between two and ten years. "It was such a new investigation; they may not know (all the facts)." She wasn't made aware when the boy involved in the Stone Bridge incident was arrested in July 2021.

Michele went on to say that she had recently reviewed all emails between us from May to October 2021. None mentioned a sexual assault at Stone Bridge. At the prosecution table, I could see that Theo was getting nervous.

When Theo Stamos began her cross-examination, she spoke quickly and loudly. At one point, she apologized for her heightened volume, saying she thought the court reporter was having trouble hearing her. The court reporter gave a puzzled shrug at this assertion.

Under questioning, Michele offered that she sent messages concerning schools to me about a half hour before her office released them to the media and public. I would show senior administration the draft releases and ask if they had any comments or suggestions.

Theo asked if this procedure was followed for the October 7, 2021, release that detailed the arrest of the boy involved in the Stone Bridge and Broad Run incidents.

Michele confirmed that this was the case.

"Was his reaction 'Don't send it?'" Theo's volume was set to "high" again.

Michele gave as devastating a one-word answer as I had ever heard.

"No."

Theo quickly took her seat.

"I have no further questions."

I've heard the first thing that first-year law students are taught is "Never ask a question you don't know the answer to." How could an experienced prosecutor like Theo Stamos have made such a stupid mistake? Not only did she make the mistake, her lightning-quick end to questions drew a bright red line under that mistake for the jury.

I turned to Jennifer and asked if Theo had just made a fatal mistake.

Maybe.

Doug Fulton and the Finland Connection

LCPS Director of School Administration Doug Fulton is a unique individual. He's always immediately recognizable by his goatee and signature bow tie. When he took the stand, Doug listed his credentials: teacher, coach, and high school principal with more than thirty-six years in education. He was also an ordained minister, but I'm guessing Doug didn't want to polish the résumé apple too much, as he failed to mention this.

Doug testified that his office didn't receive formal notice of the arrest of the boy involved in the Stone Bridge incident until late September. This was the result of Court Services sending a snail mail notification to 21000 Education Court addressed to David Spage, who had held Doug's position seven years previously.

Doug testified that he was on a train in Finland, his family's ancestral home, during October 2021 when he got an international call from me asking about how the boy involved in the Stone Bridge and Broad Run incidents had been transferred. Prior to that, Doug said he hadn't discussed the case with me.

Assistance from the Administrative Assistants

I underestimated Maria Polink.

An administrative assistant III, Maria served as my secretary starting in April 2021. To me, she seemed to be generally plagued by uncertainty and lacked self-confidence. She struck me as one of life's perpetual victims.

I had grossly underestimated her.

While she admitted to being nervous when Jennifer's questioning began, Maria confidently established facts to support my case:

- There were no phone calls to our office that or walk-in visitors who between May 28 and October 6, 2021, mentioned a "sexual assault."
- I didn't mention any sexual assaults, nor did she hear me use these words between May 28 and October 6, 2021. Since her desk was six feet outside my office door, if anyone would have heard such a remark, it would have been Maria.
- Critical race theory was the topic that dominated demonstrations outside the Administration Building that summer.
- Maria never heard Joan Sahlgren discuss a sexual assault at Stone Bridge with me.

Maria later told me that Theo Stamos approached her outside the courtroom to ask what she would be testifying about. Following her lawyer's advice, Maria declined to talk to Theo. Maria said that Theo became angry and stalked away.

I felt ashamed for underestimating Maria Polink.

Kim Goodlin is one of the world's kindest, most conscientious souls. I saw her husband, Gary, outside the courtroom prior to Kim's testimony. I asked him how Kim was doing. "Like you'd expect" was the answer. Kim internalizes the worries of the world. She's always ready to accept blame when something goes wrong, even if it's not her fault. She beats herself up over errors she didn't make or that others associated with LCPS make.

Kim, who was my executive assistant for years and who now served Joan Sahlgren in that capacity, confirmed all of the key points in Maria's testimony. She added that there was a lot of controversy surrounding Policy 8040 during the summer of 2021.

Kim was a nervous wreck on the stand, shaking as she testified. I gave her a sympathetic thumbs-up as she left the courtroom.

Saving Grandma for Last

Brenda was the final witness to testify in my defense. Jennifer wanted my wife to testify about the stress I was under during the summer of 2021. The prosecution didn't want her to do this. There was a long sidebar after Brenda was administered her witness oath. She sat nervously on the stand while I tried to send subtle signals to her that everything was OK.

It was decided that Jennifer could ask Brenda one question: Did I say anything about a sexual assault at Stone Bridge High School between May 28 and October 6, 2021?

"No."

Jennifer then snuck in two more questions. How long had we been married? Forty-two years. Did we have grandchildren? Yes.

Later in the day, we learned how this last fact resonated with the jury.

"Take your grandchildren on a trip!" a juror called out as she left the courthouse.

Nobody wanted to send grandma to jail.

As Brenda left the stand, Jennifer asked me for the last time if I wanted to testify.

No.

The Three Stooges (Minus One) Make Their Case

The prosecution's closing arguments brought to mind the 1936 Three Stooges short *Disorder in the Court*. Theo Stamos and Jason Faw couldn't have made more mistakes in their final pleas to the jury if Moe and Larry had scripted them.

Jason Faw presented the initial part of the prosecution's closing arguments and broke virtually every rule of making a good presentation:

- Faw had the bailiff dim the lights so the jurors could better see his PowerPoint. This made it difficult, if not impossible, for the jurors to take notes.
- He read the PowerPoint. You're never supposed to do this. You're not giving your audience any more information than they can read on the screen.
- Faw had his back to the jurors a good bit of the time while being sideways to them at others. The prosecutor made little eye contact with them.
- Faw's reasons for me committing perjury were overly complex and conspiratorial. He lumped the nine statements that constituted my "perjury" into one long statement through which he said that I had knowingly attempted to mislead the special grand jury. Faw said I realized the errors I had made late in my testimony of August 2, 2023, and that eventually led me to "commit the truth" by making a statement to cover my past lies.
- The motivation for my perjury? I wanted to keep the details of the May 28, 2021, incident at Stone Bridge away from

the public, "because it would have complicated the school system's attempts to implement a policy of allowing transgender students to use the bathroom that matches their gender identity."

- Oddly, Faw threw away the materiality aspect of the trial during his closing remarks. He admitted that I couldn't have put information about the sexual assault in the May 28, 2021, message to the Stone Bridge community. As an LCPS parent, Faw said he was thankful that I couldn't violate the confidentiality of student records.

After Jennifer Leffler's closing argument, Theo Stamos offered the prosecution's final summation. Compared to Theo's work, Faw's presentation looked like a masterpiece.

Theo planted herself right in front of the jury box. She noted her Greek heritage, saying, in Greece, the church is the center of the community. In America, Theo stated that the courthouse is the center of the community. The courthouse is like a church, "or mosque" Theo added, in a nod to a male juror in the front row on the far right side, who appeared to be of Indian or Pakistani descent. Her attempt at multiculturalism fell flat. The juror folded his arms across his chest, cast his eyes at the wall, and never looked back for the duration of Theo's argument. The seven jurors sitting in the back row of the jury box and the woman sitting next to the disaffected juror could clearly see that one of their members had checked out. Watching this juror's interactions with his fellow jurors, I pegged him as a possible jury foreman. Turned out, he was the alternate juror, and he was excused before the jury began deliberations. However, his reaction to Theo's "holy" oration helped my cause significantly.

Undeterred by her cultural gaffe, Theo continued with the church metaphor. The courtroom benches were like pews. Theo singled me out for the jury, saying I had committed sacrilege by lying in this sacred place.

Theo was animated as she spoke, gesturing emphatically with her hands, sometimes reaching across the wooden barrier that separated her from the jury. Later in the afternoon, I ran into Matthew Barakat, the Northern Virginia correspondent for the Associated Press, whom I had known for years. Matthew said he was in the courtroom for Theo's closing and noticed the three female jurors sitting together in the front row of the jury box recoiling when Theo reached out into their personal space.

That couldn't have been good.

Theo used the remainder of her closing argument to portray me as the tip of the spear of a grand conspiracy to cover up what happened at Stone Bridge in the promotion of a "woke" agenda. She pointed out that I was the longest-serving LCPS administrator of all the administrators that had appeared during the trial. "He knows everything that's going on . . . He asks questions and knows where the bodies are buried." Theo said that the May 28, 2021, message to the Stone Bridge community was the first act in a long cover-up of the facts. She harkened back to my journalism background, saying my job was to find out the "who, what, when, where, and how" of everything concerning LCPS. Having found out all of this about the Stone Bridge incident, I decided to cover up this knowledge.

Theo cited the heroic role of Governor Glenn Youngkin in uncovering the nefarious deeds of LCPS. Transgender rights, woke conspiracies, Republicans rushing in to own the libs; this was Fox News/MAGA red meat. The jury did not look like a Fox News/MAGA bunch.

How were they going to react to the prosecution's arguments?

Jennifer's Summation

In contrast to the prosecution's closing arguments, Jennifer Leffler kept her distance (about fifteen feet) from the jury. Mainly, she stayed behind the podium, making one brief trip to its front to use an ELMO (Electric Light Machine Organization) visual presenter.

Jennifer neatly summed up the faults in the prosecution's case, noting that the jury must find "beyond reasonable" doubt that I had intentionally lied to the special grand jury:

- She said I "gave it my best shot" in trying to tell the special grand jury what I knew and when. If my testimony appeared inconsistent, it was because I was trying to recall additional facts about the events of May 28, 2021, more than fourteen months after they occurred.
- Everybody recalled things differently, and Tim Flynn and I obviously had different recollections of May 28.
- Tavis Henry and I never discussed what happened at Stone Bridge.
- Joan Sahlgren got information about May 28 in "waves" from different sources and couldn't pinpoint what she heard from whom when.
- Michele Bowman searched all her communications and couldn't find one between May 28 and October 6, 2021, where she mentioned a sexual assault to me.
- Maria Polink and Kim Goodlin never heard the words "sexual assault" come out of my mouth in relation to Stone Bridge during the summer of 2021.
- She pointed out that there were not two witnesses or one witness with corroborating evidence who could show that I willfully lied to the special grand jury.

Using the ELMO, a device resembling an overhead projector that transfers the image of a document to a TV screen, Jennifer walked through each of the nine statements the prosecution cited as perjurious. She showed why each statement, taken separately, was true.

I noted every juror was taking notes during Jennifer's presentation.

The Final Verdict

With final arguments finished, Judge Fleming gave the jurors a lunch break with an approximate end time of 2:30 p.m. All of the trial's major participants retired to the large lobby outside the courtroom. We watched the jurors depart for, and return from, lunch; we tried not to make eye contact or utter anything that they could hear.

As part of her duty as my attorney, Jennifer had to ask Theo what sentence she would recommend if I was found guilty. Theo's answer was jarring: six months in jail and a $2,500 fine. I could imagine Glenn Youngkin speaking at a future rally outside the Administration Building should this sentence be imposed: "My administration uncovered a criminal conspiracy in Loudoun County Public Schools. We sent one of their top administrators, Wayde Byard, to jail. You remember Wayde Byard, the former public information officer for Loudoun County Public Schools. He didn't give the community information about a transgender student raping a girl in a girls' bathroom at Stone Bridge High School, and Attorney General Jason Miyares made sure he paid the price!"

Media began filtering in and occupying benches among the trial's participants. I had to warn my sister, Dale, as tactfully as I could, to stop talking to Nick Minock, who was wearing the most aggressively loud, retina-burning blue suit that I had ever seen. My sister, like myself, had my father's gift of gabbing with strangers. But gabbing with Nick Minock could be dangerous, as everything you say is on the record and could, and probably would, be used against you. Dale had been a reassuring figure throughout my trial, driving Brenda to Leesburg and monitoring the trial from the back of the courtroom.

The bailiff came out of the courtroom at 4:17 p.m. and informed us that the jury had reached a verdict. The jury had deliberated for less than two hours. Generally speaking, when juries take this little time, it's because they've reached a "not guilty" verdict. Jennifer cautioned me not to read too much into the short deliberation. The trial participants, media, and interested parties, including Brenda, Dale, Scott Smith, and Ian Prior, entered the courtroom.

Judge Fleming seated himself at the bench and issued a calm, yet very serious warning. I ranked this as his finest moment during the trial. Fleming said that the jury would soon enter the room and render its verdict. He didn't know if this verdict would be "guilty" or "not guilty." Whatever the verdict, Fleming knew that there would be an emotional reaction to it. If those in the courtroom didn't think they could control their emotions when the verdict was read, they needed to leave the courtroom. Fleming glanced at Scott Smith, who was seated with Ian Prior at the right rear of the courtroom. The judge said he would leave the bench for two minutes. When he returned, the jury would be called in and the verdict read. Fleming said he surmised anyone still in the room when he reassumed the bench would be able to control their emotions.

During Fleming's absence, extra bailiffs entered the room. I especially noticed one hulking bailiff who positioned himself at the door through which the jury entered and exited.

After Fleming's return, the jury entered through a side door and silently took its collective seat in the jury box. The jury's foreman was identified. I was heartened by the jury's selection of a leader. This gentleman, a man of my age, had occupied the last seat on the far right in the jury's second row throughout the trial. During jury selection, he said he'd previously served on a jury during the 1980s. He was the possessor of a thin, expressive face topped by thinning blond hair. I thought this man's feelings were evident throughout the trial. During prosecution presentations, he often had a "Who farted?" look on his face—eyes wide open, mouth turned down in a semi-frown—when the prosecution was trying to make a point.

Fleming asked the jury if they had reached a verdict. The foreman answered in the affirmative. Was the verdict unanimous? Yes. Did the jury need to be polled for its individual feelings? No.

That said, Fleming instructed the foreman to hand a bailiff a folded piece of paper with the verdict written on it. The bailiff walked the paper across the courtroom to the clerk of the court, who was seated at a lowered desk at Fleming's right. I felt oddly detached as the bailiff made his short journey. What was written on that paper was going to determine a large part of my future. Perhaps I was unemotional because Jennifer looked up to me just before the verdict was read and said, "We've won."

When the clerk unfolded the paper and read the verdict, we had, indeed, won.

"Not guilty." (I later learned from someone who knew one of the jurors that the jury had basically decided after the first day of the trial that the charges against me were nonsense.)

"You are free to go, sir," said Fleming in his resonant judge's voice.

After the verdict, the clerk walked over and handed the decision to me, a large smile on her face. I had had the feeling throughout the trial that the court staff was pulling for me.

Turning around, I saw Dale comforting Brenda as Brenda broke down sobbing.

Jennifer asked if she could give me a hug.

Of course she could.

Scott Smith, at least outwardly, managed to control his emotions.

PART VII

Our Lives after the Trial

The Aftermath

Having achieved a "Hollywood ending" through the verdict, I scripted a Hollywood exit from the courthouse. I concocted something to feed the media, and they ate it up—sound bites designed to go down easily. Picking up where my professional life left off, however, was something I couldn't script.

Media Madness

During my long hours of meditation at Old Stone Church, I had scripted what I would say if I was found "not guilty." I refused to contemplate a defeat by composing a "guilty speech."

Going through my mental file of semi-useful information, I looked for inspiration in crafting my words. I settled on Abraham Lincoln's second inaugural address: "With malice toward none, with charity for all . . ." You can't go wrong with Honest Abe.

During the endless hours of educational professional development that I've sat through, the need to take time for "reflection" had always been emphasized. Given endless hours to reflect, I had come to the conclusion that there was no alternative path to the high road. I wasn't going to vent the dark feelings that occasionally entered my thoughts during the past seven months.

Using my screenwriter skills, I authored a quick quote that would encompass my feelings, would make for a good sound bite, and, hopefully, would be the primary quote used in post-trial coverage: "I'm not going to put any more quarters in the outrage machine. I'm not going to make incendiary statements. I'm not going to give counterpoints to political views because that's what's gotten our community here and our nation here and I just don't want to be part of it."

I made sure I complimented Brenda about her central role in my life, which this experience had only magnified.

"It's quite a thing, after forty-two years, when your wife invests your life savings into your defense. She is courageous, and I couldn't ask for a better life partner. She's just affirmed why I love her."

I stated that I was not "happy" about the verdict, but, rather, "relieved."

"Today, I can't really say I'm happy because I expected this. Jennifer made sure this happened. She assured me every step of the way. I felt confident in this. I felt confident in Judge Fleming. I felt confident the jury would reach an impartial and fair verdict."

I made sure Jennifer Leffler was at my side as I faced the media. In a brief conference before we left the courthouse, we decided that she would answer questions about me not testifying. This question, as expected, came up. Jennifer said, "He testified before the grand jury and we felt it was truthful testimony. We knew the jury was going to see that, so we didn't see why we would put him on the stand to reiterate what he, at the time, thought was truthful."

I gave the media some insight into the thoughts behind my special grand jury testimony, starting with the fact that I had once been among their ranks. "Having done your job, and having been in this job for a long time; you have rumor, you have hearsay, you have opinion and you have fact. When a charge is levied by a law-enforcement agency, then it becomes an allegation."

I made clear that I had no animosity against Tim Flynn. "I have nothing against Tim Flynn. There is no conflict between us. We've been friends for years. We might have just remembered things differently."

Everyone asked if I would be returning to work. I replied—in a very calculated way—that my plans were now day-to-day, and I would soon talk with my colleagues to decide on my employment future. "I was a workaholic. I admit that. And for a workaholic, it's like having withdrawal when you have six months off. So I haven't figured the whole thing out." I added that my immediate plans were to attend a family birthday party and watch the Yankees game.

Luke Rosiak, wearing a blue golf shirt, stood at the back left of the scrum, occasionally lobbing in a rhetorical grenade seeking an incendiary comment. Did I think that the school board should release the Blankingship & Keith report? I replied that since this decision was not mine, it would be inappropriate for me to comment. I knew Rosiak would write a negative article, and I didn't intend on helping him. Rosiak had spent most of the trial sitting with Ian Prior. Prior, Theo Stamos, and Jason Faw departed the courthouse quickly without offering comment. Scott Smith stayed around to offer comments to those who would have them.

I didn't care.

After doing a mass press conference, I broke from the pack to do live shots for the early evening news. Facing my fear, my first live interview was with Fox 5's Tisha Lewis. Before the arrival of Nick Minock, Tisha Lewis was the terror of public information types in the metropolitan Washington area. A physically imposing Black woman, Tisha formed her journalistic style during a stint at Fox 32 in Chicago. She had an angle for every story before doing any research or interviews. Facts didn't change that angle. I remained calm as the red light on the camera flicked on and stuck to my talking points.

So far, so good.

Next up, Nick Minock.

I bantered lightly with Nick before the live broadcast threw it to him. He seemed unusually amiable. Joan Sahlgren later told me the LCPS communications staff had a "come to Jesus" moment with Nick in my absence. Joan and Dan Adams had a talk with Nick's news director, and Nick, about his past misdeeds concerning LCPS.

Apparently, the talk took.

Before going live, Nick and I chatted pleasantly about the trip he and his wife would be taking to Bora Bora the next day. Nick bantered with the anchor at WJLA before interviewing me. I knew there was only so much time before they went to commercial. I employed my talking points and used the last few seconds to wish Nick a safe journey to Bora Bora to run out the clock.

Viewing the interview later, my assessment was that no damage had been done.

Big relief.

Drew Wilder of WRC-TV, the NBC affiliate, was up next. Drew is a genuinely nice guy and a true professional. WRC is the longtime No. 1 news station in the Washington area and doesn't indulge in the hysterics of its competitors. Drew's report wasn't live, so I could repeat my talking points with a calmer demeanor.

Last up was Matthew Torres of WUSA-9. Once Washington's top-rated news station, WUSA is now a bare-bones operation. Matthew is another nice guy and a fair journalist. I asked him about the trip to Canada that he had been about to take the last time we met about a year ago. Not a live shot, I dispensed my talking points as cameras were being broken down around me.

I then joined my wife and lawyers who had been waiting patiently while I practiced my "craft."

The Attorney General, Sore Loser

Asked for comments about the verdict during the evening following the decision, Virginia Attorney General Jason Miyares's spokeswoman, Victoria LaCivita, sent this out via email: "The special grand jury indicted Mr. Byard after hearing all the evidence, and we're proud that the judge agreed with us time and time again that this case needed to be heard in front of a jury. Lying under oath undermines our justice system and must be taken seriously . . .

"While we are disappointed with the jury's decision, we're proud of our team for uncovering the truth and providing answers to concerned Virginia parents." Translation: The jury found Wayde Byard "not guilty," but he was still "guilty."

Upon reading this, several people said I should sue LaCivita for libel.

I discreetly filed a FOIA request on June 28 to see if I could view the communications trail that led to her message. I asked for "all emails, texts and written communication to and from Attorney General Spokeswoman Victoria LaCivita between January 15, 2022, and June 28, 2023, in which the words Wayde or Byard are mentioned."

As expected, I got a notice from Assistant General Counsel Tyler Barnes invoking the seven-working-day extension allowed for FOIA requests under the Code of Virginia. On Saturday, July 8, Barnes sent me an email stating my request would cost $170.46.

"How do I pay?"

Workplace Negotiations

The following Monday, June 26, I returned to the Administration Building for the first time in more than seven months to talk about my future with LCPS. Chief Human Resources Officer Lisa Boland met me at the entrance, and we allowed how this was much happier than our last meeting.

In the superintendent's office, Lisa and Interim Superintendent Daniel Smith told me that Business and Financial Services was still calculating my pay. They wanted to make sure that it was given to me in a manner that would do the least tax damage. The school board seemed amenable to paying my legal fees. At $35,000 and change, this came as a relief.

I said I wanted to come back to work in some form until my original retirement date of January 1, 2024. Daniel and Lisa were amenable to this. We decided we'd work out the details when Joan Sahlgren returned from vacation. We set a follow-up meeting for Thursday, July 6. In the meantime, I wouldn't be charged for any leave. Truth be told, I didn't mind another week off to adjust to the shock of reestablishing a work routine.

The *Washington Post* House Call

On Tuesday, June 27, Jennifer Leffler texted me to say that Karina Elwood of *The Washington Post* wanted to write a profile of me.

Karina arrived two days later promptly at the agreed meeting time of three, with her freelance photographer, Rob, not far behind. Karina let me know before she started taping and later called to confirm facts, which spoke highly of her level of professionalism. We spent two hours together. I made clear up front that I wasn't going to say anything about the trial. That was fine, she assured me, since this was a personality profile. I tried to stick to anecdotes that I'd scripted out in advance. I tried not to flinch as Rob took photos of me at close range.

We decided to travel to Old Stone Church to get some atmospheric photos.

As Karina and Rob departed, I sincerely hoped things would go as well as I felt they had.

Opening the Tomb

I had a conference with Daniel Smith, Lisa Boland, and Joan Sahlgren to discuss my return to LCPS. We agreed that I could no longer be the "Voice" or "Face" of LCPS, which was a mutual relief. I'd be referred to as a "communications coordinator" with the same level of pay. I'd concentrate on writing projects before my retirement.

I'd no longer have to attend school board meetings. Another relief.

My anger level would rise the longer these meetings went on, and the midnight rides home from these frustrating exercises in representative government often left me feeling anything short of death would be preferable.

Lisa gave me a new photo badge that provided access to the Administration Building and its offices. The first time I used it was to unlock the door to the Communications and Community Engagement suite. Entering just before lunch, I bumped into virtually the entire staff, and we held an impromptu reunion. I regaled them with some of my courtroom adventures before entering my office for the first time in more than seven months.

It was like opening the door to a tomb filled with artifacts belonging to a person who no longer existed. Something that caught my eye immediately was a small notepad with the numbers of my then attorney, Tim McEvoy, and my mom. The sight of mom's phone number generated an immediate feeling of loss more powerful than I had anticipated.

I retrieved my Yankees lanyard from my upper-right desk drawer and attached it to my new badge. I alternated my lanyards between Giants and Yankees depending on the season. The Giants hadn't finished their season or begun their playoff run when last I was here.

I discovered a small Gatorade Zero that I had left in the break room refrigerator in December. What the hell? Still good. Twinkies weren't the only things with a long shelf life.

I rebooted my computer to discover I was digitally dead. LCPS's myriad software platforms no longer recognized my existence since I hadn't logged on in more than half a year. I spent much of the next few hours proving that I existed.

With my email reestablished, I looked at messages that had begun flooding in shortly after noon on December 12, 2022. Media consultants have told the current generation of reporters that the best way to begin formal communications is with casual salutations. Most of the emails began with the words "Hi Wayde." The body of the message would then state something like, "Just heard the Attorney General took a gigantic shit on you. Can you give us a 'shocked' reaction that will allow us to seek further quotes that will extend this story beyond one news cycle?" The traditional "sincerely" is often replaced by "Best" at the conclusion of these communications. This struck me as rather British, like "Cheerio!"

I'd rather they just asked questions old-school style: blunt, formal, to the point.

A Day of Goodbyes and Hellos

I started my work day on July 7, 2023, my first full day back at work, at ten in the morning at Leesburg's Union Cemetery. LCPS staff from the upper echelons to the administration's custodial staff gathered for Hector Rodriguez's graveside service. Hector had been the longtime night security guard at the Administration Building, but he had been so much more. He was a cheerful, caring presence who had a kind word and smile for everyone. I made it a point to stop by the reception desk every day on my way home to spend a few minutes with him and share a laugh. During late-night school board meetings, he always followed the action over a speaker in the lobby and commented on the pace of the proceedings. Hector also kept an eye on the security cameras to see if any agitated souls from the public comment segment were lurking around the building.

Hector came to America from El Salvador. A graduate of Loudoun Valley High School, he worked as an inventory control clerk at the Safeway in Leesburg all day before working a 5:00 p.m. to 1:00 a.m. shift as the security guard at the Administration Building. Everyone marveled at his work ethic. Hector was so popular that when the security firm he worked for lost its contract, LCPS found a way to keep him on the job.

Everyone loved Hector like family.

He died at forty-eight from colon cancer.

It just wasn't right.

Some things stood out about Hector's funeral.

First, I hadn't known he was Jewish. I was a bit stunned when I saw the wooden Star of David atop his plain, pine coffin.

I was heartsick as his elderly mother started reciting a long prayer in Spanish to herself as the coffin was lowered into the ground at the beginning of the service. You didn't have to be fluent in Spanish to understand the anguish in her voice.

As was Jewish tradition, mourners threw a trowel of dirt upon the coffin at the service's conclusion. The sound of dirt hitting the raw pine sent a jolt through my body.

The night before, I had learned that a longtime colleague, Tim Bullis, had died at fifty-two, also of colon cancer. I'd hired Tim thirty years before as a reporter for *The Winchester Star*. He had been a cocky young man, bordering on obnoxious. But he had been willing to learn through the editing process and had become an excellent journalist before, like me, he became a school public information officer. Through the years, we'd catch up at National School Public Relations Association (NSPRA) conferences. He became a leader in school public information and, having lost his youthful cockiness, a confident pro.

After the funeral, I spent part of my afternoon reviewing the FOIA requests that had come in since my suspension. Same names seeking information for the same purpose: proving LCPS was part of a nationwide effort to indoctrinate students so that, brainwashed, they could destroy the American way of life.

I reflected on the fate of Hector and Tim as I read through this string of fear-based inquiry.

Get a life before it's gone, losers.

The (Disappointing) Answer to My FOIA Prayers

When I told LCPS Division Counsel Bob Falconi that I'd filed a Freedom of Information Act request with the attorney general, he responded that I wouldn't get the email I was looking for.

He was right.

What I got from the attorney general's office was definitely not worth $170.46.

There were a lot of routine filings seeking court documents related to my case.

Still, there were a few interesting tidbits, such as a March 29, 2023, email from Charles Homans of *The New York Times Magazine* to Ms. LaCivita. Homans said that he was writing about the 2021 sexual assault cases, the investigation that followed, and Scott Ziegler's and my upcoming trials. "I was wondering whether it would be possible to interview Attorney General Miyares?"

Ms. LaCivita replied in the negative. "Because the cases are pending, the Attorney General cannot comment."

I bet she wouldn't have said that to Nick Minock.

It was apparent that Justin Jouvenal of *The Washington Post* was on to the farcical nature of the indictments against Scott Smith and me the day they were issued. On December 12, 2022, he emailed LaCivita, setting off this email exchange.

Jouvenal: "It doesn't look like these charges are related to the sex assaults. I don't want to mislead our readers about what this is about. Can you (say) whether the charges relate to the sex assaults or something else in the case of each man charged?"

LaCivita: "We cannot make extrajudicial comment regarding the context of charges as it is prohibited by the ethics rules surrounding prosecuting."

Ethics rules? C'mon Victoria. Justin Jouvenal was calling bullshit. You'd been caught.

My friend Neal Augenstein obviously had the same opinion of Nick Minock that I did. On June 22, 2023, he sent an email to LaCivita asking if closing arguments would be that day. "Your guy Nick Minock says closings [are] today." Neal followed this sentence with a smiley face emoji. You learn something new about people you know all the time. I never saw Neal as an emoji guy, much less a smiley face emoji guy.

LaCivita confirmed that unofficial attorney general spokesman Nick Minock was correct. "Yes, just got word that the defense rested. I'm not at the courthouse. Closings are today."

My case was obviously being followed fairly closely in Richmond. I wonder how long it took before it became apparent to Miyares and company that things would not go their way?

They were obviously prepared for the worst.

I found an addendum to LaCivita's sour grapes statement of June 22. "Additionally, Louisa Commonwealth's Attorney Rusty McGuire has extensive experience prosecuting perjury cases and is available to speak on background." I had to wonder how Rusty would frame the ass-whipping taken by his colleagues at the attorney general's office.

Glenn Youngkin, Sticking His Head Back in the Toilet

On July 19, 2023, the Virginia Department of Education (VDOE) issued new guidance on how school boards should craft policies regarding the use of bathroom and locker room facilities by transgender students. It did so using the kind of rhetoric the Youngkin administration was famous for while making sure that parents were included in the mix. The title for these model policies: "Model Policies on Ensuring Privacy, Dignity, and Respect for All Students and Parents in Virginia's Public Schools." This could have been entitled: "Model Policies That Undo Everything a Democratic Governor and General Assembly Did in 2021 While Providing Further Ammunition for the Culture War We Hope Will Rage at Least Until Election Day."

The gist of the new model policies:

- Students will use bathrooms that correspond to their sex at birth.
- School personnel will only refer to each student with pronouns adhering to the sex identified on their official record. (It should be noted that such records can be changed only by parents, unless the student is over the age of eighteen.)
- Student activities will now be separated by sex rather than gender identity.

Youngkin trotted out his well-worn talking points on this subject in an interview with the Associated Press. "This is about doing what's best for the child. And oh, by the way, also recognizing that we need to ensure the privacy and dignity and respect of all children and all parents in the school system. And that's what I think we have ... very carefully constructed here."

The new model policies also prohibited school divisions from encouraging teachers to conceal a student's gender identification from their parents. In Youngkin's Brady Bunch world, parents were always at the ready to have thoughtful conversations with their offspring, no matter how difficult the problem. "What we're not saying is that trusted counselors and other trusted adult's [sic] in a child's life should be excluded. What we are ... saying is that parents just need to be involved and are the first stop. And then collectively there is ... a support mechanism around a child that can be most effective."

Obviously, the governor had never asked a school principal about how difficult it is building a support mechanism around a child with the help of their "loving" parents.

Before the new model policies were even issued, several school boards said they were not going to adhere to them. Many contentious debates were in the meeting forecasts for the fall months.

I wondered how much better off the commonwealth would be if those in state government, be they Democrat or Republican, put the effort into other problems—climate change, the fentanyl crisis, gun violence, income inequality—that they did into where less than one-tenth of 1 percent of the children in public schools pee and change their clothes.

Two-Member Dining Society

In July, I invited former Superintendent Scott Ziegler to dinner at the Italian restaurant on Berryville's main street. I didn't want to start any rumors by being spotted in Loudoun. You never know who's watching there and how influential they are on social media. Better safe than sorry.

Scott's appearance was a bit shocking, at least for Main Street in Berryville, Virginia. In addition to his two discreet earrings, Scott was wearing black fingernail polish. Coupled with the sleeve of tattoos on his right arm, this created a disconcerting look for a middle-aged man. He said he was being considered for a corporate job and would probably have to alter his look. My only, half-joking, comment was that he'd better not "let his freak flag fly in court" lest he be judged unfavorably by the jury.

Appearances aside, Scott and I compared notes about our shared experience as the objects of a political witch hunt. (The phrase "political witch hunt" hurts to even think about, since it comes out of Donald Trump's mouth so often. Unlike Trump, it fit perfectly where Scott and I were concerned.)

Scott's involuntary manifestations of rage were more dramatic than mine. He once jumped up out of a deep sleep and began pounding the wall with his fists. I urged him, based on my experience, to seek counseling. Scott said that he and his wife would probably do this after they moved to North Carolina, something that would happen in the next few weeks. Luckily, the Zieglers were able to sell their home for twice the price they had bought it for only three years earlier. The money garnered from the Loudoun sale allowed them to almost buy their new house outright. While diminished slightly, Scott's Virginia Retirement System pension was enough to live on.

Scott said that his youngest son was able to graduate from Loudoun's Woodgrove High School without any adverse incidents; no taunting, no bullying, no mention of his father's situation at all. As a formerly bullied principal's son, this made me very happy. Scott said that another former principal's son, Dr. Sam Shipp, had a lot to do with this. Sam is one of LCPS's best principals. His father, Jerry, had been Sam's principal when Sam attended Loudoun Valley High School. Simply put, Sam got it. He handled difficult situations with grace and a steady hand.

Scott said he and his wife attended their son's graduation without incident. Given the way diplomas were distributed alphabetically, their son was the last member of his class to be honored. As was Woodgrove's tradition, he was asked to remain on stage as Sam declared the class of 2023 officially graduated. The younger Ziegler held his diploma aloft and received a thunderous ovation as the ceremony concluded.

I was glad that this young man and his parents had this moment of closure. It had taken many years for me to put my high school traumas behind me. They still nip at my unconscious self in the darkest corners of my darkest dreams.

Scott's daughter had a different experience.

She stayed away from the publicity surrounding Scott and was unaware of how intensely negative it was. An uncle referenced the severity of the situation, and Scott's daughter did a Google search of her father's name. Within minutes, she called Scott sobbing about what she had found.

The damage the Commonwealth of Virginia and the vicious minority of Loudoun's citizens had done to Scott, me, and our families was tangible and, I fear, long-lasting.

Concerning his upcoming trials, Scott said his lawyer would call Tim Flynn to the stand. The prosecution had dropped the "star" witness from my trial from their list of potential witnesses in Scott's case. Scott said he and Flynn had a phone conversation on the evening of May 28, 2021, which may have been why Flynn had a recollection of the second Teams meeting. However, no matter the venue, Flynn never laid out the scenarios he so fully recalled during his interviews with prosecutors. Scott remembered Scott Smith's behavior being Flynn's primary concern. And, by the way, Flynn said the boy involved in the Stone Bridge incident was not transgender, just an extremely messed up kid seeking attention.

The unmentioned "coconspirator" who was the source of much of the political evil that enveloped Loudoun, Ian Prior, would probably be a witness at one of Scott's trials, if not both. Scott said his FOIA work had led to an admission from the Virginia Attorney General's Office that there was email correspondence from Prior to Jason Miyares. This was being withheld as part of an ongoing investigation. Scott said that the withholding was shaky legally because Prior was not an employee of the attorney general's office. Further, he thought Prior had manipulated Scott Smith and others who had sued the school division. I'd love to see this weasel finally face public scrutiny. If any past skeletons came tumbling out of his closet, even better.

I told Scott that he was the one person who shouldn't testify at his trial (he was currently on the fence on this subject). Theo Stamos, Jason Faw, or whatever minion the attorney general had in the courtroom would mercilessly attack Scott and get him to say something that a jury could misconstrue. Better to let the rogue's gallery of misfits that would parade to the witness stand do your dirty work for you. Like me, Scott could be combative. Odds were, it wouldn't end well if Scott took the stand.

When he might take the stand had become the object of legal wrangling. The prosecution was trying to move the trials back, supposedly because of the threatening atmosphere created by the Loudoun Love Warriors postings. This was a liberal Facebook group that, ignoring the Anti-Racist Parents of Loudoun County debacle, had attacked conservatives. Fuck Facebook. (I had to get that out of my system.) The real reason for a delay was, of course, that Glenn Youngkin didn't want any more legal defeats before the November 7 election.

Whenever Scott's trial took place, he would spend the night at a hotel in Brunswick, Maryland, and commute to the proceedings. His wife would not accompany him. She didn't want to set foot in Loudoun again. I couldn't blame her.

A potential future legal action that Scott mentioned intrigued me.

The legal firm that successfully sued Fox News in the Dominion Voting Systems machine case was considering launching a lawsuit for wrongful prosecution on Scott's behalf. I allowed that I might be willing to join such an effort. My reasons would be monetary, of course, because I'd suffered some concrete financial damage at the hands of Virginia's elected officials and compensation was due. Beyond that, it would cause Glenn Youngkin and Jason Miyares political embarrassment and hold them accountable for their actions in a public fashion. Any political pain that I could cause them would be well worth the effort. I'd also like to have the money to buy Brenda some of her long-deferred dreams.

As we parted on Berryville's Main Street, I urged Scott to stay in touch. For better or worse—and I would hold it was more for the better—we would be forever linked.

End of an Era

Liz Campbell shut down the Friends of Wayde Byard Facebook page on August 21, 2023.

From day one we have had a fun group of fans sharing fun memes and commiserating over another closed school day. Many charities and schools have reached out to Wayde to make public appearances or create creative tee shirts to raise money for a cause or charity . . .

This page has brought tons of laughs, snow day discussions and also a lot of joy. I hope it has made you smile from time to time

Thank you, Liz.

(Liz made one more entry, announcing my retirement, on December 14. It got 1,500 likes and 377 positive comments. Again, thank you, Liz.)

Glenn Youngkin Remembering Scott Smith

Glenn Youngkin used a Sunday-morning appearance in September on *Fox News Sunday* to pardon Scott Smith before a verdict was rendered in his upcoming obstruction of justice and disorderly conduct appeal. "We have righted a wrong," said Youngkin. "He should have never been prosecuted here. This was a dad standing up for his daughter."

Loudoun County Commonwealth's Attorney Buta Biberaj, rightly, called bullshit. "This is an unprecedented and inappropriate intervention in an active legal case. He chose to interfere in the legal process, and not for justice, but for political gain."

For his part, Scott Smith was grateful to the governor, kind of. "I wanted to win this on my own merit in court, straight up. I didn't want a pardon, and, really, one was never talked about until after my last court hearing when I made it very known to everyone that I was very disheartened about what had happened in that hearing and it was time for Youngkin to do something about this misjustice and I never heard from him until real recently."

Smith also explained some technical legal issues pertaining to his case. "It was a really complicated thing, but Youngkin couldn't pardon me unless I dropped my appeal, and I refused to do that. I just wasn't going to drop my appeal and accept responsibility for something I didn't do. My court date is two weeks out. I think Youngkin was hoping this would have been over by now and I won on my own merit."

Just guessing here, but I think Glenn Youngkin definitely wanted this over.

A Split Decision for Scott Ziegler

On September 29, 2023, a jury found Scott Ziegler guilty of a misdemeanor count of retaliation for firing a teacher, but not guilty of firing her because she appeared before the special grand jury. This split decision mystified me, as did any connection with May 28, 2021, which was what the special grand jury was supposed to be investigating.

On March 22, 2022, Ian Prior had made one of his more dramatic appearances before the Loudoun County School Board. He used the public comment portion of the meeting to state that unnamed teachers had been touched in a sexual manner and that LCPS had done nothing about it. "At an elementary school in Loudoun County, you have teachers that are being inappropriately touched, multiple times a day, for the better part of two months. The school administration has not solved that problem, despite a March 11 email to your Title IX office. This administration has not solved that problem. So that problem now becomes a Title VII problem." (Title VII prohibits sex discrimination in the workplace.)

Prior ended his comments with a rhetorical flourish, "Now, I believe I've given you all the information you need to track this down and solve it tonight. But if you don't, you know how to get in touch with me."

At a subsequent school board meeting, special education teacher Erin Brooks and a teacher assistant, Lauren Vandermuelen, revealed that they were the teachers Prior had spoken about. Brooks claimed a student exhibited "overly sexualized behaviors, including fondling, groping and facial and hand gestures." Brooks and Vandermuelen claimed LCPS retaliated against them by not renewing their contracts. They also said this retaliation was related to the fact that they testified before the special grand jury. Vandermuelen repeated these claims on Fox News.

This matter involved a nonverbal fifth-grade, special-education student with the emotional development of a three-year-old. When the inappropriate behavior occurred, Brooks and Vandermuelen were offered temporary and longer-reaching teaching strategies and equipment to discourage and mitigate the student's behavior. The equipment included a heavy apron, which covered the teacher's breasts and genitalia. The principal told me that when the student was transferred to another teacher and their Individualized Education Program (IEP) was followed closely, the student's behavior ceased.

All of which led me to issue a very unusual statement on the teachers' public statements, which was done with the consent of the student's parents.

"While we encourage all teachers and students to report any concerns about inappropriate touching or sexual assault to the proper authorities, we expect staff to do so in the process laid out in LCPS policy that is consistent with our need to protect the privacy of our students as well. The teachers inappropriately distributed student records without the consent of the family and without the knowledge of school staff for reasons that are unrelated to their job duties and this profound breach of trust to their students has been addressed appropriately by LCPS."

Brooks's appearance before the special grand jury resulted in two misdemeanor charges against Scott Ziegler: acting with a conflict of interest and penalizing an employee for appearing in court. Brooks also sued the former superintendent for $1 million for wrongful termination.

Scott's attorney, Erin Harrigan, wrote a filing stating that Brooks had inappropriate communication with Ian Prior regarding the special needs student. One of the documents presented to the court was a March 22, 2022, email from Brooks to Prior. In this email, Brooks acknowledged that Vandermuelen spoke with Prior about the groping allegations. Brooks also sought confirmation that Prior wouldn't name herself, Vandermuelen, or the school they worked at during his school board comments that night. "As you can imagine, this is a very disheartening and painful process," Brooks wrote. "As quickly as I want this addressed, I'm also still fearful of repercussions." Prior agreed to these conditions. He added that he expected Andrew Hoyler to contact him privately after his remarks.

All of this contradicted testimony Brooks gave to the special grand jury on April 26, 2022. "Laurie never shared that information with anybody. There was no intention of sharing the information with anybody."

"Despite the clear evidence of Ms. Brooks' perjury before the special grand jury, no indictment was brought against her," Harrigan stated in her filing. "The special grand jury did return two indictments against Ziegler that day, both involving Ms. Brooks."

This email chain between Brooks and Prior was forwarded to Carlton Davis on September 23, 2022. Harrigan sought to find out if Brooks was promised a plea deal for testifying against Ziegler. She sought documents to prove such a deal existed. This drew a heated denial from Theo Stamos during an August 10, 2023, hearing on Harrigan's filing. "Mr. Davis made no promises, because none were needed, because there was no perjury. To suggest Davis went rogue on me and had a conversation with a witness is preposterous."

Oh, Theo, nothing is "preposterous" when considering Carlton Davis's ability to fuck up. At the end of the day, my old friend Judge Fisher ruled against Erin and Scott, stating that their motion for possible plea-deal documents was "based on speculation."

"To grant a motion like this, I need more evidence than I've got."

Really, judge? What more did you need?

I was baffled by the split jury decision on Scott's cases, and I was sure he'd win on appeal.

On March 6, 2024, Judge Douglas Fleming demonstrated that he, too, was baffled, setting aside the verdict because of errors in the jury instructions. He set a March 28 hearing to determine the date of a retrial. The attorney general's office issued a release saying it looked forward to trying the case again. I considered that optimistic since, after two years, the attorney general had failed to secure any convictions from the work of the special grand jury—not even a misdemeanor. A five-day retrial to begin on February 3, 2025, was eventually scheduled.

I also had a little bit of survivor's guilt, given Scott's continuing legal drama.

Scott Smith, Looking for a Big Payday

Predictably, Scott Smith filed a $30 million lawsuit against the Loudoun County School Board, stating his daughter's rights had been violated because a Title IX investigation hadn't been started right after the May 28, 2021, incident at Stone Bridge High School. The lawsuit identified the people filing the complaint as John and Jane Doe, not Scott and Jessica Smith, to protect the identity of the people involved in this incident.

Scott Smith then told multiple media outlets that he was John Doe.

Making Sense of It All

I have stopped feeding quarters into the outrage machine. I will give no more currency to controversy. That's the biggest takeaway from my experience of being a "felon."

I have stopped having negative interactions with people whose minds I can't change. I've stopped feeding quotes to the media that could be interpreted as confrontational. I am adhering to the philosophy Billy Joel expressed in his 1976 epoch, "Angry Young Man."

> *I had my pointless point of view,*
> *And life went on no matter who was wrong or right*

I also noted what Billy says at the end of concerts, "Don't take any shit off of anybody."

My shit-taking days are over.

The summer after I graduated college, I decided to read some of the assigned books I should have read, but faked my way through without cracking their covers. One such work, authored by F. Lee Bailey, had been assigned in a prelaw class. Something Bailey wrote stuck with me: He preferred the English presumption of guilt over the American presumption of innocence where defendants are concerned. Bailey's thought on the American system was, "If you are innocent, why are you being charged?" If you are found to be innocent in an American court, the assumption you're guilty still sticks with a lot of people. Surely a clever lawyer employed legal chicanery to beat the charges. In England, if you're not guilty, you've shown why the state's assertion was wrong.

When I beat the perjury charge, I knew there would always be those who would claim I was guilty.

I reconciled myself to that.

I also reconciled myself to the fact that my life would henceforth be distilled to this summary paragraph that shows up in virtually every story concerning May 28, 2021, at Stone Bridge High School and the numerous legal cases it spawned: "A Loudoun jury acquitted schools spokesman Wayde Byard of lying to the special grand jury about the 2021 sexual assaults during a trial in June." The epitaph for my public life.

October 2023 found me among seventeen friends at a "gratitude dinner" I held at a local restaurant. Having seventeen true friends who reached out to me in my greatest hour of need left me humbled, as did the fact that there could have been many more seats at that table.

As I look back on the seven months encompassing my public indictment and trial, I really have trouble putting it in context. I'm too close. I find that when I write about it, visceral emotions spring out of me.

In the movie *Office Space*, one of the Bobs notes that Peter is missing a lot of work. Peter replies, "Well, I wouldn't exactly say I've been *missing* it, Bob."

Before December 2022, I hadn't taken an extended break since the summer of 1973. I recommend doing this every fifty years or so. I found out I didn't miss work. I didn't miss tedious meetings; the school board's especially. I didn't miss the commute, especially after tedious school board meetings. I didn't miss people filing idiotic, conspiracy-driven Freedom of Information Act requests. I didn't miss bitching parents and uninformed reporters with an agenda. I didn't miss the unwanted attention from people who wanted a selfie with me.

I didn't miss my former life.

At all.

When I think about it too deeply, a bit of nonsense from my early teenage years pops out of my deep memories. Whenever the football Thunderbirds of Mahwah, New Jersey, Junior-Senior High School scored a touchdown, the band would break into the Notre Dame fight song. The student body sang unauthorized lyrics that supposedly reflected our status as badass teens:

Beers, beers for old Mahwah High,
You bring the Scotch and I'll bring the rye,
Send those freshmen out for gin,
And don't let a sober sophomore in,
We never stagger,
We never fall,
We sober up on good alcohol,
When we yell, we yell like hell!
For the glory of Mahwah High

In addition to such revelry, which would probably get a high school administrator fired today, coaches gave out cigars and beer in the locker room after big victories. (That definitely would get the coaches fired, and the athletic director, principal, and even the superintendent as well.) In honor of my Thunderbirds roots, I considered lighting up my genuine Pedro Ramos cigar, which the great Yankee reliever gave me at a promotional event decades ago, after my not guilty verdict. I decided to leave Pedro untouched by flame. The last time I smoked a cigar, I threw up.

I reflected on what my greatest achievement might be in light of a long string of bizarre life events. My greatest achievement? After sixty-six-plus years—they have yet to beat the optimism out of me.

December 2023: Wrapping Things Up

The Loudoun County School Board voted to pay $35,000 for my legal expenses and $1,500 for the expungement of my indictment. This was done through anonymous items on the board's consent agenda. Ultra-conservative Tiffany Polifko was the only board member to vote against this compensation. Given the fractious nature of the Loudoun County School Board, I'll take an 8-1 vote. I was very relieved that no public debate or uproar resulted from these actions.

On December 6, 2023, Theo Stamos was named Virginia's Deputy Attorney General for Criminal Justice and Public Safety. In announcing the promotion, Attorney General Jason Miyares noted that "Theo Stamos has tirelessly pursued the truth that Virginians deserve." The news release, composed by Victoria LaCivita, went on to state, "Theo spearheaded the investigation into the Virginia Parole Board and the Loudoun County School Board, which resulted in the termination of the previous superintendent and a successful conviction for retaliatory firing." (Somehow, I didn't rate a mention.)

On December 20, the attorney general's office announced it was dropping the misdemeanor charge that Scott Ziegler lied to the School Board on June 22, 2021, when he said he didn't know about any assaults in LCPS bathrooms. The reason cited: the "significant additional resources" that would have to be devoted to the February 2024 trial. In an unusual spin, the attorney general noted the money LCPS had spent on Scott's earlier trial. "That trial lasted 5 days and required the summoning of numerous jurors and witnesses . . . LCPS spent additional taxpayer funds providing attorneys to many witnesses." (I'll note the attorney general has never revealed what his investigation, the special grand jury, and my trial cost the taxpayers of the commonwealth.)

Miyares's December announcement of the end of Scott's prosecution was a classic "news dump." Announcing a major bit of news just before Christmas virtually assures it will be lost in the holiday hoopla. The only negative that I could think of from the case being dropped is that Mike Chapman and Beth Barts would not be put on the witness stand and be held accountable for their actions.

Tim Flynn and I attended a party at a former colleague's house in mid-December. He made a hasty exit right after I arrived. He, politely, asked me if I could move aside, so he could retrieve his coat from a foyer closet. If these are the last words he utters to me, I'm fine with that.

Ian Prior resurfaced, yet again, on February 7, 2024, when former Trump advisor Stephen Miller's America First Legal filed an EEOC complaint against the NFL. America First contended that the NFL's Rooney Rule, which mandates the interviewing—not hiring—of minority candidates for head coaching jobs constitutes discrimination.

The Washington Post quoted Prior in relation to this action: "'If the National Football League truly wants to end discrimination in the employment process, then the NFL should stop discriminating in the employment process, follow the meritocratic system it displays on the field, and eliminate the Rooney Rule,' said Ian Prior, a senior adviser with America First Legal."

It was good to see Prior move on to bigger things after cleaning up Loudoun County.

On the same date, I checked the Fight For Schools Facebook page. The first thing I noted was that Facebook correctly labeled Fight For Schools as a "political organization." The next thing that I noted is that there had not been a posting since May 6, 2023. That posting concerned the Loudoun County commonwealth's attorney's race.

Following a link to Fight For School's website, I noted there hadn't been a posting since December 7, 2022. That post detailed the firing of Scott Ziegler. I also noted that the donation buttons, including the option for monthly recurring donations, still appeared to be active.

I have found no evidence that Ian Prior and Fight For Schools had any influence—philosophical or monetary—on the 2023 election of the Loudoun County School Board.

I'm not the only one to notice this.

On December 12, the 2020–2023 Loudoun County School Board, the most embattled in American history, held its final meeting. Outgoing Chair Ian Serotkin gave the best summation of what happened to this much-maligned group of elected officials in his parting comments.

"No one else has been through what we've been through. No one else; the seven of us who have been up here since 2020. It was a novel strategy, politicizing a local school board to a national level and trying to use it to influence election results statewide. It turns out that's a trick that works exactly once. We had millions of dollars try to influence what happened in our board room in 2021, and it was effective in influencing the gubernatorial election in that year. But those same efforts completely failed in 2022 and failed again in 2023 because the people who live here in Loudoun County and around the commonwealth were smart enough to see those efforts for what they were.

"And the end result here, after everything, is that we're going to see the exact same partisan split on the next board as we have on the current one. I am hoping for the next board's sake that that is the nail in the coffin for the national hyper-politicization of the Loudoun County School Board, but time will tell."

Well said.

ACKNOWLEDGMENTS

I would like to acknowledge Jennifer Leffler and Mary Herbert, who embody the spirit of justice behind the law.

I also would like to acknowledge Ned Waterhouse, Jim Person, Asia Jones, Dianne Shipe, Sharen Gromling, Don Butler, Jim and Michelle Noland, Bent Ferrell, Bill Collins, Billy Grubbs, John Brewer, Eric Stewart, Dave Stewart, Charles Barrett, Jim Barnes, and all of the personal and professional friends who were there in my hour of need.

They taught me that I was rich beyond measure, beyond any monetary designation of wealth. Thanks to all of my LCPS family who bent the rules a little to express their support.

ABOUT THE AUTHOR

Wayde B. Byard served for more than twenty years as a public information officer for Loudoun County Public Schools. In a previous professional life as an award-winning journalist with *The Winchester Star*, he reported on crime, government (sometimes government-related crime), and sports.

He is a graduate of the University of Missouri's famed School of Journalism and lives in Winchester, Virginia, with his wife.

He is the author of six books, including *Spottswood Poles: A Baseball and American Legend*; *L.A. Football Confidential: The Definitive Guide to the History of Football in Los Angeles*; and *The Burgundy and Gold Standard* about the history of the team formerly known as the Washington Redskins.